How to (Not) Lie with Data:
Creating Effective Data Visualizations with Python

by Alex Kenan

Use Matplotlib, Seaborn, and Plotly to learn data visualization concepts to derive valuable, intuitive insight.

How to (Not) Lie with Data: Creating Effective Data Visualizations with Python

Ebook ISBN 978-1-7360606-4-3

Paperback ISBN 978-1-7360606-5-0

Hardcover ISBN 978-1-7360606-6-7

https://www.alexkenan.com/pyviz/

Cover by Aaesha Zahra, @aaeshazahra on Fiverr

Table of Contents

Introduction

We have entered the age of big data: there are terabytes and terabytes of information available for analysis in every field imaginable. With all of this information, it is necessary to make summaries that adequately convey the story behind the data, portray patterns, and show any outliers. That need has led to the enhancement of the field of data visualization, which seeks to create effective graphical representations and to tell a story with data. Though data visualization has been around since the 1800s, "Big Data" has vastly increased the scope of data visualization. In the age of Big Data, everyone wants to make data-driven decisions, and data visualization is essential to understanding your data.

Our eyes are drawn to color, and our brains can segment and discern different patterns. An effective data visualization makes use of the natural human ability to recognize patterns and intuitive understanding to convey a message. It is the difference between staring at rows on a spreadsheet and staring at a graph: one conveys a clear message, and one does not.

Effective data visualization is important for all industries; unfortunately, most people do not have any formal training in data visualization. This leads to a lot of misunderstanding and not using the right type of chart for the right message. Relying on Excel's graphing templates is how most people create charts. Excel's default bar chart template used to be an awful 3D wood-colored bar chart that made its way into "official" reports like investor presentations, company SEC 10Q and 10K filings, and more. These charts can be unintentionally deceiving; at other times, the charts have been deliberately curated to "show" the truth but be misleading and lead to incorrect conclusions. That is the context and background for this book: to show the readers how to make effective data visualizations. To *not* lie with data. To do so, you need to learn the rules and the suggestions of data visualizations. You need to see how *to* lie with data so that you *don't* lie with data.

Most people will only think of bar charts and line charts when they think of chart types; this book will show you how to make scatter plots, line plots, various histograms, bar charts, pie charts, choropleths, and variations of line plots. The first part of this book covers the basics, and the second part of this book will show you how to create effective visualizations using a variety of datasets like New York SAT testing data, US state populations, TSA passenger throughput numbers, and more. Since data visualization applies to almost all industries, we will use data from a wide variety of industries.

Almost every analytical tool comes with built-in graphical tools: MATLAB, Excel, Tableau, Python, Power BI, and others. We will use Python in this book; its utility as a programming language provides for some advantages that are difficult to replicate in standalone tools like Excel and Tableau. This book assumes that you, the reader, have basic knowledge of Python, meaning that you are comfortable with the syntax, able to import default libraries and install third-party libraries, and have a basic understanding of the language. If this is not the case, you should take advantage of some of the free resources at the /r/learnpython subreddit (https://www.reddit.com/r/learnpython/wiki/index). As such, this book assumes that you already have your Python setup tweaked to your preferences. This book was written using a mix of PyCharm and Spyder Integrated Development Environments (IDEs) with Python versions 3.7, 3.8, and 3.9, but the Python code should work in any IDE or even from the command line.

We will focus on three Python libraries in this book: Matplotlib, Seaborn, and Plotly. These three libraries have extensive documentation for creating specific charts, but they do not explain when you should use that chart type, how you can enhance them, or what you should watch out for. This book builds on a lot of the library documentation to create a good reference book for effective data visualization. The goal is to *not* lie with data visualization: by avoiding the common data "viz" pitfalls, you can create beautiful, effective charts that help you make data-driven decisions.

Matplotlib is a comprehensive library for creating static, animated, and interactive visualizations in Python, and it is one of the most popular Python graphing libraries. It can create almost any type of visualization, but you have to build it yourself with some unintuitive keywords and commands. Seaborn extends Matplotlib and provides color palettes, wrapper functions to make complicated Matplotlib figures in a few lines, and overall improvements and enhancements to Matplotlib. Both of these libraries generate plot figures in your IDE. Plotly is a departure from the first two libraries; it uses a JavaScript engine that renders in web browsers. A lot of the concepts are the same, but since the plots are rendered in a browser, the figures have more default interactivity. Plotly has a high-level API called Plotly Express (PX) that has pre-built figures for common chart types. If you need more customization, there is the Plotly Graph Objects (GO) library that allows you to customize almost every parameter and facet. Since there are advantages and disadvantages to all three libraries, being able to create similar charts in all three libraries gives you maximum flexibility.

You will need to have the following libraries installed:

- Matplotlib (version 3.2.0 or higher)
- Seaborn (version 0.11.0 or higher)
- Plotly
- NumPy
- Pandas
- Scipy
- Requests

These libraries may ship with bundled IDEs, especially one like Spyder from the Anaconda distribution. Otherwise, you will have to install them yourself with:

```
pip install matplotlib seaborn plotly numpy pandas scipy
    requests --upgrade
```

Each chapter in this book will explain the chart type, show a common lie for the first several chapters, review the necessary import statements, develop the chart type in Matplotlib, Seaborn, and Plotly as appropriate, finish with some concluding remarks, have a "full code" section with examples that were developed with each library, and link to further documentation. Each chapter builds on the last; Matplotlib, Seaborn, and Plotly are introduced and expanded on as different chart types are explored. Therefore, it is recommended to read each chapter in order.

To start, let's discuss the two main categories of data.

- *Categorical data* is data that is separated into discrete categories. There are several subcategories:

  - Nominal categories could be Fast, Medium, and Slow for how long it took people to run one mile, or Small/Medium/Large for penguin flipper size
  - Binary categories could be True or False, or Profit or Loss
  - Interval categories are like nominal categories, but there is a ranking involved. For example: Very Satisfied, Satisfied, Neutral, Dissatisfied, Very Dissatisfied. Very Satisfied is typically better than Dissatisfied
- *Numerical data* is data that is composed of meaningful numbers. Be careful! Just having numbers does not make the data numerical. For example, sometimes interval categories can be arranged as 1 to 5, such as 1 and 5 star reviews for a product (this book, perhaps?). This is still an interval, categorical description even though it has numbers. A dataset with the population of each US state would be numerical data.

We will be working with these two data types, but there are a few other categories of data. Now that we have explained the types of data that we will be working with, let's get to the first type of data visualization: the scatter plot.

Scatter Plots

Introduction

Scatter plots use markers (typically dots, sometimes other marker styles) to represent and show relationships between two numerical variables. Oftentimes, marker color can be used to show a third, categorical variable. Scatter plots are often used to determine if a correlation exists between the two variables. The x-axis is typically an independent variable, and the y-axis is typically a dependent variable; however, this convention does not always have to be followed. Scatter plots can be used for cluster analysis (seeing if there are groups of markers close together) and closeness to the mean analysis to look for outliers.

Scatter plots can become busy if there is too much data; our eyes need to be able to discern distinct markers and not one blob. If you have a lot of data that you want to plot, consider some of the following:

- Limiting the amount of data that is shown (be aware of selection bias)
- Using a contour or density plot
- Plotting with some opacity to show the density of data
- Using a heatmap

We will use the `mpg` dataset from Seaborn to demonstrate the use of scatter plots. `Mpg` has 9 columns:

Column Name	**Datatype**	**Description**
mpg	`float`	Miles per gallon efficiency of the car
cylinders	`int`	Number of cylinders that the car's engine has
displacement	`float`	Car's displacement (which is a measure of engine cylinder volume)
horsepower	`float`	Car's horsepower
weight	`int`	Car's weight
acceleration	`float`	Car's acceleration (as a 0-60 time)
model_year	`int`	The model year of the car as a two-digit number
origin	`str`	Car's manufacturing country. One of `usa`, `japan`, or `europe`.
name	`str`	Car's model name

The Lie

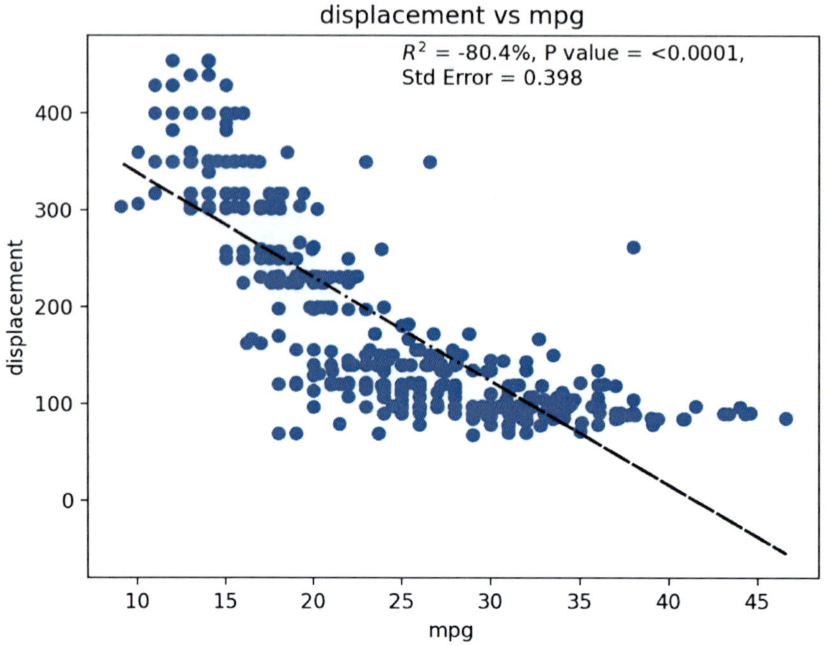

By itself, this scatter plot is not a lie; however, correlation coefficients and linear regressions should be properly evaluated and not immediately taken as gospel. The oft-repeated saying that correlation does not imply causation still holds true, and it can be very tempting to assume that since the magnitude of the R^2 value is high, the linear regression will accurately predict the dependent variable. In this case, it is very tempting to assume that mpg and displacement are inversely correlated. The coefficient of determination (R^2) is highly negative, the p value is low, and the standard error is pretty low. Scatter plots can tell you a lot about relationships and the appearance of relationships, but it takes care to determine that there is a causal relationship. Just showing this graph and concluding that mpg and displacement are inversely correlated is a lie.

Imports

```
import matplotlib.pyplot as plt
import seaborn as sns
import plotly.express as px
import plotly.graph_objects as go
import numpy as np
from scipy import stats
import plotly.io as pio
pio.renderers.default = "browser"
mpg = sns.load_dataset('mpg')
plt.style.use('default')
```

These lines go at the very top of your program. The `pio` lines ensure that notebook IDEs like Spyder render any Plotly graphs in a browser instead of in the Plots pane or in-line in the Notebook area.

Matplotlib

We can pass two `List`-like variables to Matplotlib's `plt.scatter()` function, and it will create a scatter plot. The last line we need for any plotting is `plt.show()` so that Matplotlib renders the plot. Let's show a basic `mpg` and `acceleration` scatter plot:

```
plt.scatter(mpg['mpg'], mpg['acceleration'])
plt.show()
```

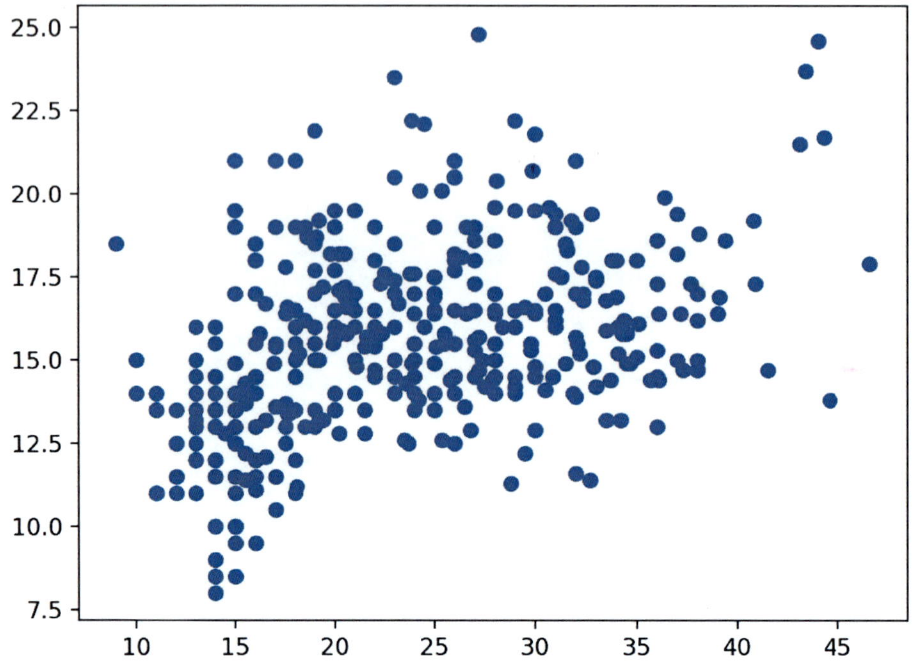

It's hard to tell what is going on in this scatter plot. Luckily, Matplotlib gives us options for labelling axes and titles. Instead of just `plt.scatter()` and `plt.show()`, we can add labels:

```
plt.scatter(mpg['mpg'], mpg['acceleration'])
plt.xlabel('MPG')
plt.ylabel('Acceleration (0-60 time)')
plt.title('Acceleration (0-60 time) vs MPG')
plt.show()
```

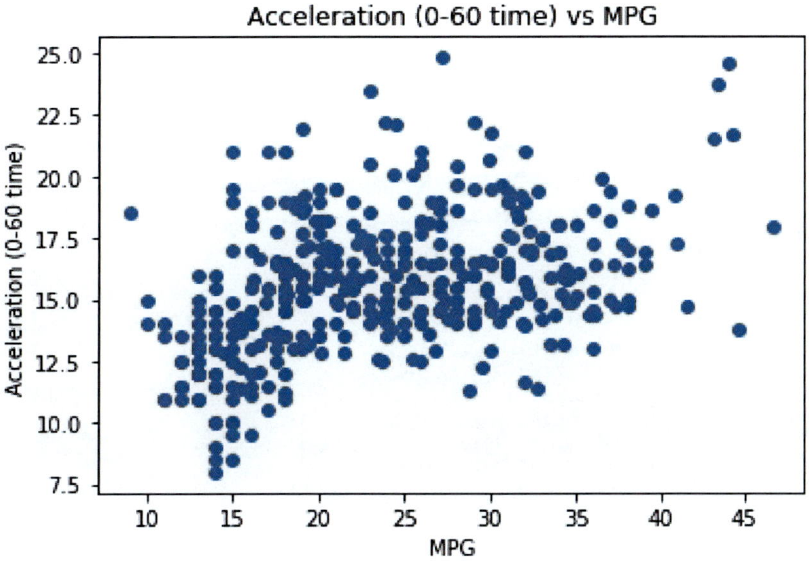

We can customize the marker color and marker style with `color` and `marker`, respectively. There are many ways to select a color [1]:

- Matplotlib's default colors (`color='k'`)
- Matplotlib's Tableau color palette (`color='tab:blue'`)
- Cascading Style Sheets (CSS) named colors (`color='navajowhite'`)
- Hex color codes (`color='#FF0022'`)

We will start by using Matplotlib's default colors:

Color	**Matplotlib code**
Blue	`'b'`
Green	`'g'`
Red	`'r'`
Cyan	`'c'`

Magenta	`'m'`
Yellow	`'y'`
Black	`'k'` (k)
White	`'w'`

There are also many marker styles available [2]. The default scatter plot option is a circle, but here are some of the most popular marker styles:

Style	**Matplotlib code**
Circle	`'o'`
Point	`'.'`
Plus	`'+'`
X	`'x'`
Diamond	`'D'`

Let's see how to make a scatter plot with the datapoints as gray pentagons.

```
plt.scatter(mpg['mpg'], mpg['acceleration'], color='slategrey',
            marker='p')
plt.xlabel('MPG')
plt.ylabel('Acceleration (0-60 time)')
plt.title('Acceleration (0-60 time) vs MPG')
plt.show()
```

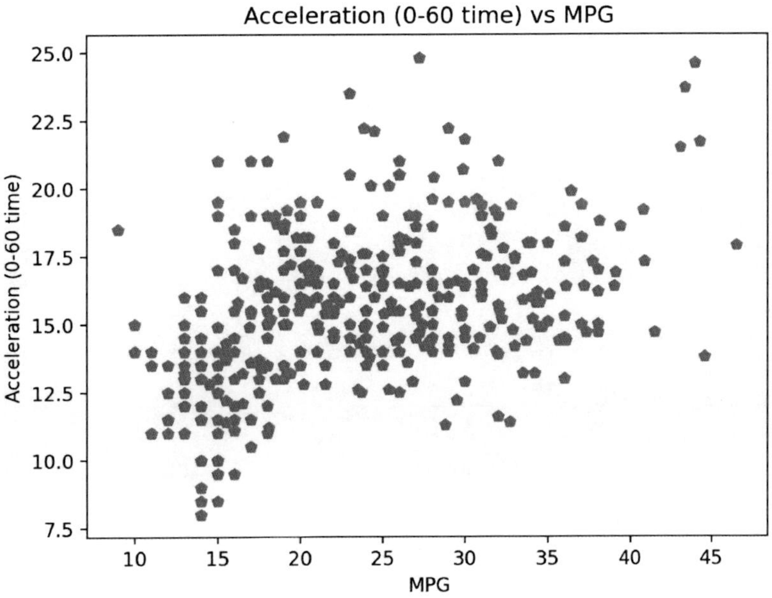

It's still hard to see the relationship, so let's use the numerical Python library Numpy to add a trendline. Note that we can keep adding elements to `plt`: we have been using `plt.scatter()`, and now we'll use `plt.plot()` to plot a trendline on top of the scatter plot. Making a trendline gives us access to the `linestyle` options [3] as well:

Linestyle	**Description**
`'-'` or `'solid'`	solid line
`'--'` or `'dashed'`	dashed line
`'-.'` or `'dashdot'`	dash-dotted line
`':'` or `'dotted'`	dotted line
`'None'` or `' '` or `''`	draw nothing

There are also options for creating custom variants of the above linestyles, but we won't use them in this book.

Now, onto the trendline creation. We will use Numpy's `polyfit` function to calculate a trendline from the `mpg` and `acceleration` columns, and we pass `1` to indicate that we are looking for an x^1 or linear relationship. This function should work for non-linear relationships, too: just change the `1` to a different number to indicate the order of the function being generated.

```
plt.scatter(mpg['mpg'], mpg['acceleration'])
polyfunction = np.polyfit(mpg['mpg'], mpg['acceleration'], 1)
trendline_function = np.poly1d(polyfunction)
plt.plot(mpg['mpg'], trendline_function(mpg['mpg']), "k-.")
plt.xlabel('MPG')
plt.ylabel('Acceleration (0-60 time)')
plt.title('Acceleration (0-60 time) vs MPG')
plt.show()
```

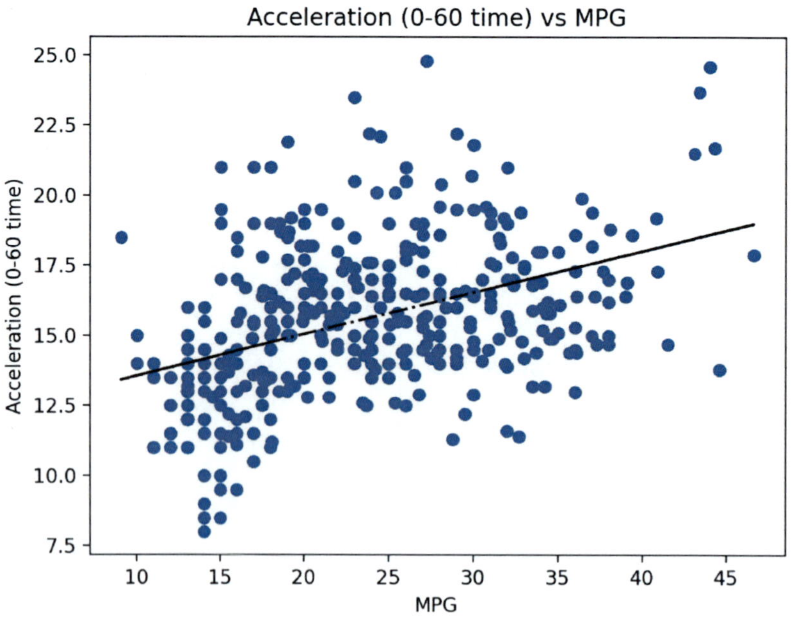

We would be remiss to have a trendline without R^2, the linear regression equation, and other regression details. We can use Scipy's `stats` library to calculate these details for us. We can also use `plt.annotate()` to add a text annotation to the plot. All we need for the annotation is `text` and a `xy` position, but we could also add `xytext` and an arrow to indicate the annotated point. For now, let's use the `xy` coordinates of `(10, 27)`. Since that point is off of the plot given Matplotlib's default boundary behavior, we can use `plt.ylim(lower, upper)` to move the bounds. If we enclose anything that is "equation-like" in `$` within the text annotation, Matplotlib will render it with LaTeX (pronounced lah-teck) to provide clean equations; `$R^2$` will become R^2 on the canvas.

```
plt.scatter(mpg['mpg'], mpg['acceleration'])
polyfunction = np.polyfit(mpg['mpg'], mpg['acceleration'], 1)
trendline_function = np.poly1d(polyfunction)
plt.plot(mpg['mpg'], trendline_function(mpg['mpg']), "k-.")
slope, intercept, r_value, p_value, std_err =
            stats.linregress(mpg['mpg'],mpg['acceleration'])
if p_value <= 1E-3:
    p_value_str = '<0.0001'
else:
    p_value_str = '{:.3f}'.format(p_value)
details = """Acceleration = {:.3f}*MPG + {:.2f}
$R^2$ = {:.1%}, P value = {}, Std Error = {:.3f}""".format(
         slope, intercept, r_value, p_value_str, std_err)
plt.annotate(details, xy=(10, 27))
plt.ylim(7, 30)
plt.xlabel('MPG')
plt.ylabel('Acceleration (0-60 time)')
plt.title('Acceleration (0-60 time) vs MPG')
plt.show()
```

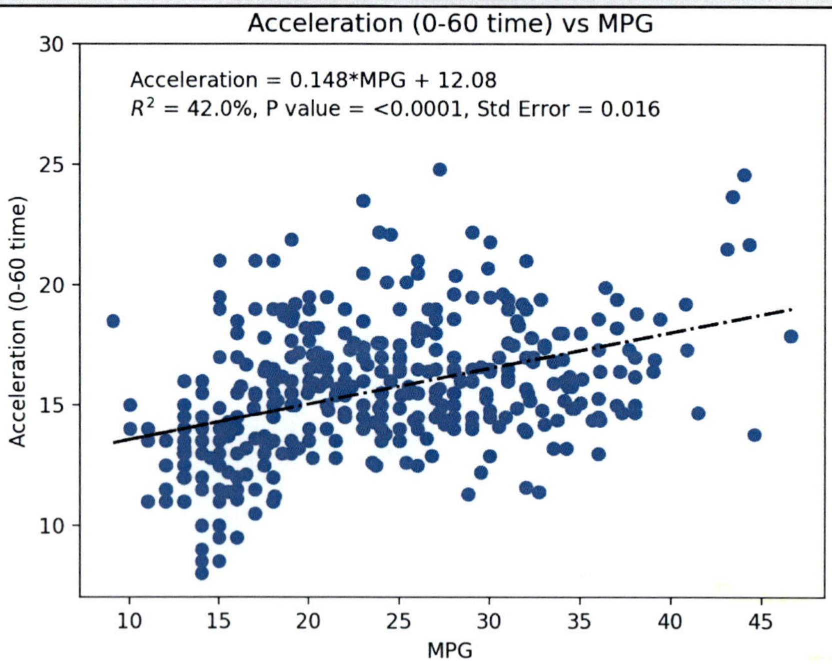

Lastly, we can plot the *origin* parameter in *mpg* using color as the third dimension of the scatter plot. This requires using Pandas Boolean indexing to create groups for the *usa*, *europe*, and `japan` groups. Pay attention to the locations of the brackets; if you get `KeyError: True` or `KeyError: False`, you probably misplaced brackets. We will also use the `label` plot parameter to create a legend.

```
usa = mpg[mpg['origin'] == 'usa']
japan = mpg[mpg['origin'] == 'japan']
europe = mpg[mpg['origin'] == 'europe']
plt.scatter(usa['mpg'], usa['acceleration'],
            label="USA", color='b')
plt.scatter(japan['mpg'], japan['acceleration'],
            label="Japan", color='r')
plt.scatter(europe['mpg'], europe['acceleration'],
            label="Europe", color='k')
plt.xlabel('MPG')
plt.ylabel('Acceleration (0-60 time)')
plt.title('Acceleration (0-60 time) vs MPG')
plt.legend()
plt.show()
```

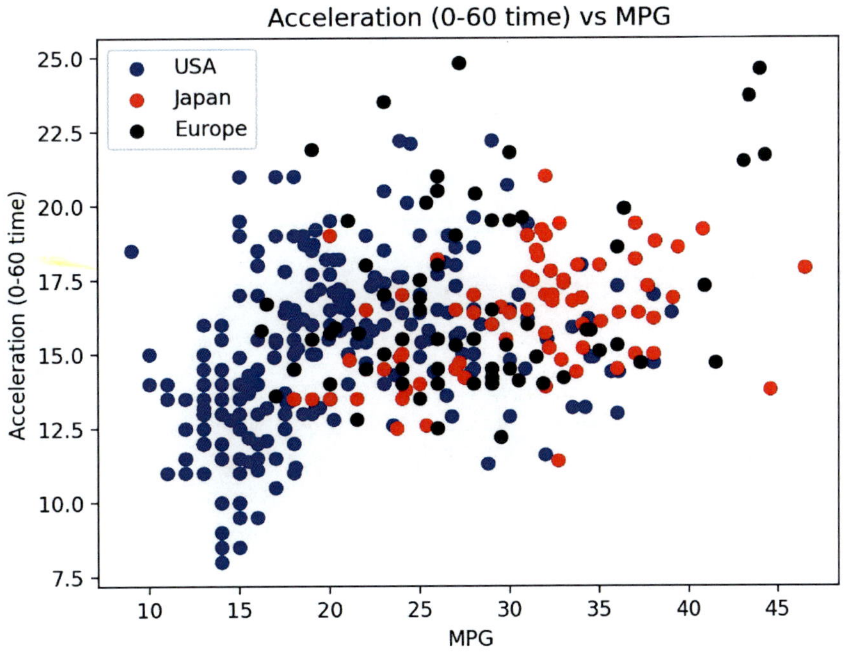

The use of three colors makes the scatter plot a little busy. We could change colors or opacity in Matplotlib to make the plot easier to read, but let's see how Seaborn can make our plotting lives easier. As a reminder, Seaborn wraps Matplotlib to make more complicated graphs easier to create.

Seaborn

The Seaborn basic scatter plot has two lines:

```
sns.scatterplot(data=mpg, x='mpg', y='acceleration')
plt.show()
```

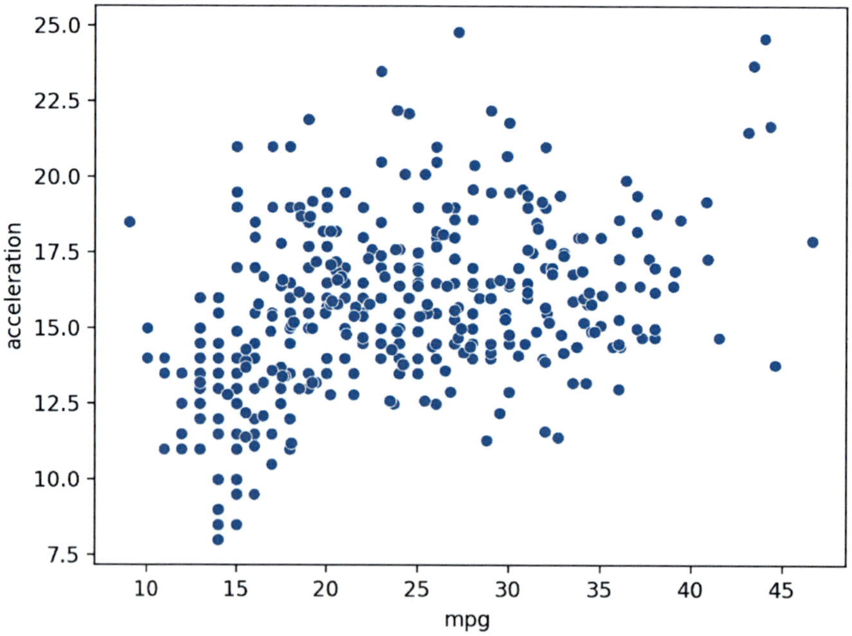

By default, Seaborn plots the column names on their respective axes. Since we are working with a Pandas DataFrame (a custom datatype that is like a table or spreadsheet), it is very easy to add the third dimension of color. Seaborn will use default colors unless we specifically pass in color arguments.

```
sns.scatterplot(data=mpg, x='mpg', y='acceleration', hue='origin')
plt.show()
```

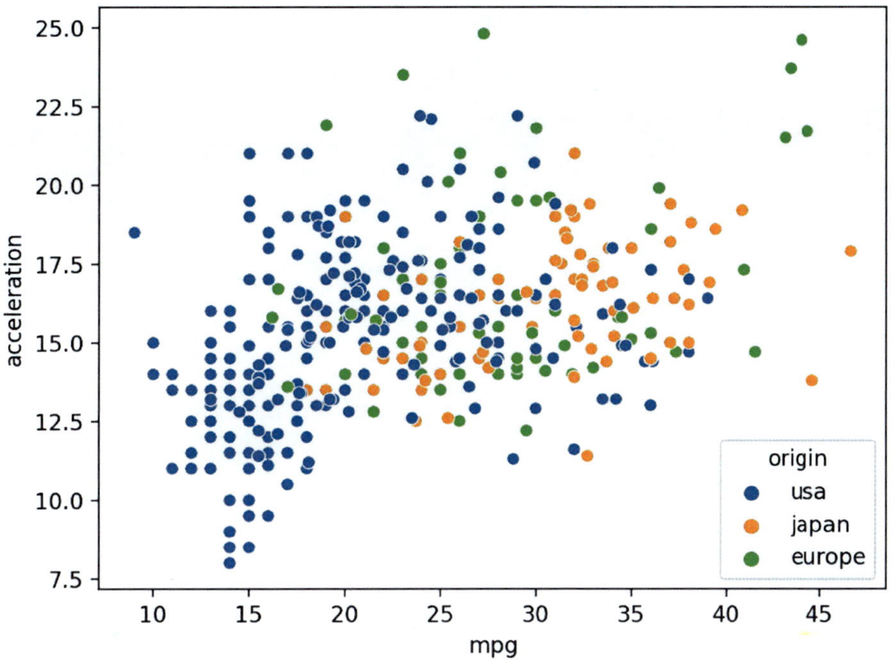

We can also change the marker style to better differentiate the different clusters, and we can still use `plt` to set a title or override the default axis labelling:

```
sns.scatterplot(data=mpg, x='mpg', y='acceleration', hue='origin',
                style='origin')
plt.xlabel('MPG')
plt.ylabel('Acceleration (0-60 time)')
plt.title('Acceleration (0-60 time) vs MPG')
plt.show()
```

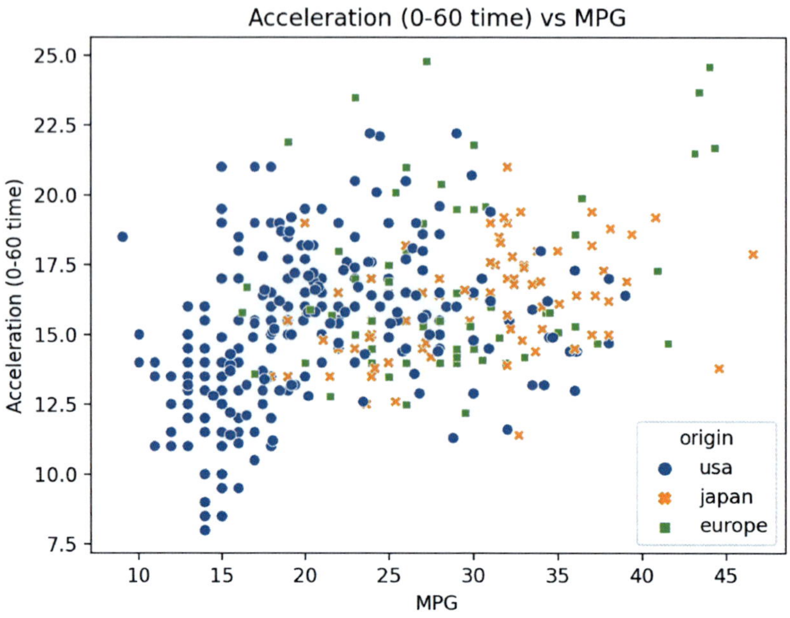

The chart starts to look pretty cluttered, but what took several more lines in Matplotlib can be done with just a few more parameters in Seaborn.

We can choose different color palettes for Seaborn plotting. Seaborn has six variations of the Matplotlib color palette (from lightest to darkest: *`pastel`*, *`bright`*, *`muted`*, *`deep`*, *`colorblind`*, and *`dark`*), and a few custom palettes (*`Set2`* and *`Paired`*). These palettes are good for categorical variables, which is what we are currently working with. There is functionality for creating custom palettes and custom sequential/diverging palettes [4], but we will not create any palettes in this book.

```
sns.scatterplot(data=mpg, x='mpg', y='acceleration', hue='origin',
                style='origin', palette='deep')
plt.xlabel('MPG')
plt.ylabel('Acceleration (0-60 time)')
plt.title('Acceleration (0-60 time) vs MPG')
plt.show()
```

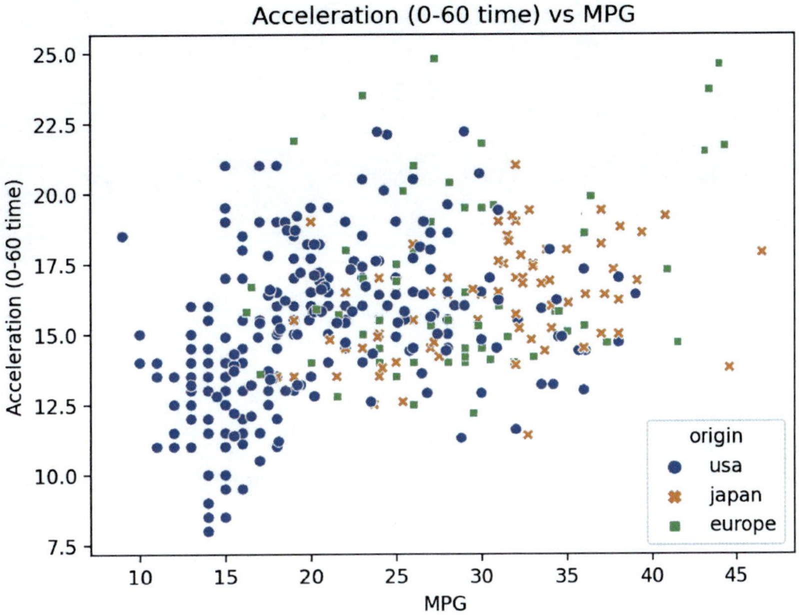

Seaborn also has a customized plot interface called `regplot`, which stands for regression plot. It has a sibling called `lmplot` which shares a lot of the same functionality. These functions create a scatter plot of x and y variables, fit a linear regression model y = f(x), and plot the resulting regression trendline and 95% confidence interval.

```
sns.regplot(data=mpg, x='mpg', y='acceleration')
plt.xlabel('MPG')
plt.ylabel('Acceleration (0-60 time)')
plt.title('Acceleration (0-60 time) vs MPG')
plt.show()
```

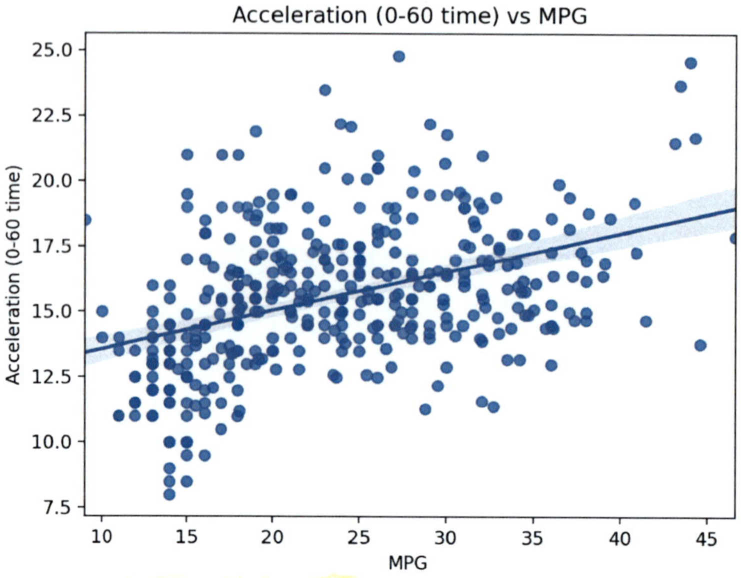

We lose the ability to quickly add color, but it makes a lot of the regression modeling easier.

Lastly, Matplotlib and Seaborn provide subplotting functionality with the syntax `plt.subplot(x, y, z)`, where `x` is the number of rows, `y` is the number of columns, and `z` is the index or current subplot that you want to edit. Matplotlib also allows us to adjust the x and y axes with `plt.xlim()` and `plt.ylim()`, respectively. We will create two subplots with 1 column and 2 rows:

```
plt.subplot(2, 1, 1)
sns.scatterplot(data=mpg, x='mpg', y='acceleration', alpha=0.60,
                hue='origin', palette='deep')
plt.xlim(7, 60)
plt.subplots_adjust(hspace=0.30)
plt.subplot(2, 1, 2)
sns.scatterplot(data=mpg, x='horsepower', y='weight', alpha=0.60,
                hue='cylinders', palette='Paired')
plt.xlim(30, 300)
plt.ylim(1300, 5300)
plt.show()
```

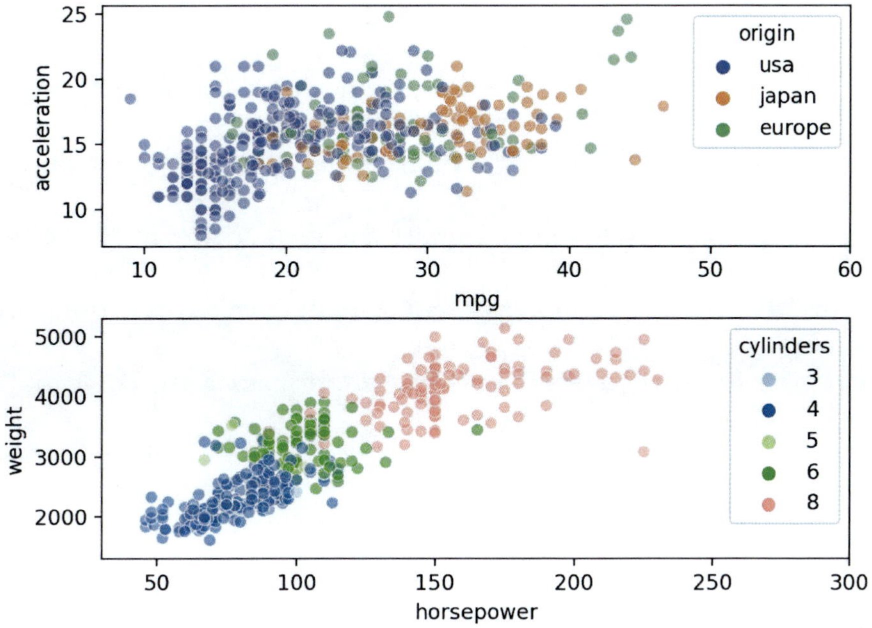

There is a lot of data overlap which makes the chart a little cluttered, but the subplotting functionality allows us to create multi-faceted scatter plots. Just because you *can* doesn't mean that you *should.*

Plotly

Plotly is different from Matplotlib and Seaborn because it uses an underlying JavaScript engine to render charts in a web browser. This means that we can create details on demand with interactive hover information, and it means that we can save files as HTML pages to share with others. The formatting syntax and overall figure philosophy are different from that of Matplotlib and Seaborn, but Plotly allows for different figure creation that addresses some of Matplotlib's weaknesses.

There are three submodules for visualization creation in Plotly: Graph Objects [5], Figure Factory [6], and Plotly Express [7]. Graph Objects are the lowest level in Plotly and are the base layer of plot types. Plotly Express is a higher-level module that is used for quickly creating common figures that consist of Graph Objects. Plotly Express on top of Graph Objects can be thought of like Seaborn on top of Matplotlib. Figure Factory was created before Plotly Express, but it performed a similar function of wrapping Graph Objects in an easier-to-manipulate format. Figure Factory still exists, but it is generally only around for backwards compatibility. For each Plotly section, we will start with Plotly Express and then transition to Graph Objects for more customization.

Let's again get started with a basic scatter plot:

```
fig = px.scatter(mpg, x='mpg', y='acceleration')
fig.show()
```

Remember, this plot will render in your web browser; the browser should snap to the foreground on your computer. If it doesn't, you will have to click on your browser application. You should see this:

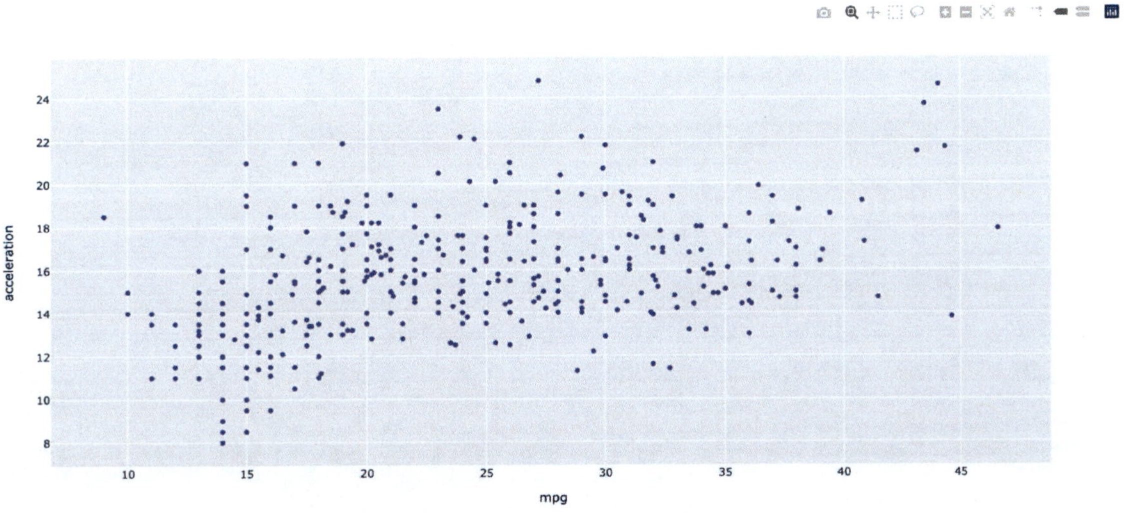

Plotly has its own toolbar that allows for saving as a PNG, zooming, panning, lasso selecting, autoscaling, resetting to defaults, toggling spike lines on hover, and comparing info if more than one dataset is shown. Play with the spike lines and hover over datapoints. Look ma, interaction!

We can add origin with color like we did with Seaborn, and we can update the axes and plot titles. Each time the program is re-run, a new browser tab should open up.

```
fig = px.scatter(mpg, x='mpg', y='acceleration', color='origin')
fig.update_xaxes(title="MPG")
fig.update_yaxes(title='Acceleration (0-60 time)')
fig.update_layout(title="Acceleration (0-60 time) vs MPG")
fig.show()
```

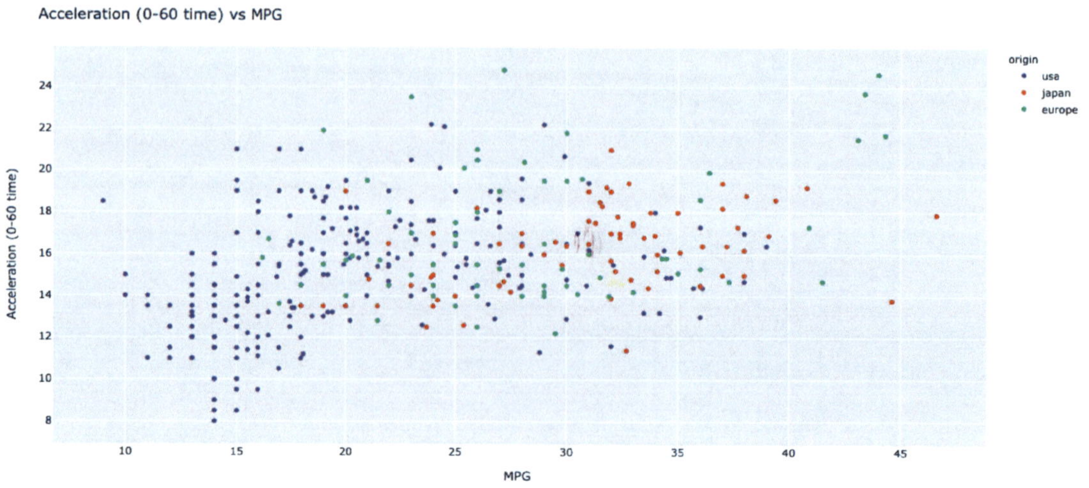

Let's look at adding hover data. If we pass a `List` to the parameter `hover_data`, it will show that information in addition to the x and y variables. There is another, more concise, way to update the axis labels and plot title:

```
fig = px.scatter(mpg, x='mpg', y='acceleration', color='origin',
                 hover_data=['name', 'model_year', 'cylinders'],
                 title="Acceleration (0-60 time) vs MPG",
                 labels={"mpg": "MPG",
                         "acceleration": "Acceleration (0-60) time"})
fig.show()
```

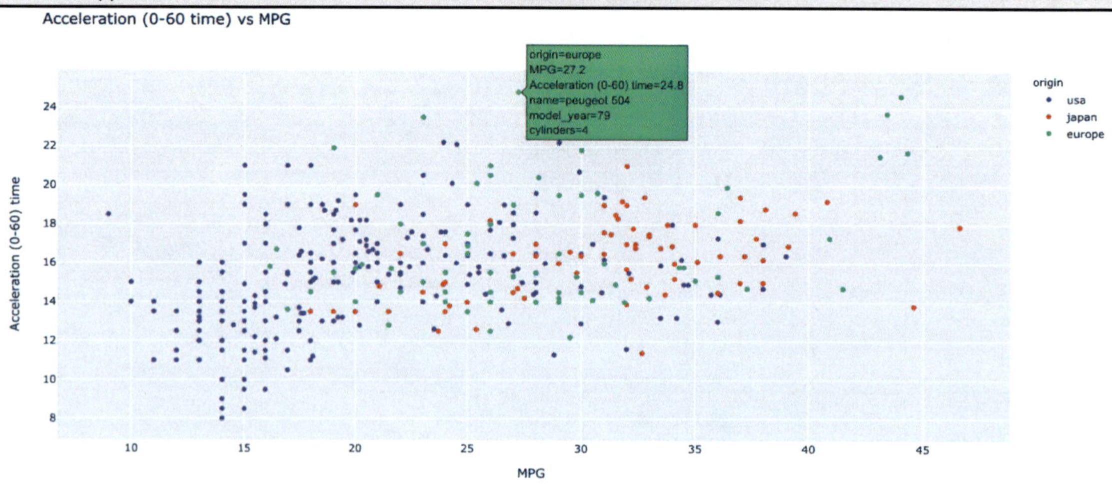

Changing marker style is a little different. You can update the marker style for all points with `fig.update_traces(marker={'symbol': 'star'})`, but to update each individual trace's marker style requires Graph Objects.

You can save Plotly charts as an HTML file with the syntax `fig.write_html('/path/to/file.html')` for Mac or `fig.write_html(r'\path\to\file.html')` on Windows.

Plotly supports linear and nonlinear trendlines with Ordinary Least Squares (OLS) and Locally Weighted Scatterplot Smoothing (LOWESS), respectively. Adding a trendline to a Plotly Express plot is as easy as passing `trendline="ols"` to `px.scatter()`:

```
fig = px.scatter(mpg, x='mpg', y='acceleration', trendline="ols",
                 hover_data=['name', 'model_year', 'cylinders'],
                 title="Acceleration (0-60 time) vs MPG",
                 labels={"mpg": "MPG",
                         "acceleration": "Acceleration"})
fig.show()
```

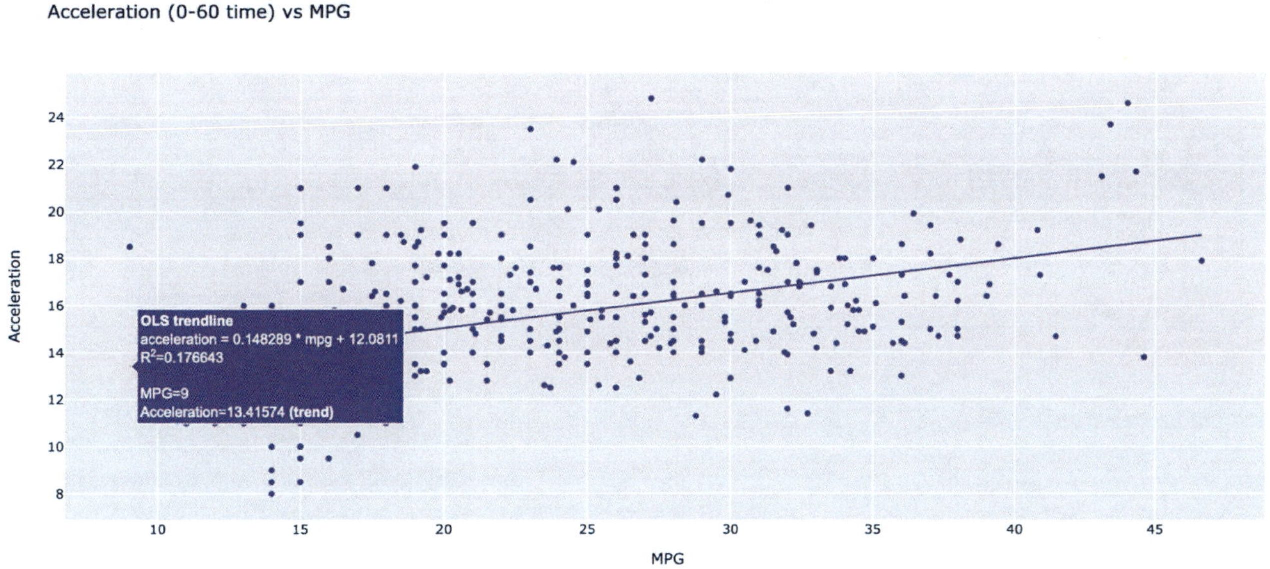

The hover tooltip shows us the regression coefficients, R^2, and regression equation.

A similar chart can be made with the `go.Scatter` Graph Object:

```
usa = mpg[mpg['origin'] == 'usa']
japan = mpg[mpg['origin'] == 'japan']
europe = mpg[mpg['origin'] == 'europe']

fig = go.Figure(data=go.Scatter(x=usa['mpg'],
                                y=usa['acceleration'],
                                mode='markers',
                                marker={'color': 'blue'},
                                name="usa",
                                hovertemplate="MPG: %{x}
                                   <br>Acceleration: %{y}"))
fig.add_trace(go.Scatter(x=japan['mpg'],
                         y=japan['acceleration'],
                         mode='markers',
                         marker={'color': 'red'},
                         name="japan",
                         hovertemplate="MPG: %{x}
                            <br>Acceleration: %{y}"))
fig.add_trace(go.Scatter(x=europe['mpg'],
                         y=europe['acceleration'],
                         mode='markers',
                         marker={'color': 'green'},
                         name="europe",
                         hovertemplate="MPG: %{x}
                            <br>Acceleration: %{y}"))
fig.update_layout(title="Acceleration (0-60 time) vs MPG",
                  xaxis_title="MPG",
                  yaxis_title="Acceleration (0-60) time")
fig.show()
```

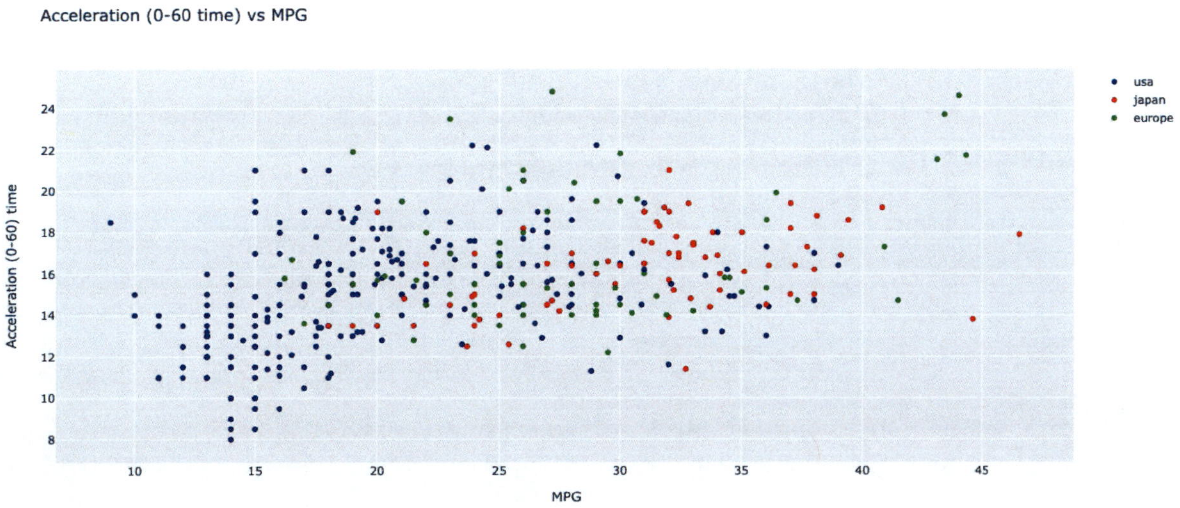

The hover text took a little more work with the `hovertemplate` parameter to drop in `x` and `y` tags, and we had to create DataFrames of each origin to plot separately. To add separate marker styles for each trace, add `'symbol': 'triangle-ne'` to the `marker` dictionary for each new scatter plot trace. To change the marker size, add a `'size': 20` to the same `marker` dictionary. For a basic scatter plot, Plotly Express made it easy to plot `acceleration` vs `mpg`.

Plotly also supports subplotting in two different ways. For Plotly Express, you can pass a column name to `facet_row` or `facet_col` for subplotting according to the column. For Graph Objects, you need to use `from plotly.subplots import make_subplots`.

```
# Plotly Express example
fig = px.scatter(mpg, x='mpg', y='acceleration',
                 facet_row="origin",
                 hover_data=['name', 'model_year', 'cylinders'],
                 title="Acceleration (0-60 time) vs MPG",
                 labels={"mpg": "MPG",
                         "acceleration": "Acceleration"})
fig.show()
```

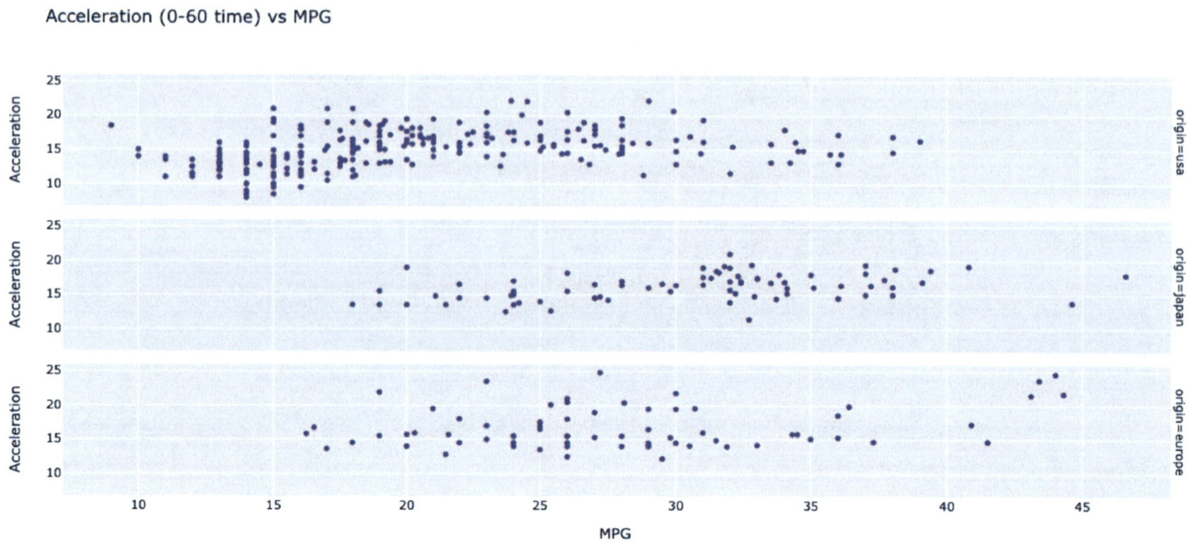

Summary

Scatter plots are used for showing relationships (or non-relationships) between two sets of numerical variables. Optionally, a third, categorical variable can be shown as color or size of markers. Messing with marker size can detract from the visualization's message, and it can quickly approach "chart junk" status, where your message gets distorted because of making the graph a little too cute.

Matplotlib, Seaborn, and Plotly offer different ways to display scatter plots. Matplotlib offers the basics, with many customizable parameters under the hood. The downside is that you have to do all of the work yourself. Seaborn offers wrappers on top of Matplotlib, and it has a one-stop-shop `regplot` with Pandas DataFrame integration. Plotly offers interactive displays and Pandas integration with ready-made objects in Plotly Express, or more customizable figures in

Graph Objects. Scatter plots are relatively simple, and they offer a good way to introduce the three graphing libraries.

Examples for Each Library

```
import matplotlib.pyplot as plt
import seaborn as sns
import plotly.express as px
import plotly.graph_objects as go
import numpy as np
from scipy import stats
import plotly.io as pio
pio.renderers.default = "browser"
mpg = sns.load_dataset('mpg')
plt.style.use('default')

# matplotlib scatterplot with color by origin
usa = mpg[mpg['origin'] == 'usa']
japan = mpg[mpg['origin'] == 'japan']
europe = mpg[mpg['origin'] == 'europe']
plt.scatter(usa['mpg'], usa['acceleration'],
            label="USA", color='b')
plt.scatter(japan['mpg'], japan['acceleration'],
            label="Japan", color='r')
plt.scatter(europe['mpg'], europe['acceleration'],
            label="Europe", color='k')
plt.xlabel('MPG')
plt.ylabel('Acceleration (0-60 time)')
plt.title('Acceleration (0-60 time) vs MPG')
plt.legend()
plt.show()

# seaborn scatterplot with origin/marker with color
sns.scatterplot(data=mpg, x='mpg', y='acceleration', hue='origin',
                style='origin', palette='deep')
plt.xlabel('MPG')
plt.ylabel('Acceleration (0-60 time)')
plt.title('Acceleration (0-60 time) vs MPG')
plt.show()
```

```
# plotly express with different color and size options
fig = px.scatter(mpg, x='mpg', y='acceleration', color='origin',
                 hover_data=['name', 'model_year', 'cylinders'],
                 title="Acceleration (0-60 time) vs MPG",
                 labels={"mpg": "MPG",
                         "acceleration": "Acceleration (0-60)
time"})
fig.show()

# Plotly GO scatter with different markers
usa = mpg[mpg['origin'] == 'usa']
japan = mpg[mpg['origin'] == 'japan']
europe = mpg[mpg['origin'] == 'europe']

fig = go.Figure(data=go.Scatter(x=usa['mpg'],
                                y=usa['acceleration'],
                                mode='markers',
                                marker={'color': 'blue'},
                                name="usa",
                                hovertemplate="MPG: %{x}
                                    <br>Acceleration: %{y}"))
fig.add_trace(go.Scatter(x=japan['mpg'],
                         y=japan['acceleration'],
                         mode='markers',
                         marker={'color': 'red'},
                         name="japan",
                         hovertemplate="MPG: %{x}
                             <br>Acceleration: %{y}"))
fig.add_trace(go.Scatter(x=europe['mpg'],
                         y=europe['acceleration'],
                         mode='markers',
                         marker={'color': 'green'},
                         name="europe",
                         hovertemplate="MPG: %{x}
                             <br>Acceleration: %{y}"))
fig.update_layout(title="Acceleration (0-60 time) vs MPG",
                  xaxis_title="MPG",
                  yaxis_title="Acceleration (0-60) time")
fig.show()
```

View this code on GitHub at https://github.com/alexkenan/pyviz/

Resources

[1] https://matplotlib.org/stable/gallery/color/named_colors.html

[2] https://matplotlib.org/stable/api/markers_api.html - module-matplotlib.markers

[3] https://matplotlib.org/stable/gallery/lines_bars_and_markers/linestyles.html

[4] https://seaborn.pydata.org/tutorial/color_palettes.html#palette-tutorial

[5] https://plotly.com/python/graph-objects/

[6] https://plotly.com/python/figure-factories/

[7] https://plotly.com/python/plotly-express/

[8] https://plotly.com/python/marker-style/#custom-marker-symbols

Line Plots

Introduction

Line plots connect points with lines to represent changes over time. They are very closely related to connected scatter plots, and any unit of time is usually on the x axis. In general, this type of chart emphasizes a trend over time. Connecting points (even if the points are not shown) implies a relationship, so do not connect unrelated points. For example, in a line plot for two different companies' stock price performance over a calendar year, it wouldn't make sense to connect dots between the two companies; rather, it makes the most sense to connect all of the points for Company A and all of the points for Company B, etc. Sparklines are line plots with no gridlines, markers, or axes ticks. They provide a good "pulse" to get a feel for performance by directionality (up, flat, or down). Sparklines are sometimes used to show stock price performance over the last 30 days, year, or other timeframe.

We will use the `flights` dataset from Seaborn to visualize line plots. Note that these date categories are not `datetime` objects; we will use Pandas functions to transform them into `datetime` objects later.

Column Name	**Datatype**	**Description**
year	`int`	Year as an integer
month	`str`	Month as a string
passengers	`int`	The number of passengers carried in that month and year

The Lie

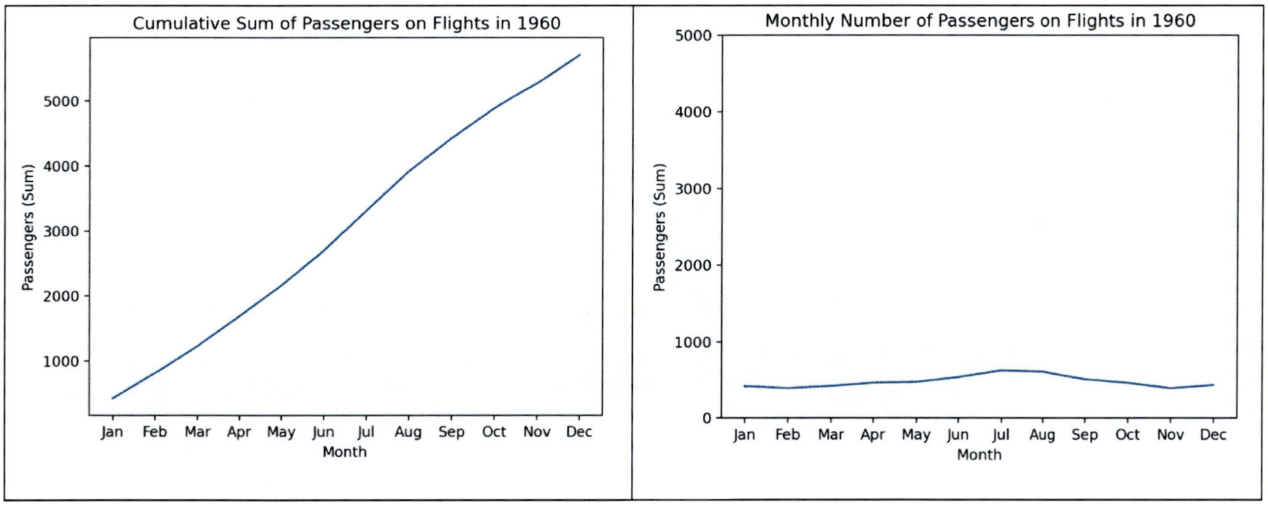

Line plots can be manipulated by adjusting axis limits, which manifests itself in two different ways: cumulative sums (left) and plain axis adjusting (right). On the left, the use of cumulative sum makes the data look like the passenger totals are relatively consistent month-over-month because the slope of the line is not easily discerned. Unless you have a specific reason, using cumulative sums forces a determined reader to try to analyze the change in the slope of the line to determine how much change has occurred in a specified time period. Depending on the field, a lot of your graph readers will have forgotten calculus, so this is an undesirable chart characteristic. On the right, the use of generous y-limits seems to reinforce the notion that the passenger totals are flat month-to-month.

Imports

```
import datetime
import matplotlib.pyplot as plt
import seaborn as sns
import plotly.express as px
import plotly.graph_objects as go
import plotly.io as pio
pio.renderers.default = "browser"
flights = sns.load_dataset("flights")
```

Matplotlib

In its simplest form, Matplotlib's `plt.plot()` only needs two points (or two `List`-like objects) passed as x coordinates and y coordinates to plot a line. Let's start by plotting `month` and `passengers`:

```
plt.plot(flights['month'], flights['passengers'])
plt.xlabel('Month')
plt.ylabel('Passengers')
plt.title('Flights')
plt.show()
```

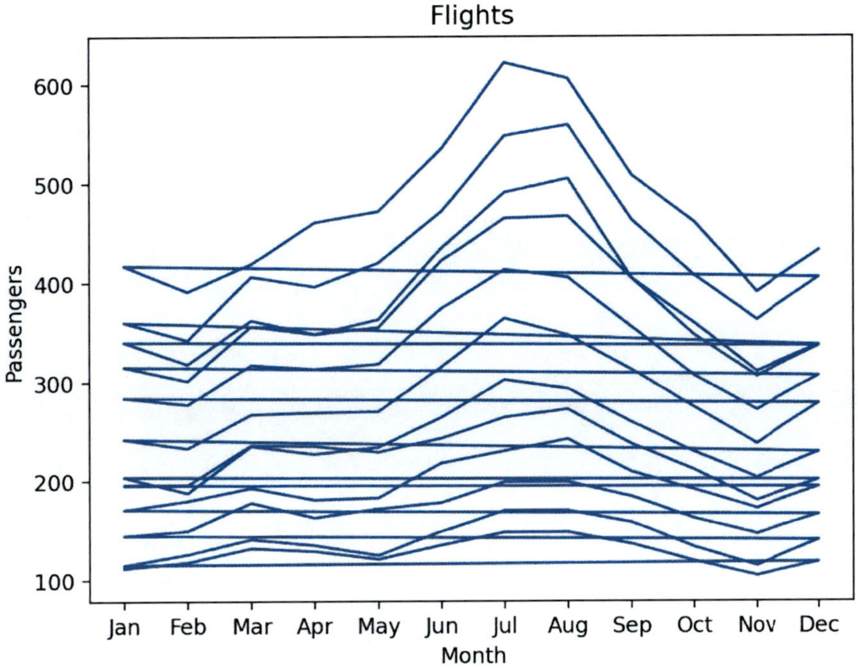

What happened? Remember, the `flights` dataset is a `list` of years, months, and passengers, so `plt.plot()` just saw a big `list` of `['Jan', 'Feb', 'Mar' … 'Dec', 'Jan', 'Feb', 'Mar', … 'Dec']` from 1949 to 1960. If it didn't try to connect December and January, we would have lines for each year. Let's look at only the last year, 1960:

```
flights_1960 = flights[flights['year'] == 1960]
plt.plot(flights_1960['month'], flights_1960['passengers'],
         label="1960")
plt.xlabel('Month')
plt.ylabel('Passengers')
plt.title('Flights')
plt.show()
```

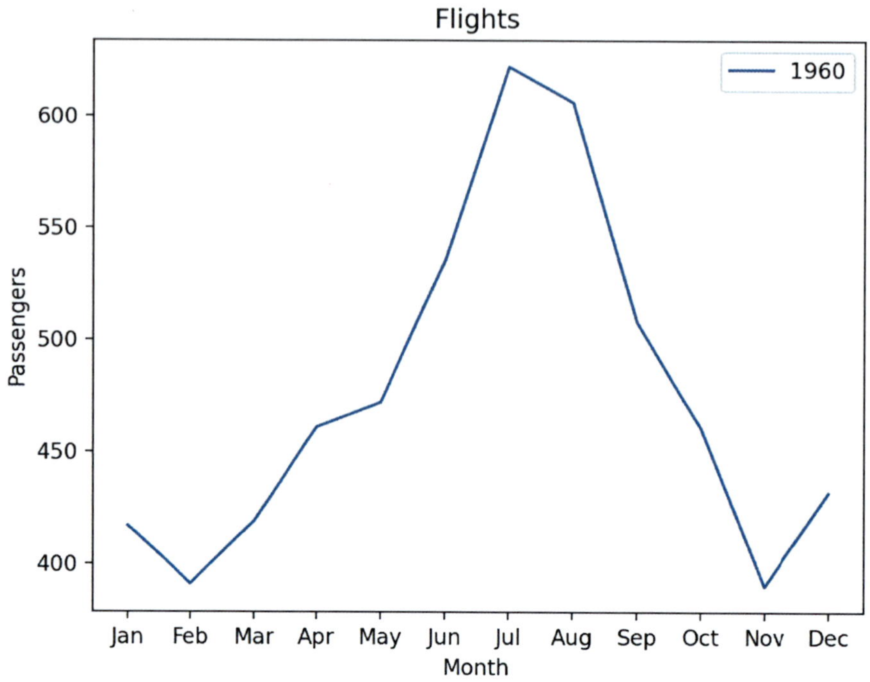

This chart is a zoomed-in version of the upper-most line on the last chart, and it is the same data shown in **The Lie** section. See how the visualization can lie? You could also argue that excessively zooming in is another lie since it emphasizes small changes. Often, the default axis ranges in Matplotlib are sufficient to show data without over- or under-emphasizing changes.

We can use the same slicing to get the passenger counts for 1956, 1957, 1958, and 1959. That way, we can compare the trend in passengers over the course of the year and over the course of the four years. We can also specify color and linestyle options to differentiate each line.

```
one = flights[flights['year'] == 1956]
two = flights[flights['year'] == 1957]
three = flights[flights['year'] == 1958]
four = flights[flights['year'] == 1959]
plt.plot(one['month'], one['passengers'], 'k-', label="1956")
plt.plot(two['month'], two['passengers'], 'b:', label="1957")
plt.plot(three['month'], three['passengers'], 'g--', label="1958")
plt.plot(four['month'], four['passengers'], 'r-.', label="1959")
plt.xlabel('Month')
plt.ylabel('Passengers')
plt.title('Flights')
plt.legend()
plt.show()
```

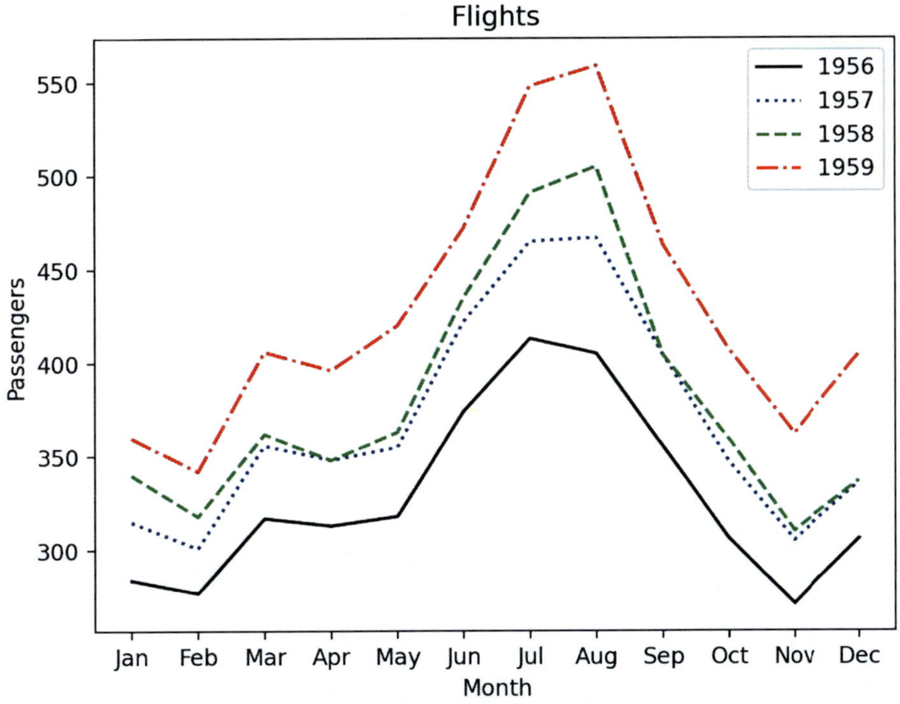

An area chart, which shades the area under a line, can be used to compare at least two lines. The area chart is an extension of line plots, and we can use them to compare the first year

(1949) to the last year (1960). We will use Matplotlib's `plt.fill_between()` function to fill between the line and the x axis (y=0).

```
first = flights[flights['year'] == 1949]
last = flights[flights['year'] == 1960]
plt.plot(last['month'], last['passengers'], 'b-', label="1960")
plt.fill_between(last['month'], last['passengers'],
                 color="b", alpha=0.30)
plt.plot(first['month'], first['passengers'], 'g-', label="1949")
plt.fill_between(first['month'], first['passengers'],
                 color="g", alpha=0.30)
plt.legend()
plt.xlabel('Month')
plt.ylabel('Passengers')
plt.title('Flights')
plt.show()
```

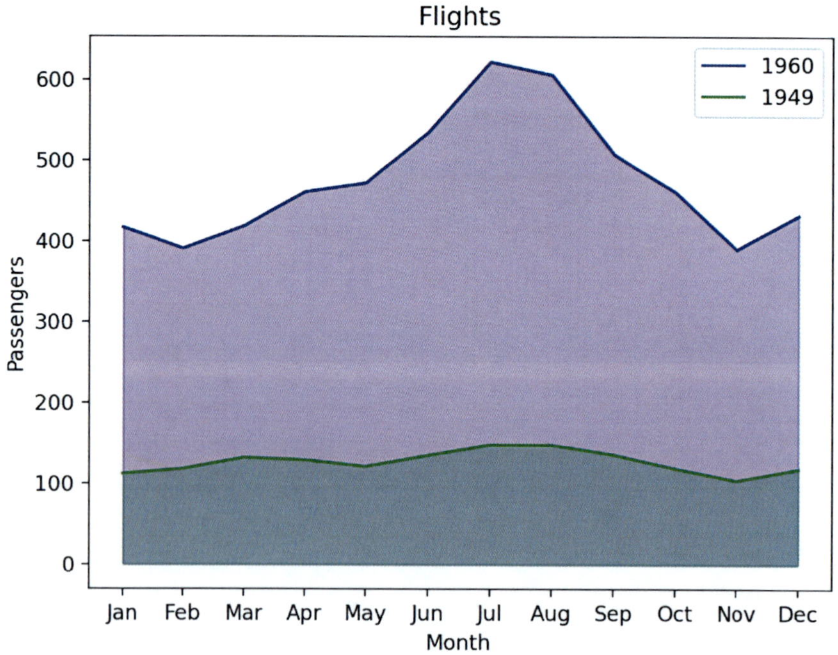

Area charts are also a good way to see a decline; for example, if we just showed 1960, we could highlight the July peak and February and November troughs. Let's move on to Seaborn.

Seaborn

We can see how Seaborn handles the first scenario we tested with Matplotlib by again just passing *month* as the x value:

```
sns.lineplot(data=flights, x='month', y='passengers')
plt.title('Flights')
plt.show()
```

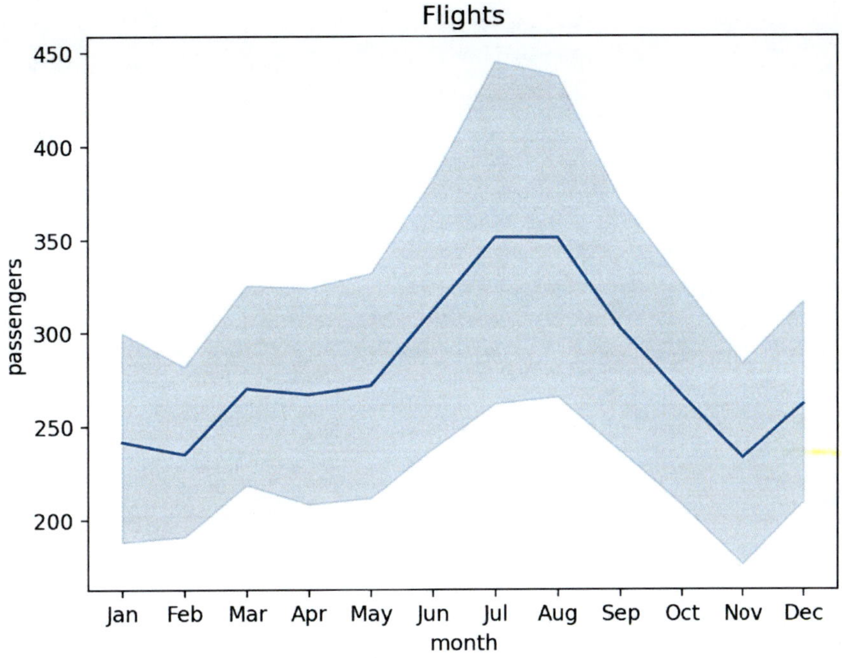

Seaborn treats the multiple values for the same month almost like error bars: the median year 1955 with the dark line, and shades through the rest of the years as the 95% confidence intervals.

Let's see how Seaborn handles displaying all of the years by month and passengers. You will see why this is not a recommended visualization! Since we are working with a DataFrame, adding color is as easy as passing `hue='year'` to `lineplot()`. We also need to adjust the x axis limits; otherwise, the legend will overlap with November and December.

```
sns.lineplot(data=flights, x='month', y='passengers', hue='year',
             palette='muted')
plt.xlim(-0.25, 14)
plt.title('Flights')
plt.show()
```

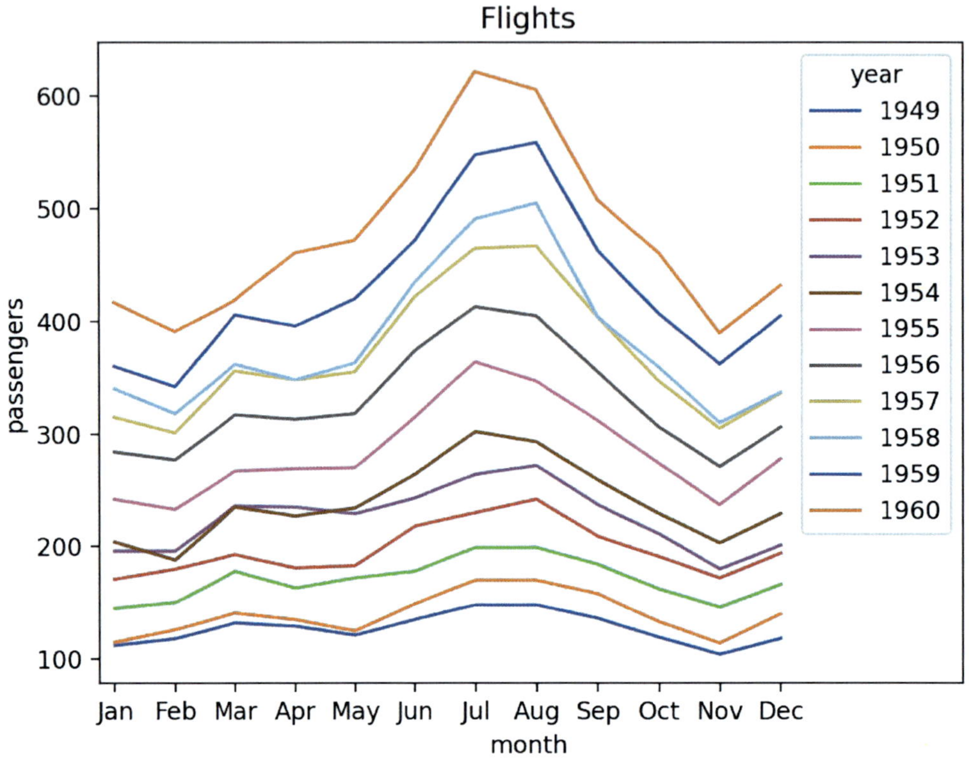

This visualization is busy, has too many (and repeated) colors, and does not intuitively and quickly convey the message that passengers go up over time. But, it shows that, when working with a DataFrame, Seaborn makes it easy to add color.

So far, we have not been able to make one continuous line from January 1949 to December 1960. Let's use Pandas' `apply` function and Python's `datetime` module to convert the month and year into a `datetime` object for plotting. (The `return` line should all be on one line; refer to the GitHub site if you can't get it to work.)

```
def create_date(row):
    return datetime.datetime.strptime('{}
        {}'.format(row['month'], row['year']), %b %Y').date()
```

This function uses datetime's `strptime()` function, which takes text and converts it to a datetime object. It creates a `str` with the month and the date and then converts it to a datetime. With the `create_date()` function created, we need to `apply` it across the entire DataFrame.

```
flights['date'] = flights.apply(create_date, axis=1)
```

Now, we can plot the `date` column as the x variable and keep `passengers` as the y variable:

```
flights['date'] = flights.apply(create_date, axis=1)
sns.lineplot(data=flights, x='date', y='passengers')
plt.title('Flights')
plt.show()
```

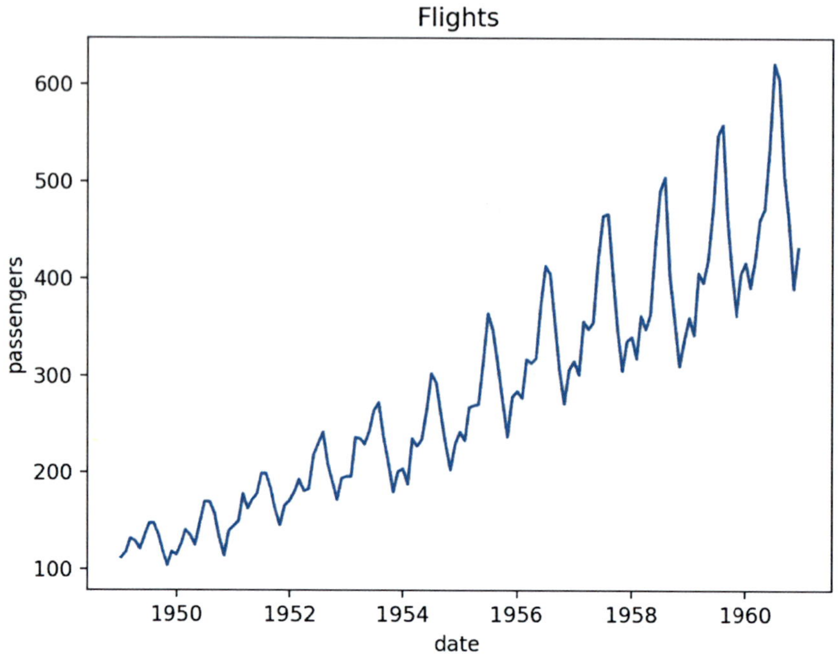

Seaborn does not have a built-in area plot function. There is a way to "cheat" by having Matplotlib use a Seaborn style template and use a Pandas `DataFrame.plot.area()` method, but this requires pivoting `flights`, creating new columns to get the stack order correct, and manually building a legend. You could also use the `plt.fill_between()` method we used earlier. Instead, we can use another Matplotlib plot method `plt.stackplot()` which accepts an x argument as a 1D array, a y argument as a 2D array, and an optional color array to plot an area plot.

```
first = flights[flights['year'] == 1949]
last = flights[flights['year'] == 1960]
y = [first['passengers'], last['passengers']]
plt.stackplot(first['month'], y, labels=['1949', '1960'],
              colors=['b', 'g'], alpha=0.30)
plt.legend()
plt.xlabel('Month')
plt.ylabel('Passengers')
plt.title('Flights')
plt.show()
```

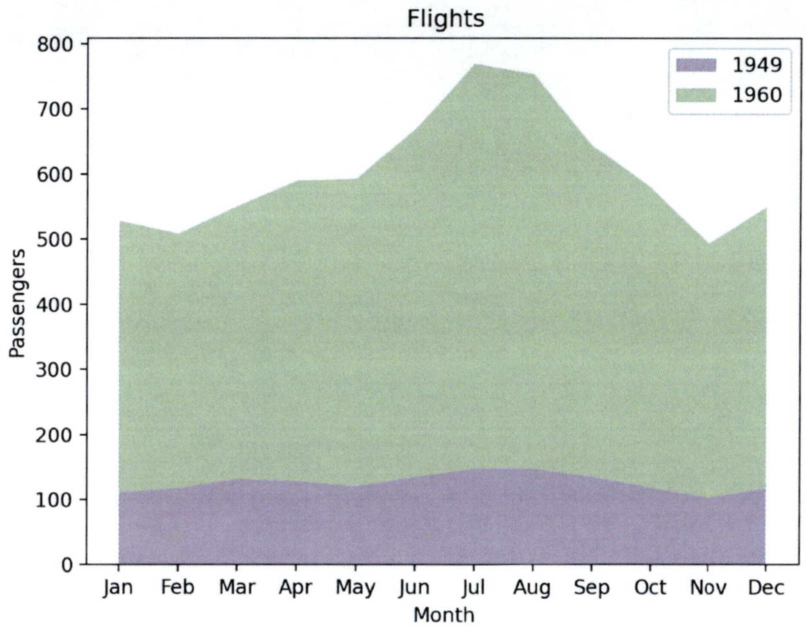

In general, area plots are fancy line plots, so you should almost always be able to create an area plot from a line plot. Next, we move to Plotly.

Plotly

Plotly Express has a `line()` function for basic line plots. For our `flights` dataset, Plotly Express has the same issue as Matplotlib if we just pass the basics:

```
fig = px.line(flights, x='month', y='passengers', title="Flights",
              hover_data=['year'])
fig.show()
```

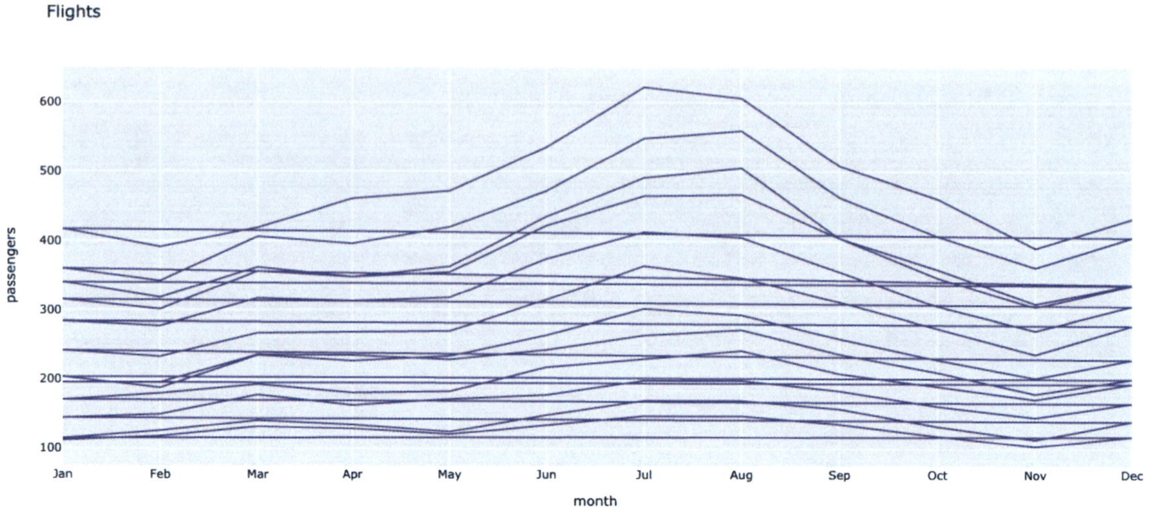

We need to fix the dates and pass `x='date'`, or we can pass `color='year'`:

```
fig = px.line(flights, x='month', y='passengers',
              title="Flights", hover_data=['year'], color='year')
fig.show()
```

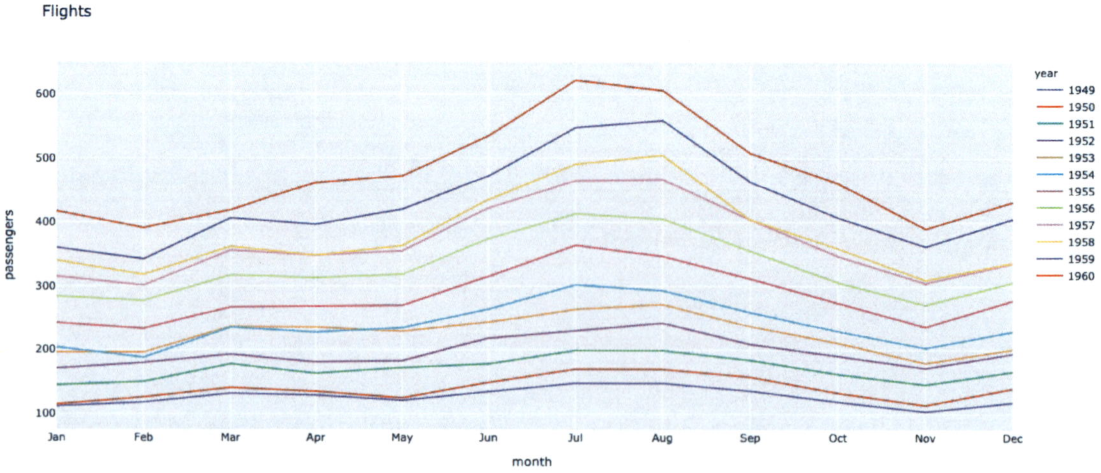

We can use the same reformatted dates to plot a continuous line from January 1949 to December 1960 (partially reproduced from earlier in the chapter):

```
def create_date(row):
    return datetime.datetime.strptime('{}
          {}'.format(row['month'], row['year']), '%b %Y').date()
flights['date'] = flights.apply(create_date, axis=1)
fig = px.line(flights, x='date', y='passengers', title="Flights")
fig.show()
```

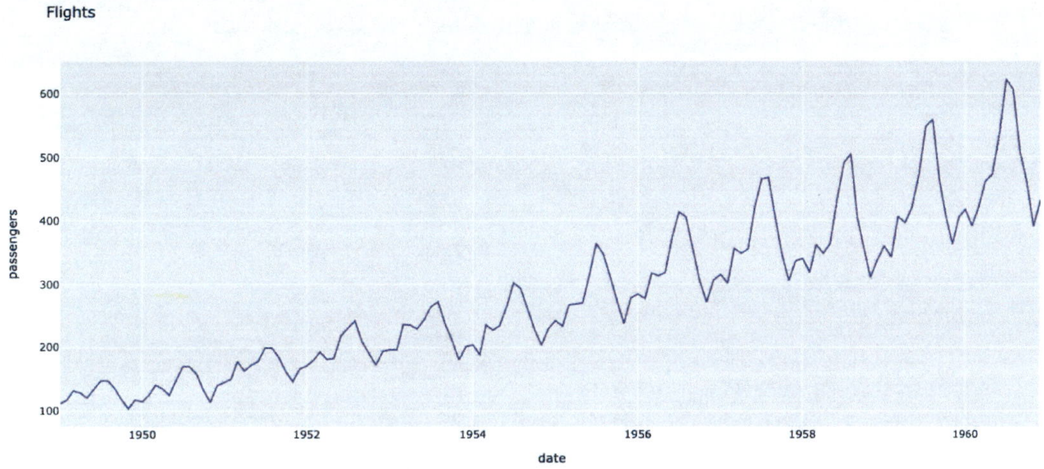

Plotly Express has an *area()* function for plotting areas. In our case, we need to create a new DataFrame with just data for the years 1949 and 1960.

```
first = flights[flights['year'] == 1949]
last = flights[flights['year'] == 1960]
new_df = first.append(last, ignore_index=True)
fig = px.area(new_df, x='month', y='passengers', line_group='year',
              title="Flights", color="year")
fig.show()
```

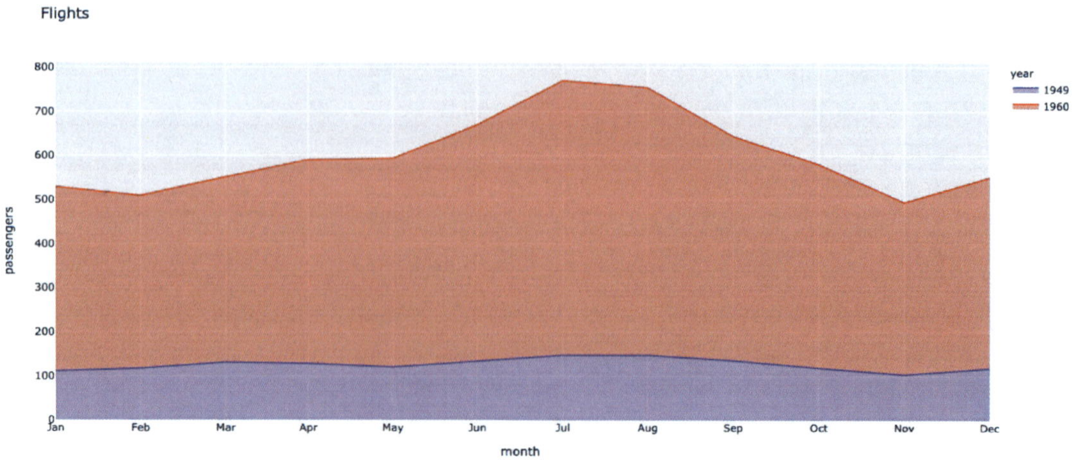

Plotly Graph Objects does not have a ready-made line function. Instead, we create a scatter plot with lines and no markers. Let's try showing the years 1952 and 1955 with different color options:

```
year1952 = flights[flights['year'] == 1952]
year1955 = flights[flights['year'] == 1955]
fig = go.Figure()
fig.add_trace(go.Scatter(x=year1952['month'],
                         y=year1952['passengers'],
                         mode='lines',
                         line={'color': '#2882BD',
                               'width': 2},
                         name="1952"))
fig.add_trace(go.Scatter(x=year1955['month'],
                         y=year1955['passengers'],
                         mode='lines',
                         line={'color': '#434343',
                               'width': 2},
                         name="1955"))
fig.update_layout(title='Flights',
                  xaxis_title="Month",
                  yaxis_title="Year")
fig.show()
```

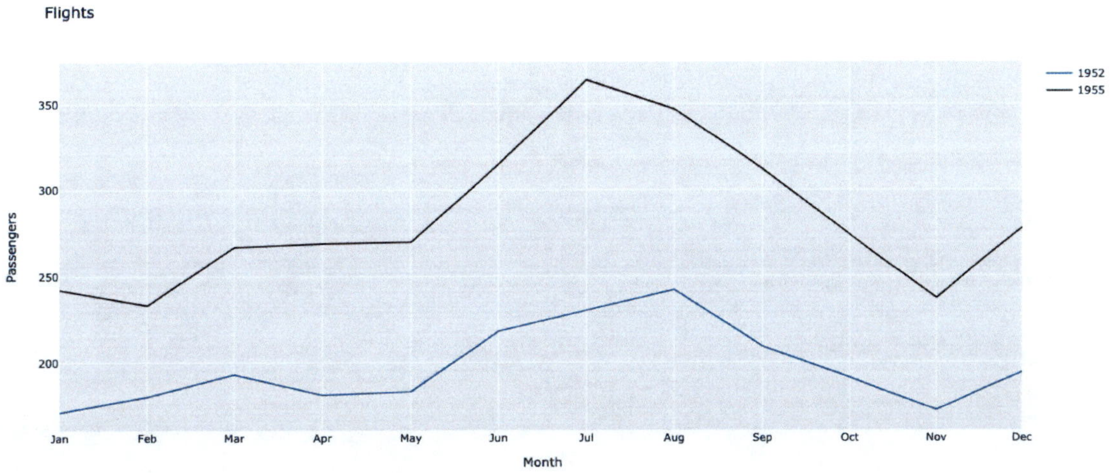

Lastly, we can fill down to the next y (`tonexty`) or to zero y (`tozeroy`) to create a filled area plot. Let's keep the years 1952 and 1955 and create the filled area plot:

```
year1952 = flights[flights['year'] == 1952]
year1955 = flights[flights['year'] == 1955]
fig = go.Figure()
fig.add_trace(go.Scatter(x=year1952['month'],
                         y=year1952['passengers'],
                         mode='lines',
                         line={'color': '#2882BD',
                               'width': 2},
                         name="1952",
                         fill="tozeroy"))
fig.add_trace(go.Scatter(x=year1955['month'],
                         y=year1955['passengers'],
                         mode='lines',
                         line={'color': '#434343',
                               'width': 2},
                         name="1955",
                         fill="tozeroy"))
fig.update_layout(title='Flights',
                  xaxis_title="Month",
                  yaxis_title="Passengers")
fig.show()
```

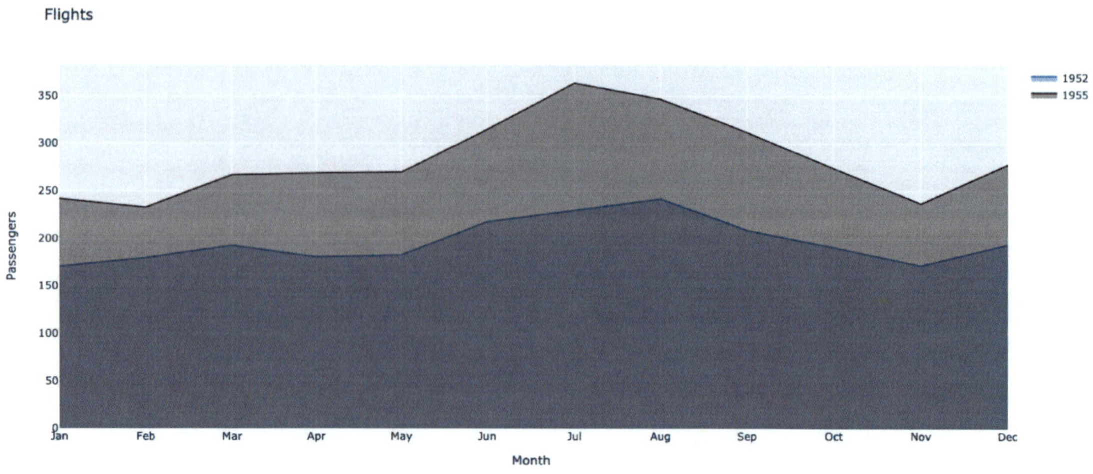

Summary

Line plots are mostly used to track a continuous variable over time. In Plotly's case, the line plot is a specific version of a scatter plot with no markers and a defined line. Sparklines can be created by removing any axis tick markers and keeping the default x and y axis limits.

Another potential downside of line plots is that zooming in or out can dilute the message. Zooming too far in may make small perturbations look very large, and zooming too far out may make large changes look very small. Usually, the default zoom is sufficient, but watch out for the deceptive zoom pitfall. Finally, don't use cumulative sums unless you have a good reason. If you use cumulative sums, this can have the effect of hiding downward trends because it forces the reader to analyse the change in slope, not just the upwards and "rightwards" direction of the line.

```
import datetime
import matplotlib.pyplot as plt
import seaborn as sns
import plotly.express as px
import plotly.graph_objects as go
import plotly.io as pio
pio.renderers.default = "browser"
flights = sns.load_dataset("flights")
plt.style.use('default')

def create_date(row):
        return datetime.datetime.strptime('{}
                 {}'.format(row['month'],
                 row['year']), '%b %Y').date()

# Matplotlib linestyles
one = flights[flights['year'] == 1956]
two = flights[flights['year'] == 1957]
three = flights[flights['year'] == 1958]
four = flights[flights['year'] == 1959]
plt.plot(one['month'], one['passengers'], 'k-', label="1956")
plt.plot(two['month'], two['passengers'], 'b:', label="1957")
plt.plot(three['month'], three['passengers'], 'g--', label="1958")
plt.plot(four['month'], four['passengers'], 'r-.', label="1959")
plt.xlabel('Month')
plt.ylabel('Passengers')
plt.title('Flights')
plt.legend()
plt.show()

# Seaborn with fixed dates
flights['date'] = flights.apply(create_date, axis=1)
sns.lineplot(data=flights, x='date', y='passengers')
plt.title('Flights')
plt.show()

# Plotly Express with corrected dates
flights['date'] = flights.apply(create_date, axis=1)
```

```
fig = px.line(flights, x='date', y='passengers', title="Flights")
fig.show()

# Plotly Graph Objects
year1952 = flights[flights['year'] == 1952]
year1955 = flights[flights['year'] == 1955]
fig = go.Figure()
fig.add_trace(go.Scatter(x=year1952['month'],
                         y=year1952['passengers'],
                         mode='lines',
                         line={'color': '#2882BD',
                               'width': 2},
                         name="1952"))
fig.add_trace(go.Scatter(x=year1955['month'],
                         y=year1955['passengers'],
                         mode='lines',
                         line={'color': '#434343',
                               'width': 2},
                         name="1955"))
fig.update_layout(title='Flights',
                  xaxis_title="Month",
                  yaxis_title="Passengers")
fig.show()
```

View this code on GitHub at https://github.com/alexkenan/pyviz/

Resources

[1] https://matplotlib.org/tutorials/introductory/pyplot.html

[2] https://seaborn.pydata.org/generated/seaborn.lineplot.html

[3] https://plotly.com/python/line-charts/

Histograms

Introduction

A histogram is a representation of the distribution of numerical data that is typically grouped into ranges called bins. These bins are typically consecutive and non-overlapping (e.g. 1-3, 4-6, etc); for a horizontal (standard) histogram, bins are usually placed on the x axis, and the count of values in each bin is displayed on the y axis as a bar. For a vertical histogram, the axes are flipped. Some histograms use the area of the bar for each bin to represent data. This can get confusing for a reader, and it relies on a reader understanding the differences in the area between two rectangles that look similar; therefore, it is a best practice to use bins of the same width. This way, the height of the bar is the only indicator of how frequently or infrequently data in that bin occurs.

Some histograms have multiple categories overlaid onto the same graph using color to differentiate categories. This technique can make histograms crowded, so this chapter will focus on single, continuous variables represented by a histogram. Next chapter, we will discuss box plots and violin plots, which are applied histograms.

We will use the `tips` dataset from Seaborn to explore histograms. This dataset contains information from a waiter in a restaurant about the tips that he received over two to three months in 1990:

Column Name	Datatype	Description
total_bill	`float`	Total bill including cost of the meal, tax, and tip, in USD
tip	`float`	The tip left by the diners
sex	`str`	The sex of the diner. Either `Male` or `Female`
smoker	`str`	Whether the diner was seated in the smoking section. Either `Yes` or `No`
day	`str`	Day of the week that the meal occurred. Either `Thur`, `Fri`, `Sat`, or `Sun`
time	`str`	Time of day that the meal occurred. Either `Lunch` or `Dinner`
size	`int`	The size of the party that ate the meal

The Lie

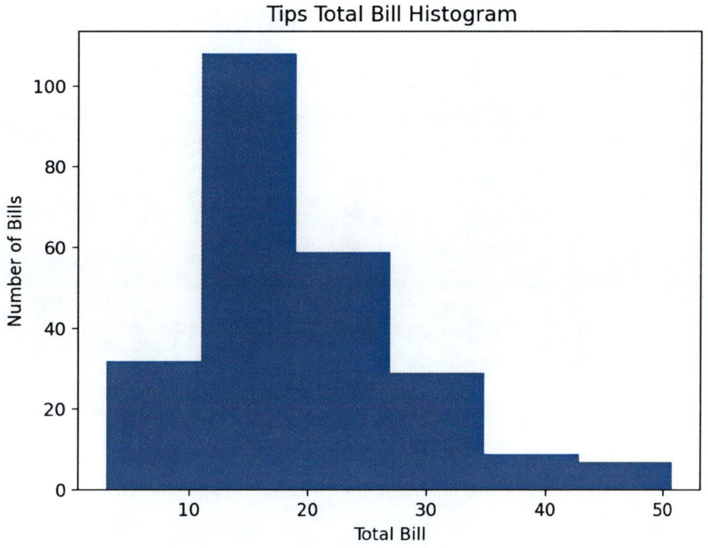

Bin size can have a big effect on a histogram. Here, the histogram shows a slightly left-skewed normal distribution of `tips`. Bin size can hide interesting quirks, though. If we make the bin size larger, we see some small jumps:

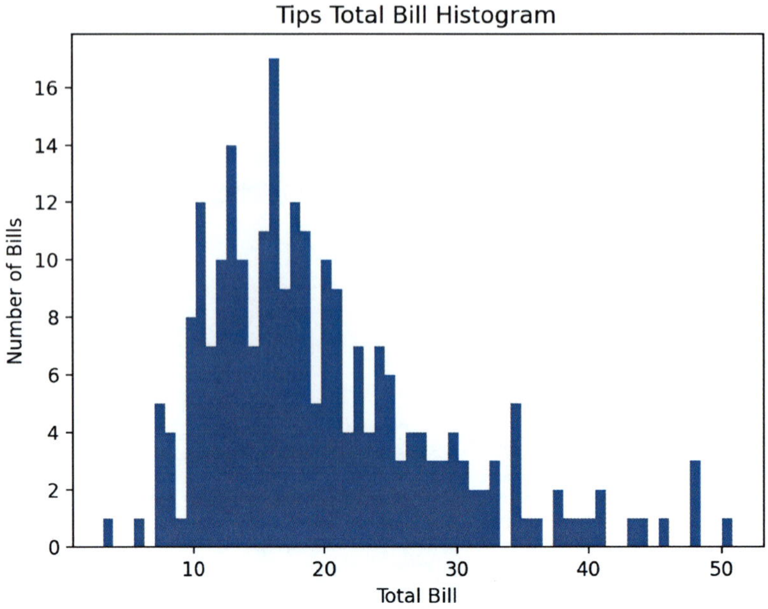

The total bill has more frequency at $35 and $48 than previously expected; our original forced bin size smoothed over this data to fit the small bin size constraint. It is often worthwhile to experiment with a histogram's bin size to strike a good balance between smoothing data, hiding data, and telling a compelling story. Missing the $35 and $48 amounts is not that significant here, but there could be more bimodal distributions hiding in your histograms if you aren't careful with bin size!

Imports

```
import matplotlib.pyplot as plt
import seaborn as sns
import plotly.express as px
import plotly.graph_objects as go
import plotly.io as pio
pio.renderers.default = "browser"
tips = sns.load_dataset('tips')
```

Matplotlib

Matplotlib's histogram function is called `plt.hist()`. At minimum, we can pass a single `list`-like object, and Matplotlib will automatically create a histogram with 10 bins as a default. We can use the parameter `bins` to select the number of bins; let's see a histogram of `total_bill` with 20 bins:

```
plt.hist(tips['total_bill'], bins=20)
plt.xlabel('Total Bill')
plt.ylabel('Number of Bills')
plt.title('Tips Total Bill Histogram')
plt.show()
```

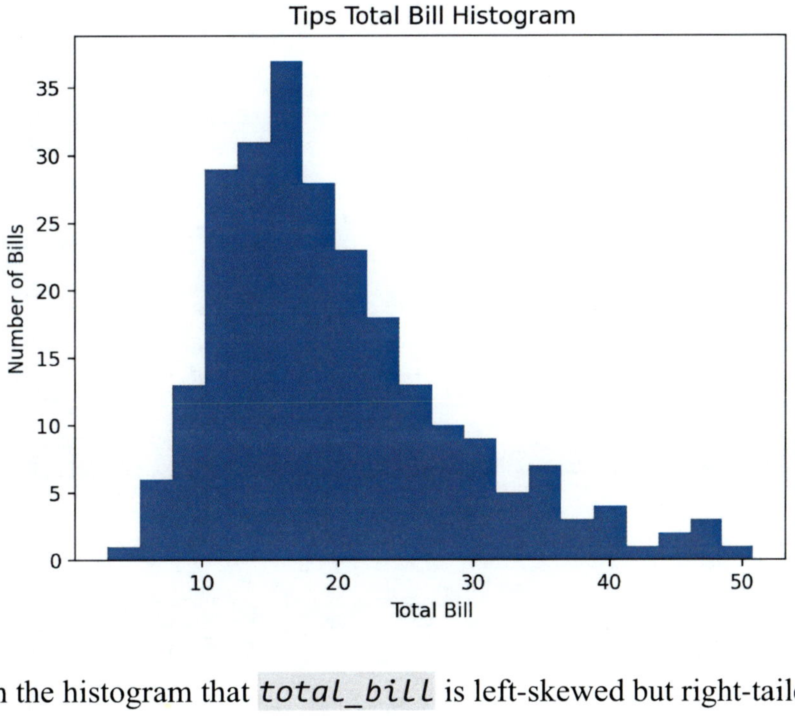

We can see from the histogram that `total_bill` is left-skewed but right-tailed; most bills come out to around \$17, but some can be in the \$40-\$50 range.

Matplotlib's histogram function also has the ability to create distribution functions. For each bin in a cumulative distribution function (CDF), the CDF shows the summed probability of that bin and all of the bins before it. A distribution or density function shows the probability of that particular bin occurring. Let's see both:

Distribution Function

```
plt.hist(tips['tip'],
         cumulative=False,
         density=True, bins=20)
plt.xlabel('Tip')
plt.ylabel('Probability')
plt.title('Tips Histogram')
plt.show()
```

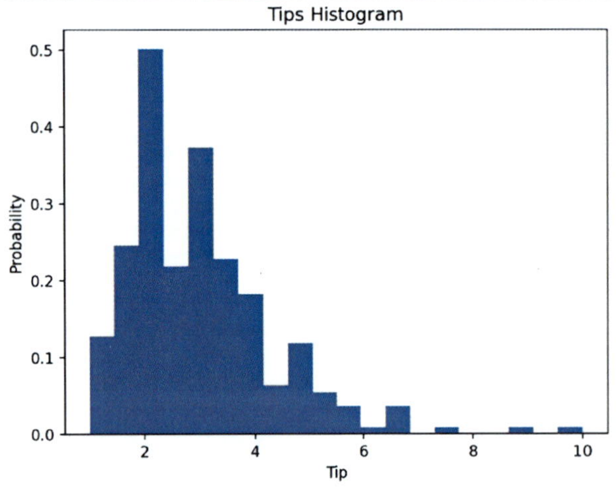

Cumulative Distribution Function

```
plt.hist(tips['tip'],
         cumulative=True,
         density=True, bins=20)
plt.xlabel('Tip')
plt.ylabel('Probability')
plt.title('Tips Histogram')
plt.show()
```

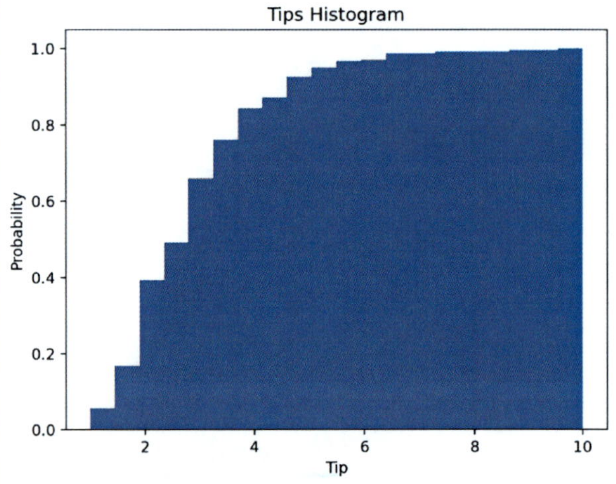

The left figure shows that a $2.25 tip is likely to occur about 50% of the time, and the figure on the right shows that 80% of tips are below $4.

There are several other parameters that we did not use [1]:

`histtype`	The type of histogram. One of `bar`, `barstacked`, `step`, `stepfilled`
`align`	The alignment of the bars. One of `left`, `center`, `right`
`orientation`	The orientation of the histogram. Either `vertical` or `horizontal`
`log`	Sets a log scale if `True`
`color`	Either a single color or a color sequence
`stacked`	Stacks bars on top of each other if there are multiple histograms with overlapping data

Seaborn

Seaborn has a function called `histplot()` that plots histograms for us. Reminder: Seaborn needs to be version 0.11.0 or higher; if you see an error like

`AttributeError: module 'seaborn' has no attribute 'histplot'`

you will need to `pip install seaborn --upgrade` to get the latest version.

Let's get to the basic Seaborn histogram:

```
sns.histplot(data=tips, x='total_bill')
plt.xlabel('Total Bill')
plt.title('Tips Total Bill Histogram')
plt.show()
```

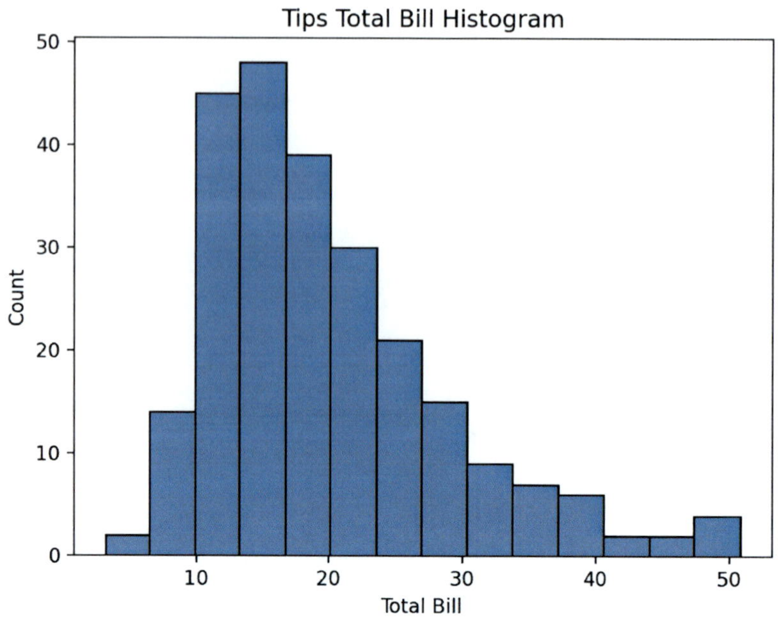

The Seaborn histogram function gives us a nice, thin border on each bar which helps to differentiate the bars.

We can overlay the lunch and dinner data with color with the *hue* parameter:

```
sns.histplot(data=tips, x='total_bill', hue="time")
plt.xlabel('Total Bill')
plt.title('Tips Total Bill Histogram')
plt.show()
```

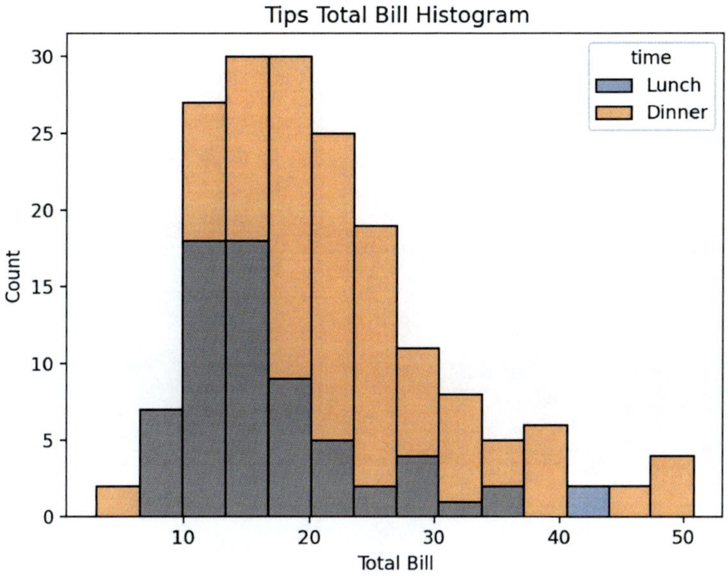

We could add a `multiple="stack"` parameter to eliminate the weird overlap color, but this would put Lunch on top of Dinner and imply that Lunch had a bigger occurence than Dinner, which is not true.

Seaborn can also display density functions. Up to now, we have been using `histplot()`; this function manipulates `displot()` for us under the hood. Using `displot()` directly, we can customize more parameters:

```
sns.displot(tips, x='total_bill', kind="kde", fill=True)
plt.xlabel('Total Bill')
plt.ylabel('Probability')
plt.title('Tips Total Bill Histogram')
plt.show()
```

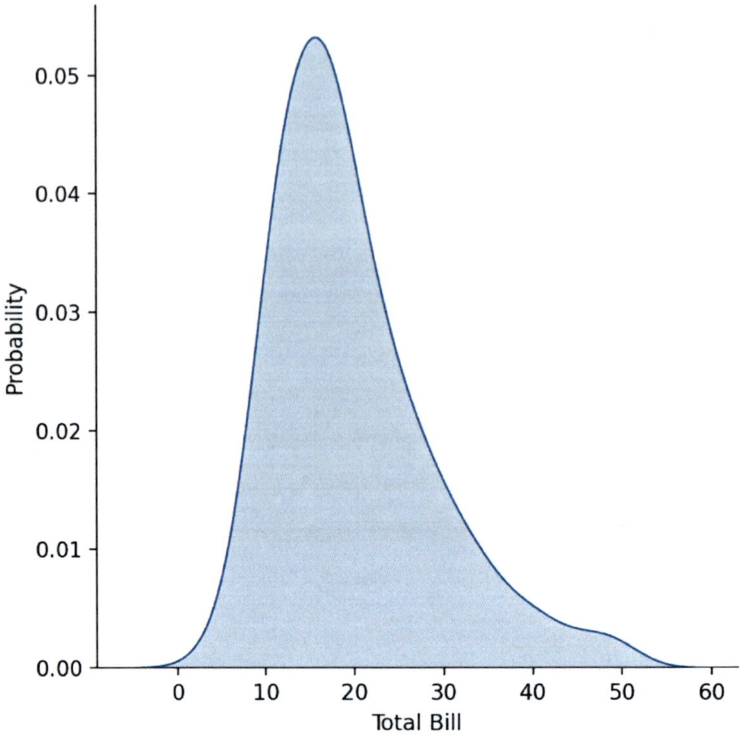

Seaborn shows a continuous function rather than plotting bars like Matplotlib does. It can even show two or more density functions on the same graph:

```
sns.displot(tips, x='total_bill', hue="sex", multiple="stack",
            kind="kde", fill=True)
plt.xlabel('Total Bill')
plt.ylabel('Probability')
plt.show()
```

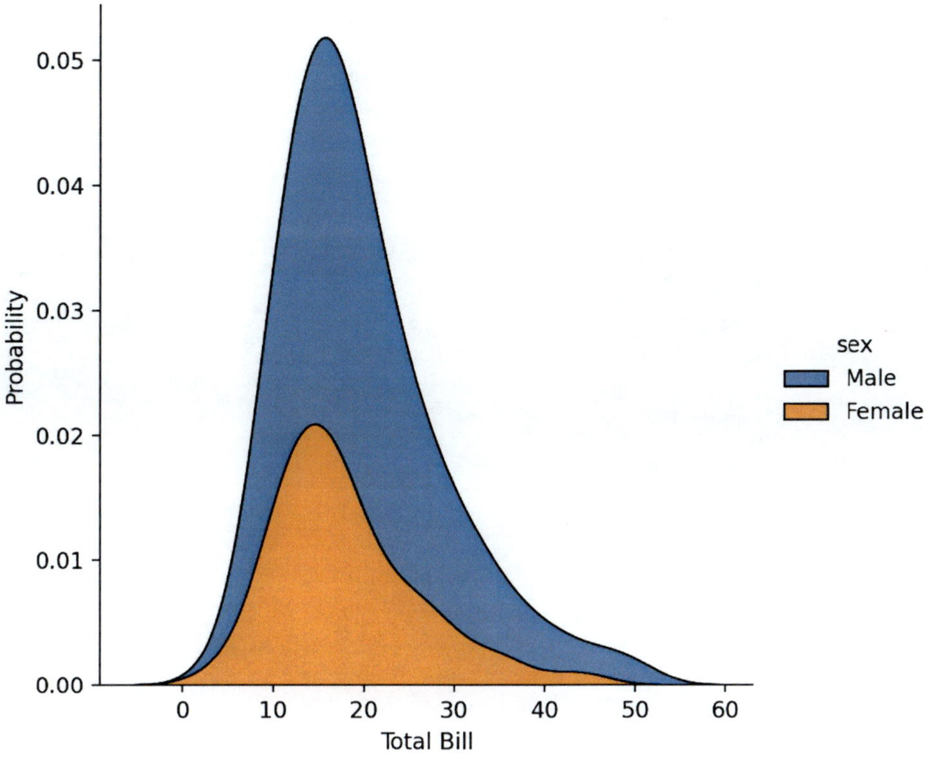

Seaborn offers lots of combined plotting options with *displot()* that we will explore in a later chapter. For now, let's move on to Plotly. For a more in-depth tutorial on histograms, visit Seaborn's distribution tutorial [2].

Plotly

Plotly Express has a *histogram()* method that almost exactly mirrors Seaborn's *histplot()* method. Here is a basic histogram:

```
fig = px.histogram(tips, x='total_bill', nbins=20)
fig.update_layout(title='Tips Total Bill Histogram',
                  xaxis_title="Total Bill",
                  yaxis_title="Count")
fig.show()
```

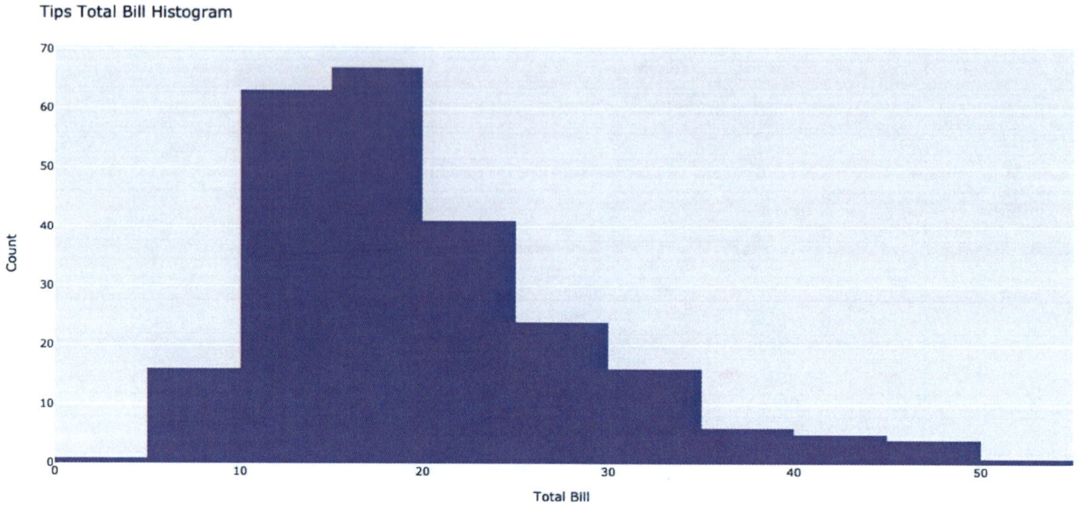

Plotly offers similar CDF functionality as well; you can pass different parameters to `histnorm`:

Nothing	Default behavior of counting samples in the bin
`percent` or `probability`	Represents the fraction or percent of samples in each bin
`density`	Sums all of bar areas to equal the total number of sample points, not the probability
`probability density`	Calculates the probability density function for all points

```
fig = px.histogram(tips, x='total_bill', nbins=20,
                   histnorm="probability")
fig.update_layout(title='Tips Total Bill Histogram',
                  xaxis_title="Total Bill",
                  yaxis_title="Probability")
fig.show()
```

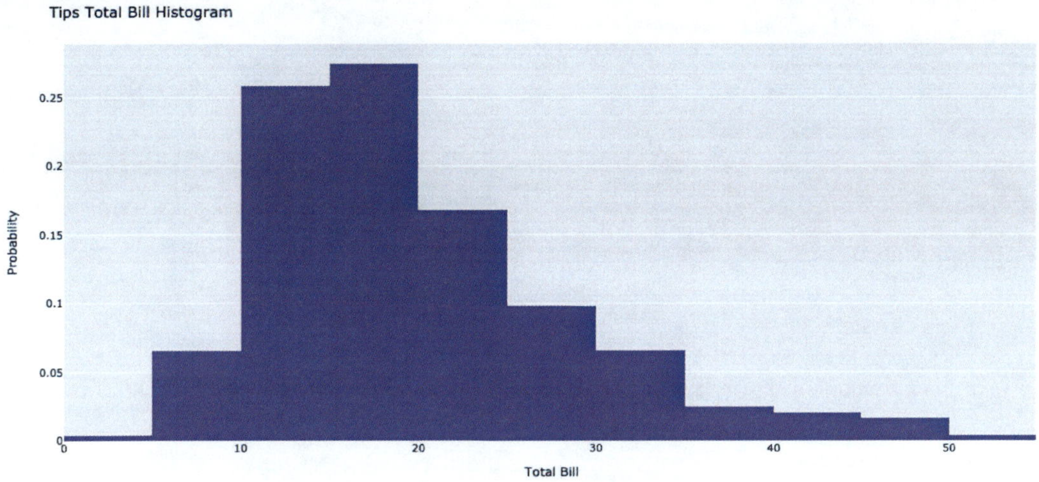

Plotly Express can also overlay two or more histograms:

```
fig = px.histogram(tips, x='tip', color='time')
fig.update_layout(barmode='overlay',
                  title='Tips Total Bill Histogram',
                  xaxis_title="Total Bill",
                  yaxis_title="Count")
fig.show()
```

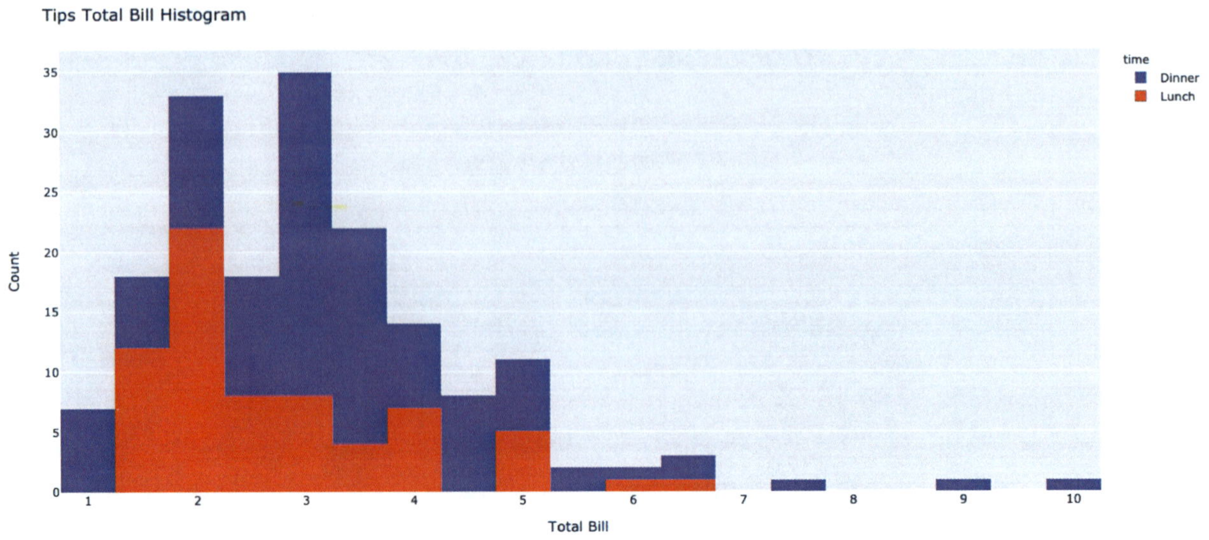

Double-clicking on Dinner or Lunch in the legend allows you to isolate to just that trace; this confirms that Lunch is laid on top of Dinner and not stacked.

Lastly, Graph Objects are available for a more customized histogram. Plotly Express is likely to have most tools you will need for histograms, so we won't spend much time on histograms via Graph Objects.

```
fig = go.Figure(data=[go.Histogram(x=tips['total_bill'])])
fig.update_layout(title='Tips Total Bill Histogram',
                  xaxis_title="Total Bill",
                  yaxis_title="Count")
fig.show()
```

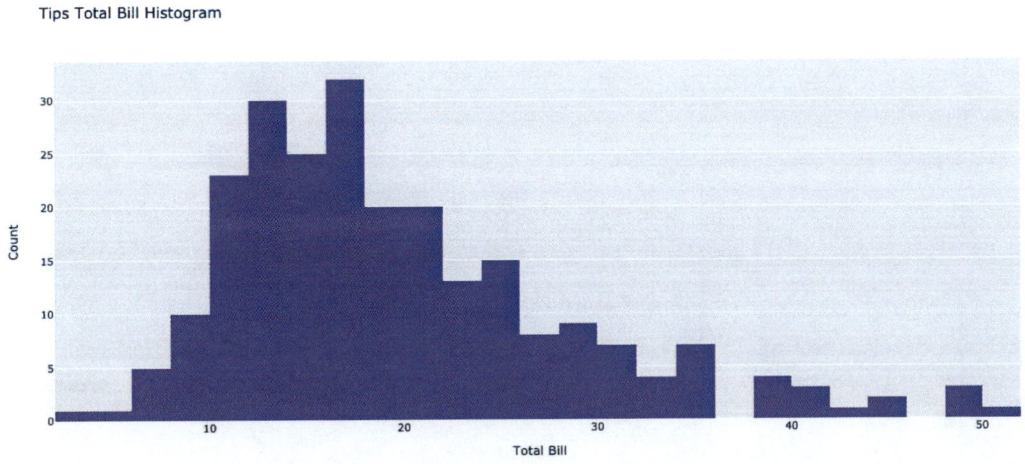

Plotly also offers chart options that combine scatter plots, bar charts, histograms, and more. We will cover those combined plots in a later chapter.

Summary

Histograms are used for showing the distribution of a numerical variable. This distribution can be grouped by a categorical variable, and color can be used to overlay different distributions on the graph. A histogram is like a bar chart for one numerical variable, with the bin ranges representing one axis, and the count within the bin representing the height of the bar on the other axis. Be careful to not go overboard with showing too much data: you want to show enough information that your readers can glance at the visualization and interpret the message.

Examples for Each Library

```
import matplotlib.pyplot as plt
import seaborn as sns
import plotly.express as px
import plotly.graph_objects as go
import plotly.io as pio
pio.renderers.default = "browser"
tips = sns.load_dataset('tips')
plt.style.use('default')

# Matplotlib
plt.hist(tips['total_bill'], bins=20)
plt.xlabel('Total Bill')
plt.ylabel('Number of Bills')
plt.title('Tips Total Bill Histogram')
plt.show()

# Seaborn multiple probability function histograms
sns.displot(tips, x='total_bill', hue="sex", multiple="stack",
            kind="kde", fill=True)
plt.xlabel('Total Bill')
plt.ylabel('Probability')
plt.show()

# Plotly Express histogram
fig = px.histogram(tips, x='total_bill', nbins=20)
fig.update_layout(title='Tips Total Bill Histogram',
                  xaxis_title="Total Bill",
                  yaxis_title="Count")
fig.show()

# Plotly Graph Objects histogram
fig = go.Figure(data=[go.Histogram(x=tips['total_bill'])])
fig.update_layout(title='Tips Total Bill Histogram',
                  xaxis_title="Total Bill",
fig.show()
```

View this code on GitHub at https://github.com/alexkenan/pyviz/

Resources

[1] https://matplotlib.org/stable/api/_as_gen/matplotlib.pyplot.hist.html

[2] https://seaborn.pydata.org/tutorial/distributions.html

[3] https://plotly.com/python/histograms/

Box Plots and Violin Plots

Introduction

Histograms are nice, but sometimes we need to show more of the data spread to tell our story. For this requirement, we can use the box plot and/or the violin plot. A box plot is an applied histogram that shows the five summary statistics: minimum value, 25th percentile, median, 75th percentile, and maximum value. A box plot is sometimes called a box-and-whisker plot because it looks like a box (showing the 25th percentile, median, and 75th percentile) with whiskers (showing the minimum and maximum value). Oftentimes, a box plot is drawn to remove outliers (typically those that are 1.5x higher than the 75th percentile or 1.5x lower than the 25th percentile). A violin plot is like a box plot with a histogram (or, more precisely, a kernel density plot) drawn on the side to show the actual distribution; a violin plot also usually shows the actual maximum and minimum values in the dataset without filtering any potential outliers.

We will use a dataset of 2012 SAT results for various New York high schools [1].

Column Name	Datatype	Description
DBN	`str`	A school identifier unique to each school
School Name	`str`	The name of the school
Number of Test Takers	`int`	Total number of test takers
Critical Reading Mean	`int`	The average Critical Reading section score
Mathematics Mean	`int`	The average Mathematics section score
Writing Mean	`int`	The average Writing section score

The Lie

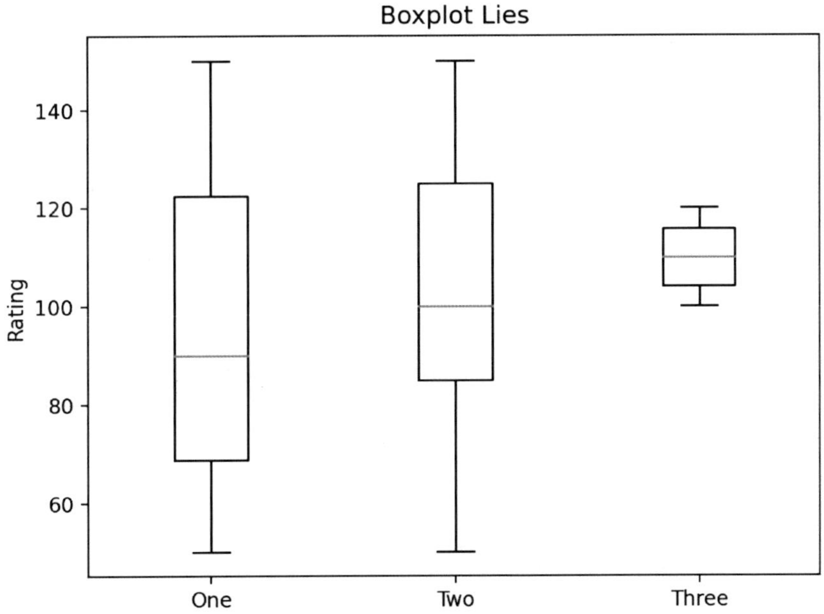

A box plot is a summary of information; by definition, this means that we are losing the granularity of some of the data. Because we just see the range and potential outliers, we have no idea what a box plot's sample size is. Box Plot One and Box Plot Two look roughly the same, but they are both hiding secrets. Which one has a larger sample size? Of the three box plots, which data do you think is the best?

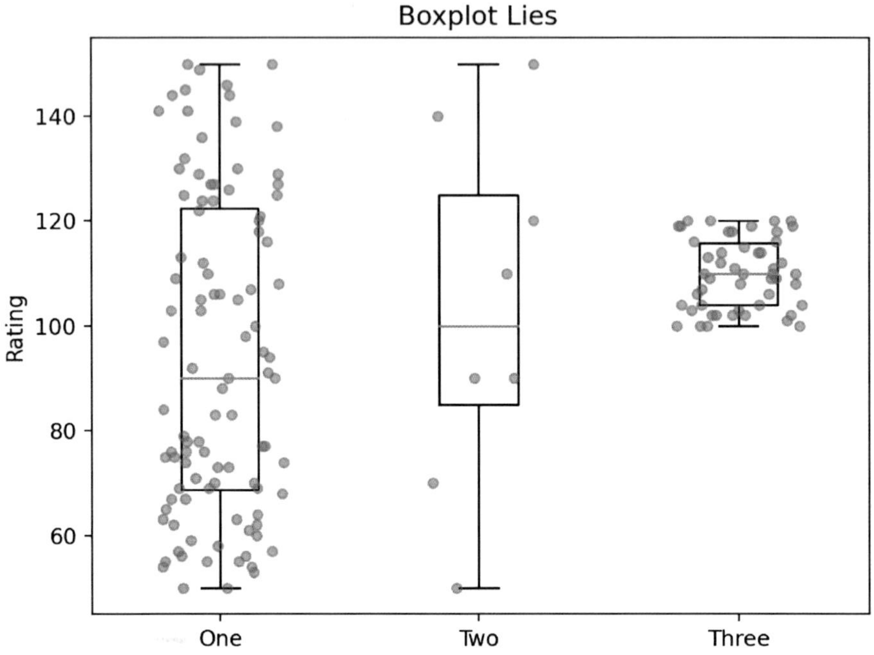

Box Plot Three has the tightest data distribution, Box Plot One has the most spread and the most datapoints, and Box Plot Two is somewhere in the middle. Be careful if you only receive box plot data summaries because they can hide crucial data distribution information in the name of simplicity and statistical representation. Even though Box Plot One and Box Plot Two look very similar, you should be more suspicious of Box Plot Two given its smaller sample size.

Imports

```
import matplotlib.pyplot as plt
import seaborn as sns
import plotly.express as px
import plotly.graph_objects as go
import pandas as pd
import plotly.io as pio
pio.renderers.default = "browser"

df = pd.read_csv('https://raw.githubusercontent.com/
                 alexkenan/pyviz/main/datasets/sat.csv')
df.dropna(inplace=True)
```

There are some blank entries in the data, so let's `drop` them with Pandas' `dropna()` function. We could edit the spreadsheet to remove these blanks, but it is always good practice to clean data since you can't always control the data source! The `pd.read_csv()` URL should be on one line in your program; the line break is for page formatting purposes.

Matplotlib

Matplotlib's `boxplot()` function will create a box plot for us. There are a few customizable parameters, but let's see a basic box plot first:

```
data = [df['Critical Reading Mean'],
        df['Mathematics Mean'],
        df['Writing Mean']]
plt.boxplot(data)
plt.xticks(ticks=[1, 2, 3], labels=['Reading', 'Math', 'Writing'])
plt.title('Boxplots for NY SAT Testing')
plt.ylabel('Score')
plt.show()
```

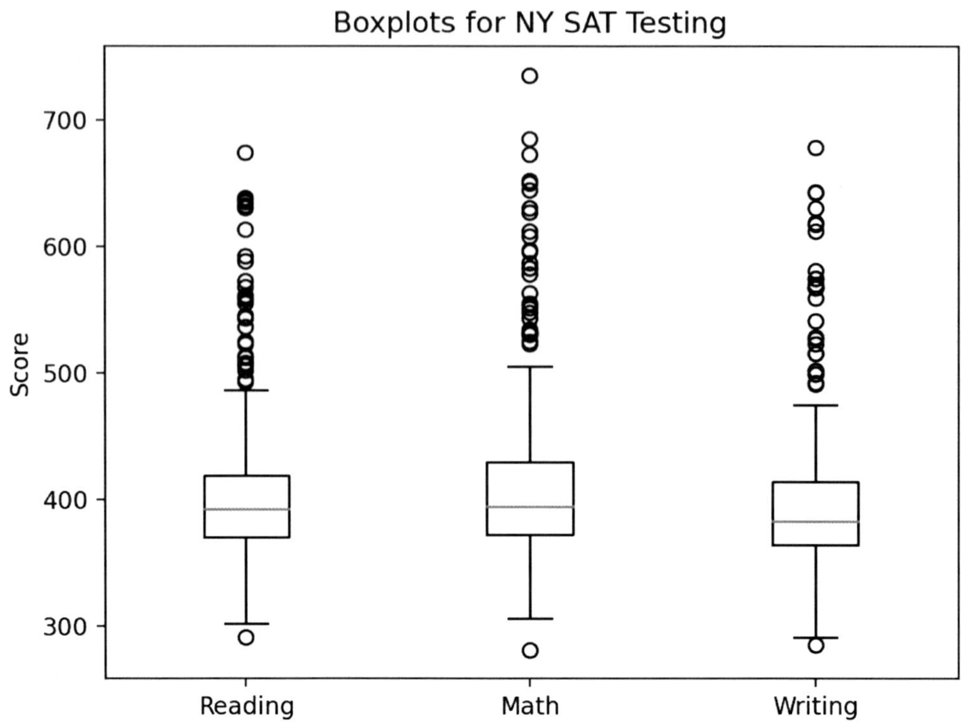

If we didn't mess with the x axis, the plot would show 1, 2, 3 instead of Reading, Math, Writing. It wouldn't be the end of the world, but we can make it look nice regardless. There are a few customizable parameters to highlight: `notch=True` sets a notch (or belt) around the box, we can change the outlier symbol with `sym`, and we can adjust the outlier range (default is that an outlier is 1.5x above or below the 75th or 25th percentile, respectively) with `whis`. We can also pass `vert=False` to get horizontal box plots, but then we would have to change our y axis ticks.

```
data = [df['Critical Reading Mean'],
        df['Mathematics Mean'],
        df['Writing Mean']]
plt.boxplot(data, notch=True, sym='+', whis=3.5)
plt.xticks(ticks=[1, 2, 3], labels=['Reading', 'Math', 'Writing'])
plt.title('Boxplots for NY SAT Testing')
plt.ylabel('Score')
plt.show()
```

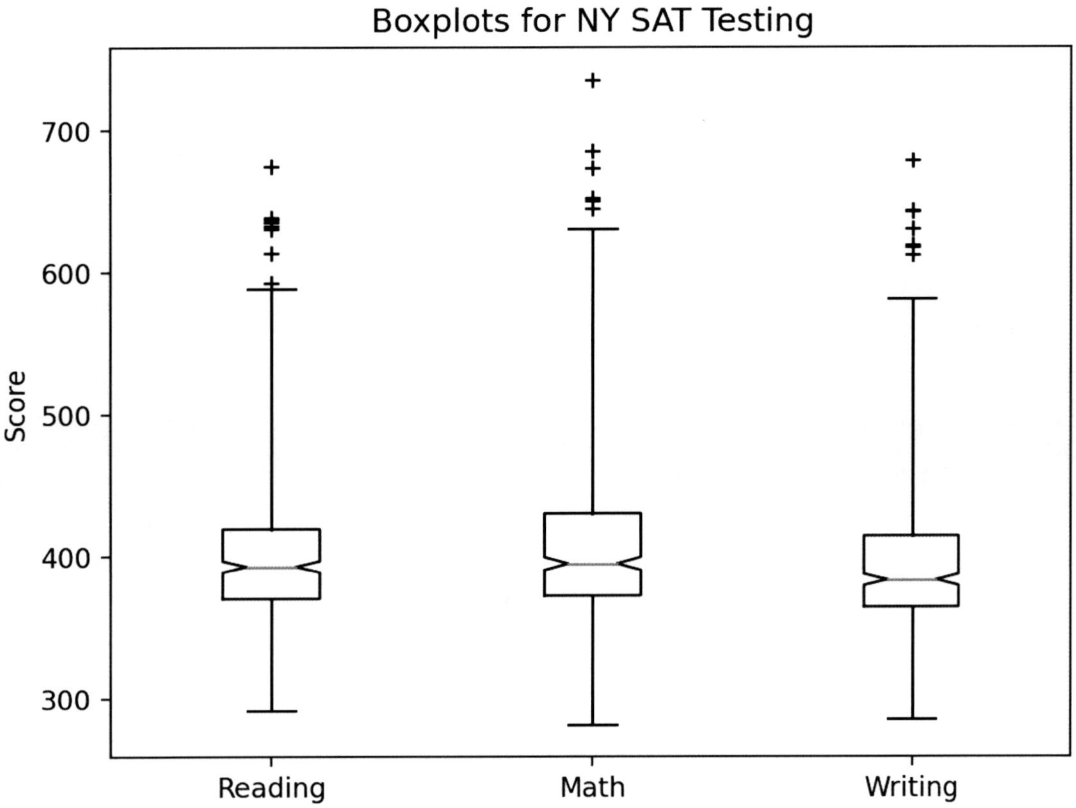

Let's move on to violin plots with Matplotlib. Shockingly, the function is called `violinplot()`.

```
data = [df['Critical Reading Mean'], df['Mathematics Mean'],
        df['Writing Mean']]
plt.violinplot(data)
plt.xticks(ticks=[1, 2, 3], labels=['Reading', 'Math', 'Writing'])
plt.title('Violin Plot for NY SAT Testing')
plt.ylabel('Score')
plt.show()
```

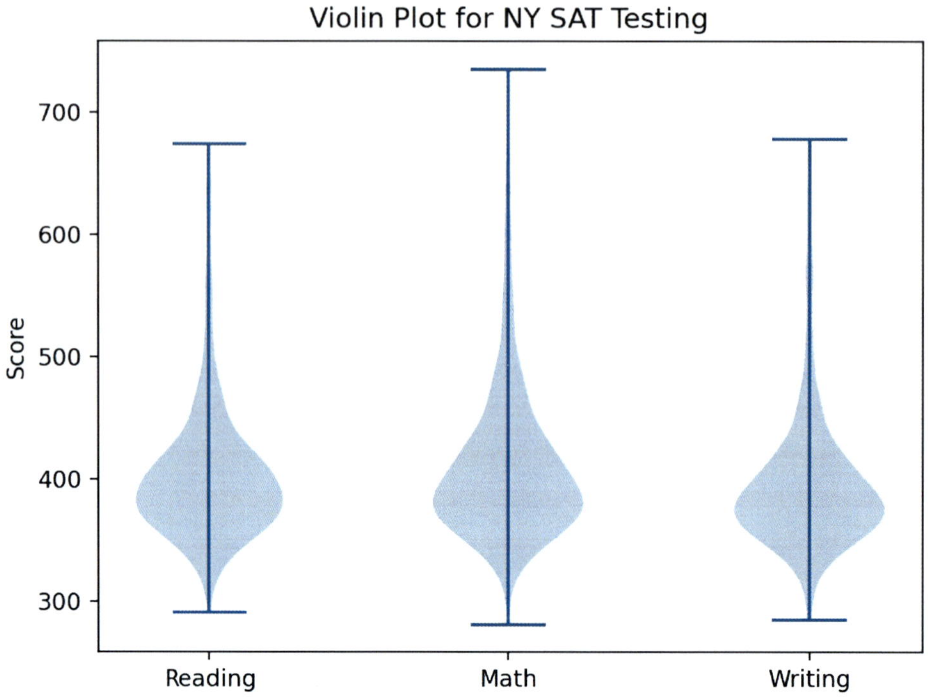

This is a slight improvement on the box plot; we gained the ability to see the distribution, but we lost the quartiles and median. Fortunately, we can pass those parameters to `violinplot()` to get a box plot with a distribution. Note that you need to have Matplotlib version 3.2.0 or higher to pass the `quantiles` parameter.

```
data = [df['Critical Reading Mean'], df['Mathematics Mean'],
        df['Writing Mean']]
plt.violinplot(data, vert=True, showmedians=True,
               quantiles=[[0.25, 0.75], [0.25, 0.75], [0.25, 0.75]],
               showextrema=False)
plt.xticks(ticks=[1, 2, 3], labels=['Reading','Math', 'Writing'])
plt.title('Violin Plot for NYC SAT Scores')
plt.ylabel('Score')
plt.show()
```

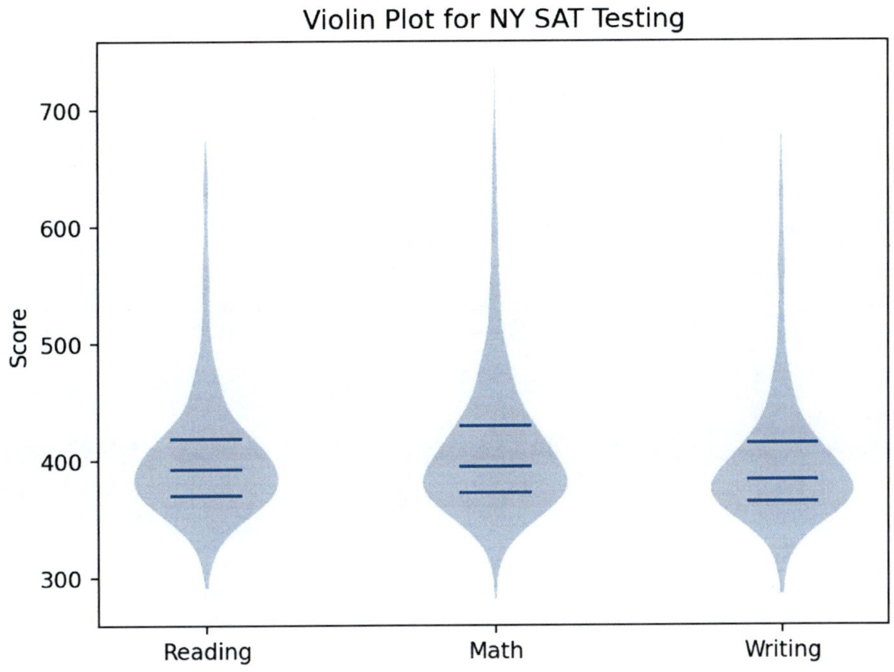

Let's move on to Seaborn to learn about a blended scatter plot/histogram/box plot/violin plot called a swarm plot.

Seaborn

First, let's make a box plot by using Seaborn's `boxplot()` method. We have to delete the `Number of Test Takers` column, or else Seaborn will try to make a box plot out of that column, too. We specify a vertical orientation, the color palette, and the box width. Since Seaborn will plot the column names as the category labels on the x axis, an alternative to changing the x ticks is to rename the columns.

```
del df['Number of Test Takers']
df.rename(columns={'Critical Reading Mean': 'Reading',
                   'Mathematics Mean': 'Math',
                   'Writing Mean': 'Writing'}, inplace=True)
sns.boxplot(data=df, orient='v', palette="Set2", width=0.25)
plt.ylabel('Score')
plt.title('Boxplots for NY SAT Testing')
plt.show()
```

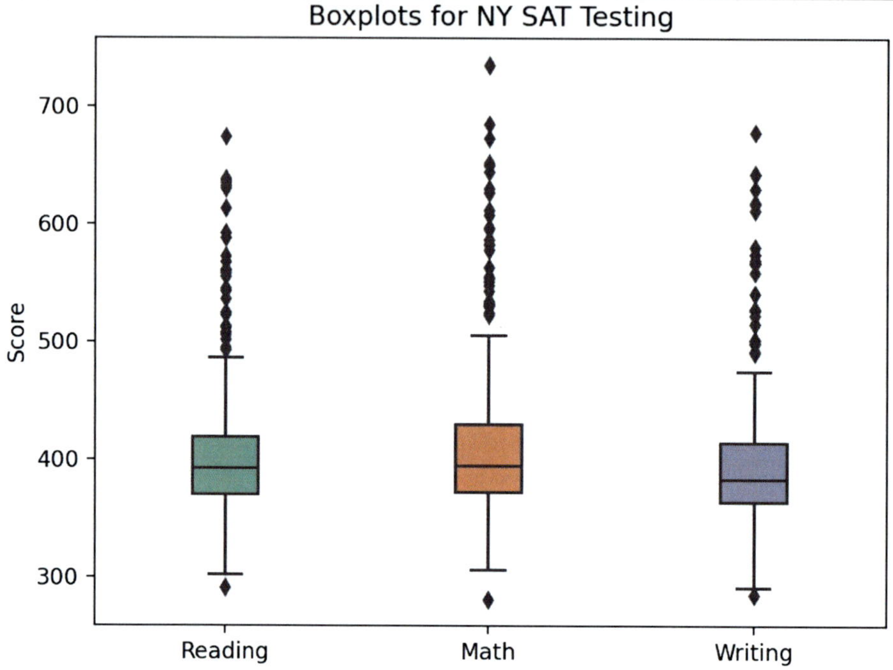

Since Seaborn wraps Matplotlib's box plot, you can pass any parameters like `notch`, `whis`, etc to Seaborn's `boxplot()` method and achieve the same customization.

Violin plots are remarkably similar for Seaborn:

```
sns.violinplot(data=df, orient='v', palette='Set2', width=0.25)
plt.title('Violinplot for NY SAT Testing')
plt.ylabel('Score')
plt.show()
```

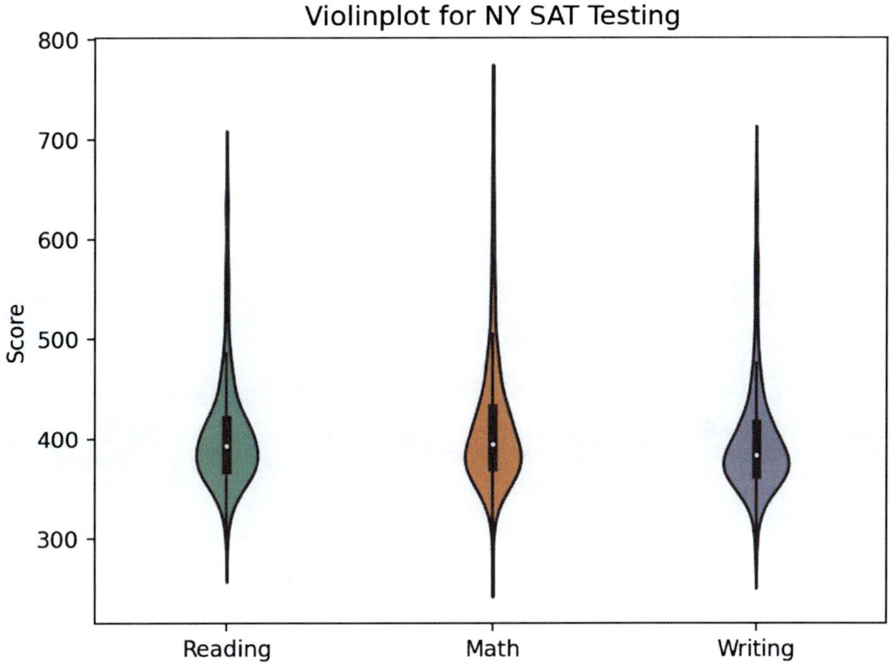

A swarm plot is a sort of applied scatter plot that takes the shape of a violin plot; rather than showing a histogram-like distribution, a swarm plot shows each dot like a scatter plot but aligns like a violin plot. Let's see an example:

```
sns.swarmplot(data=df, orient='v', palette="Set2", size=3)
plt.ylabel('Score')
plt.title('Swarmplot for NY SAT Testing')
plt.show()
```

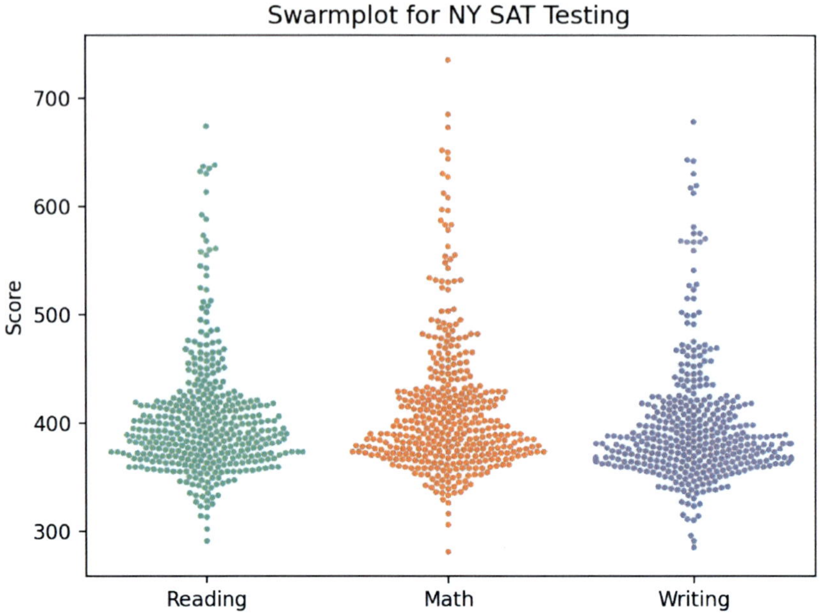

Since this is still a `plt` figure, we can draw the median line ourselves:

```
sns.swarmplot(data=df, orient='v', palette="Set2", size=3)
plt.plot([-0.33, 0.33], [df['Reading'].median(),
                          df['Reading'].median()], 'k-')
plt.plot([0.67, 1.33], [df['Math'].mean(),
                        df['Math'].mean()], 'k-')
plt.plot([1.67, 2.33], [df['Writing'].mean(),
                        df['Writing'].mean()], 'k-')
plt.ylabel('Score')
plt.title('Swarmplot for NY SAT Testing')
plt.show()
```

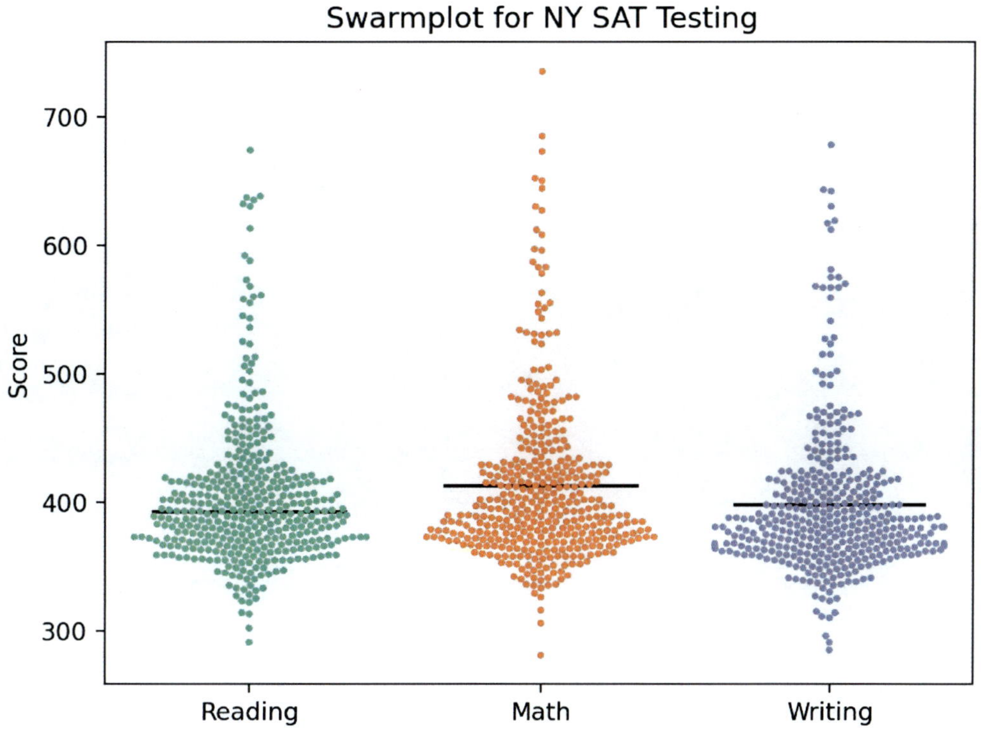

There are some other customized plot types that we won't cover; read through the Resources at the end of this chapter for more information.

Plotly

With Plotly, we gain the ability to name and shame (or name and praise) particular schools with hover data. The basic Plotly Express box plot looks like this:

```
fig = px.box(df, y=["Reading", 'Math',
                    'Writing'],
             labels={'variable': "", "value": 'Score'},
             title='Boxplots for NY SAT Testing',
             hover_data=['School Name'])
fig.show()
```

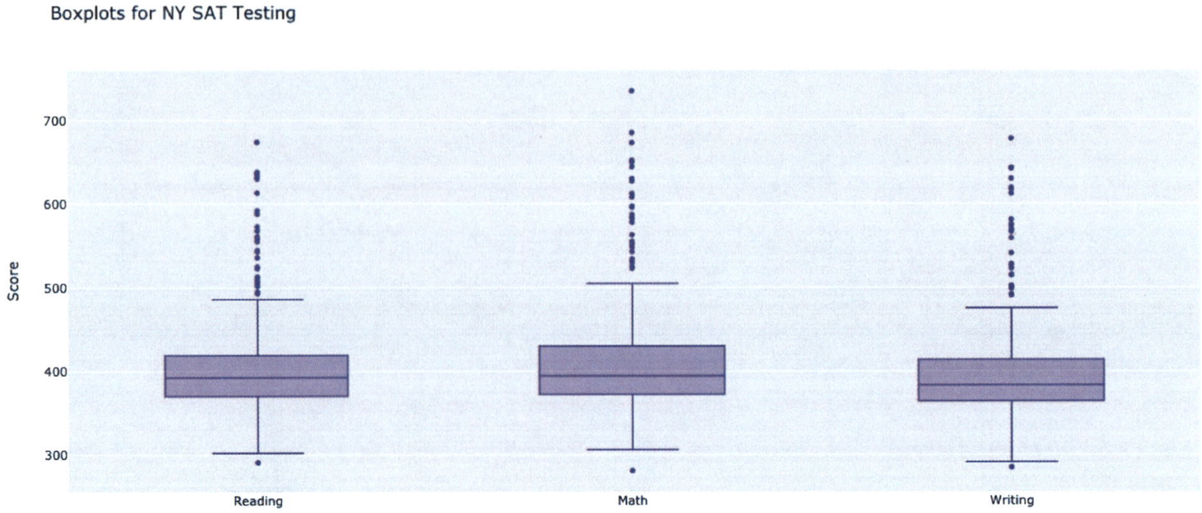

Some optional parameters that can really make your visualizations pop. You can show different points option with `points`: `'all'` shows all points with no filtering, `'outliers'` shows only the outliers, `'suspectedoutliers'` highlights suspected outliers (points that are less than 4Q1-3Q3 or greater than 4Q3-3Q1) with the `outliercolor` marker parameter, and `False` shows no points. This means that some points close to (but still outside of) the interquartile range will be highlighted. This is how to highlight suspected outliers as red on a box plot:

```
fig = px.box(df, y=['Reading', 'Math', 'Writing'],
             points="suspectedoutliers",
             labels={'variable': "", 'value': 'Score'},
             title="New York School System SAT Scores")
fig.update_traces(marker={'outliercolor': 'red'})
fig.show()
```

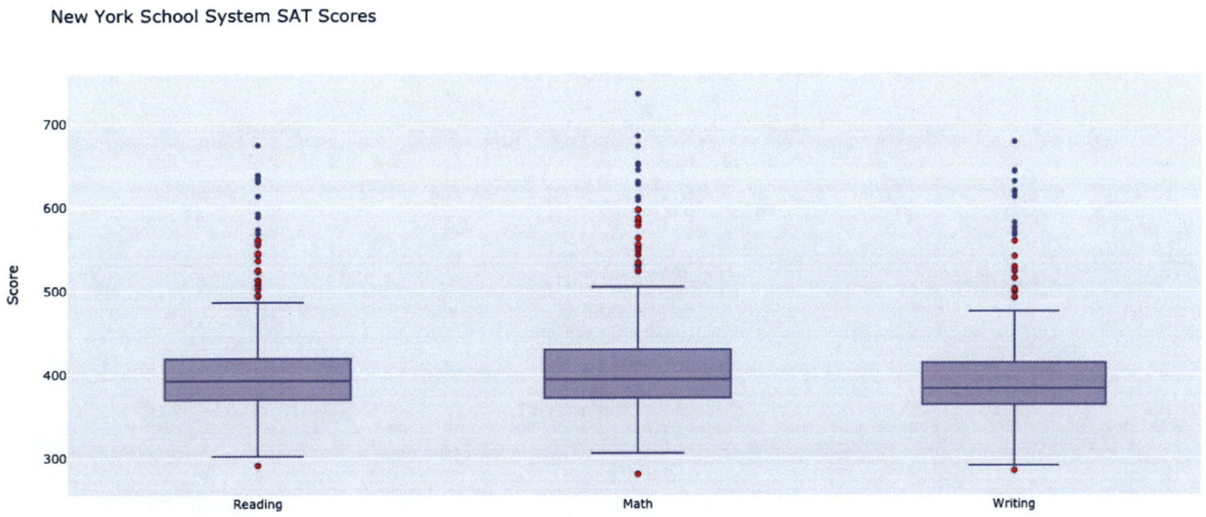

Box plots can also be overlaid with the `boxmode='overlay'` parameter. Using `points='all'` gives you both a box plot and a swarm plot:

```
fig = px.box(df, y=['Reading', 'Math', 'Writing'], notched=True,
             points="all", labels={'variable': "", 'value':
'Score'},
             title="New York School System SAT Scores")
fig.show()
```

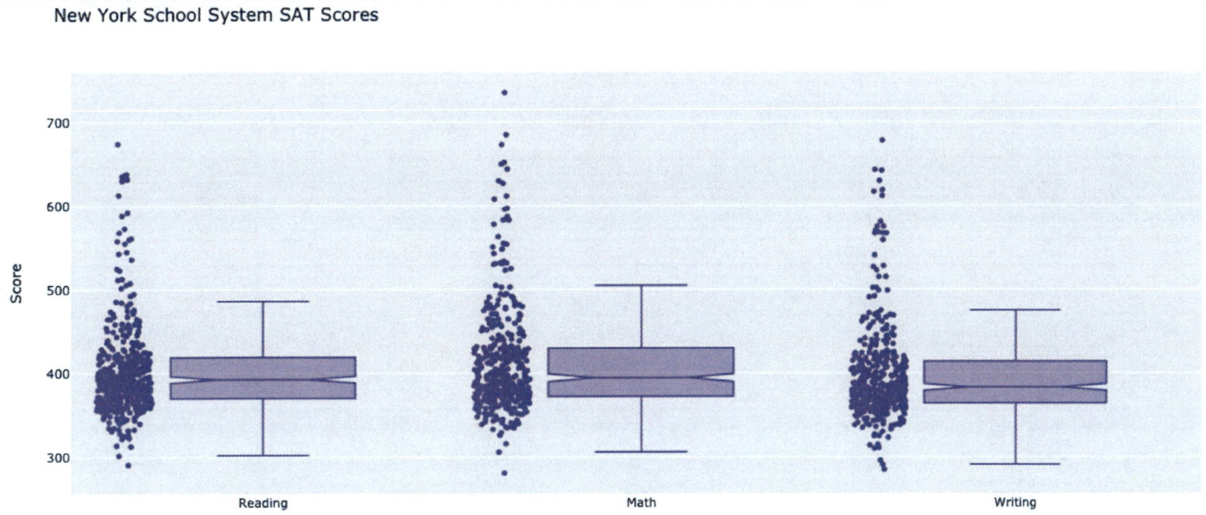

Violin plots behave similarly:

```
fig = px.violin(df, y=['Reading', 'Math', 'Writing'],
                title="New York School System SAT Scores",
                points=False,
                labels={'variable': "", 'value': 'Score'})
fig.show()
```

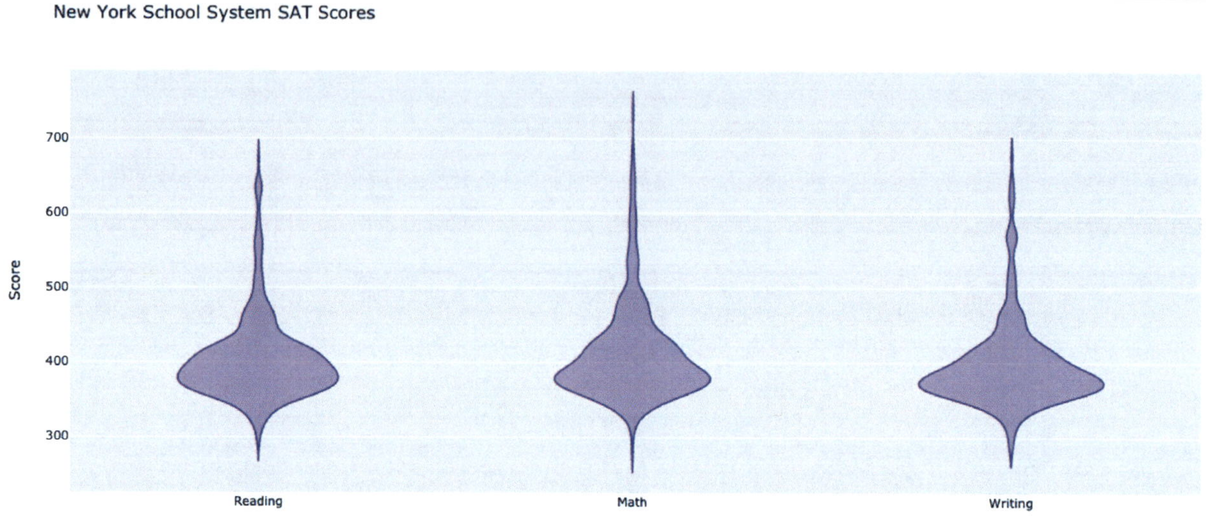

We can plot suspected outliers onto violin plots as well:

```
fig = px.violin(df, y=['Reading', 'Math', 'Writing'],
                points="suspectedoutliers",
                labels={'variable': "", 'value': 'Score'},
                title="New York School System SAT Scores")
fig.update_traces(marker={'outliercolor': 'red'})
fig.show()
```

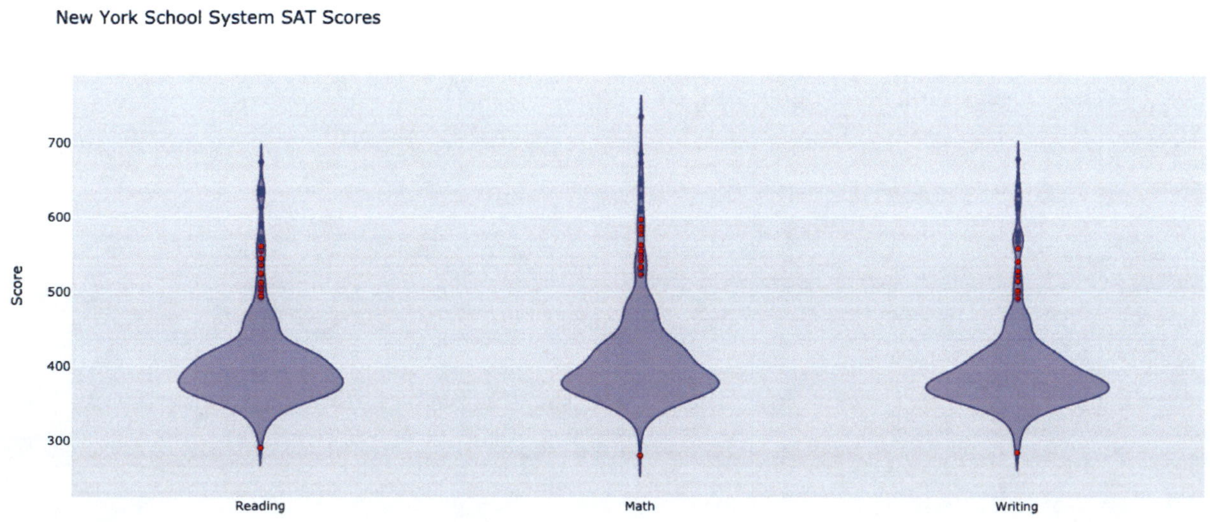

Of course, there are Graph Objects for box plots and violin plots; they are `go.Box()` and `go.Violin()`, respectively. Plotly Express should handle all of your needs, so we won't go into the Graph Objects in any greater detail.

Summary

Box plots, violin plots, and swarm plots can provide the efficacy of a histogram and include summary statistics or a greater understanding of how the data may be distributed. There are some other ways to show how a column in a dataset is distributed, but box plots and violin plots can provide advantages over histograms.

Box plots can hide the number of datapoints within the interquartile range, so it is usually recommended to annotate the graph with the number of observations, use a swarm plot, jitter the data, or otherwise inform your reader of the sample size. Violin plots can also make up for the box plot's shortcomings. These types of charts can be used to improve upon simple histograms to show the underlying observations and clustering of data.

Examples for Each Library

```
import matplotlib.pyplot as plt
import seaborn as sns
import plotly.express as px
import plotly.graph_objects as go
import pandas as pd
import plotly.io as pio
pio.renderers.default = "browser"

df = pd.read_csv('https://raw.githubusercontent.com/
                 alexkenan/pyviz/main/datasets/sat.csv')
df.dropna(inplace=True)
del df['Number of Test Takers']
df.rename(columns={'Critical Reading Mean': 'Reading',
                   'Mathematics Mean': 'Math',
                   'Writing Mean': 'Writing'},
          inplace=True)

# Matplotlib box plot with customized parameters
data = [df['Reading'],
        df['Math'],
        df['Writing']]
plt.boxplot(data, notch=True, sym='+', whis=3.5)
plt.xticks(ticks=[1, 2, 3], labels=['Reading', 'Math', 'Writing'])
plt.title('Box plots for NY SAT Testing')
plt.ylabel('Score')
plt.show()

# Matplotlib violin plot with custom parameters
data = [df['Reading'],
        df['Math'],
        df['Writing']]
plt.violinplot(data, vert=True, showmedians=True,
               quantiles=[[0.25, 0.75], [0.25, 0.75], [0.25, 0.75]],
               showextrema=False)
```

```
plt.xticks(ticks=[1, 2, 3], labels=['Reading', 'Math', 'Writing'])
plt.title('Violin plot for NY SAT Testing')
plt.ylabel('Score')
plt.show()

# Seaborn box plot
sns.boxplot(data=df, orient='v', palette="Set2", width=0.25)
plt.ylabel('Score')
plt.title('Boxplots for NY SAT Testing')
plt.show()

# Seaborn violin plot
sns.violinplot(data=df, orient='v', palette='Set2', width=0.25)
plt.title('Violinplot for NY SAT Testing')
plt.ylabel('Score')
plt.xticks(ticks=[0, 1, 2], labels=['Reading','Math', 'Writing'])
plt.show()

# Seaborn swarm plot
sns.swarmplot(data=df, orient='v', palette="Set2", size=3)
plt.plot([-0.33, 0.33], [df['Reading'].median(),
                         df['Reading'].median()], 'k-')
plt.plot([0.67, 1.33], [df['Math'].mean(),
                        df['Math'].mean()], 'k-')
plt.plot([1.67, 2.33], [df['Writing'].mean(),
                        df['Writing'].mean()], 'k-')
plt.ylabel('Score')
plt.title('Swarm plot for NY SAT Testing')
plt.show()

# Plotly Express box plot customized
fig = px.box(df, y=["Reading", 'Math', 'Writing'], notched=True,
             color=["Reading", 'Math', 'Writing'],
             labels={'variable': "", "value": 'Score'},
             title='Box plots for NY SAT Testing',
             hover_data=['School Name'])
fig.update_traces(quartilemethod="inclusive")
fig.show()

# Plotly Express violin plot
```

```
fig = px.violin(df, y=['Reading', 'Math', 'Writing'],
                title="New York School System SAT Scores",
                points=False,
                labels={'variable': "", 'value': 'Score'})
fig.show()

# Plotly express more advanced swarm plot and violin plot
fig = px.violin(df, y=['Reading', 'Math', 'Writing'],
                points="suspectedoutliers",
                labels={'variable': "", 'value': 'Score'},
                title="New York School System SAT Scores")
fig.update_traces(marker={'outliercolor': 'red'})
fig.show()
```

View this code on GitHub at https://github.com/alexkenan/pyviz/

Resources

[1] https://catalog.data.gov/dataset/sat-results-e88d7

[2] https://matplotlib.org/stable/api/_as_gen/matplotlib.pyplot.boxplot.html

[3] https://matplotlib.org/stable/api/_as_gen/matplotlib.pyplot.violinplot.html

[4] https://seaborn.pydata.org/generated/seaborn.boxplot.html

[5] https://seaborn.pydata.org/generated/seaborn.violinplot.html

[6] https://seaborn.pydata.org/generated/seaborn.swarmplot.html

[7] https://plotly.com/python/box-plots/

[8] https://plotly.com/python/violin/

Bar Charts

Introduction

Bar charts are used to represent categorical variables and numerical variables. This visualization type uses rectangular bars for each category to quantify the numerical variable; the length of each bar corresponds to the numerical variable's value. This value can be an average, sum, count, or other summary of quantity. Bar charts can also be used as a line plot for time series data, and these charts can be grouped to compare categorical variables on numerical ones.

Bar charts have the potential to be grossly misused. To avoid this, some good practices include maintaining 2D rectangular shapes for your bars (do not use 3D shapes and avoid the temptation to use chart junky images for bars) and zooming in or out to the appropriate scale. As a reminder, the default Matplotlib/Seaborn/Plotly scales are often okay. It is also a good practice to order and sort the bars from largest to smallest or vice versa to improve clarity and understanding if you are not representing time on the x axis. It is much easier for a reader to identify a trend or an outlier this way.

We will use the `mpg` dataset from earlier, and we will use Boolean indexing to focus on particular car models to track over the model years.

The Lie

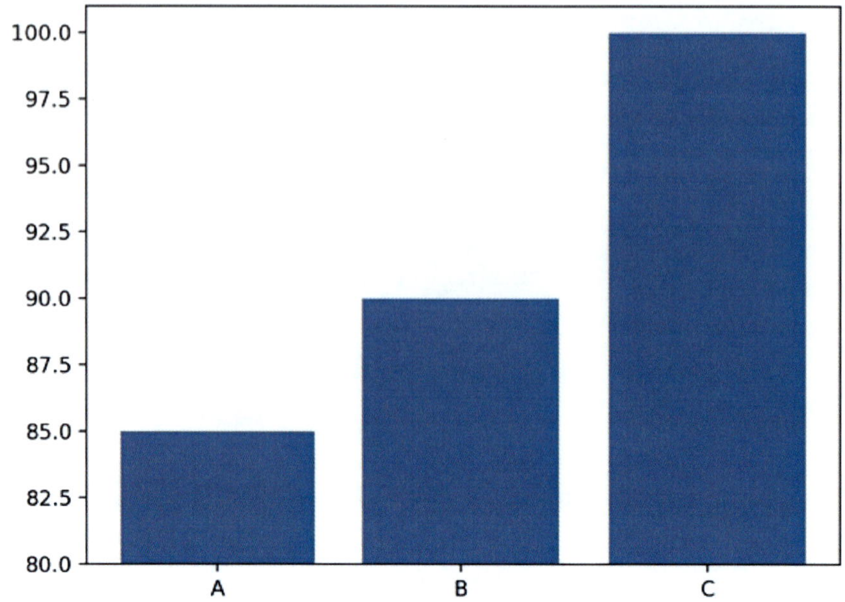

What in the world is going on with A? It's performing terribly! Unfortunately, this is a common lie. Not starting the y axis at 0 is called "truncating the y axis," and truncating the y axis has the same effect as unnecessarily zooming in; it makes the difference between A, B, and C appear much larger than it actually is. If we set the y axis limit floor as 0, the differences do not seem so large after all:

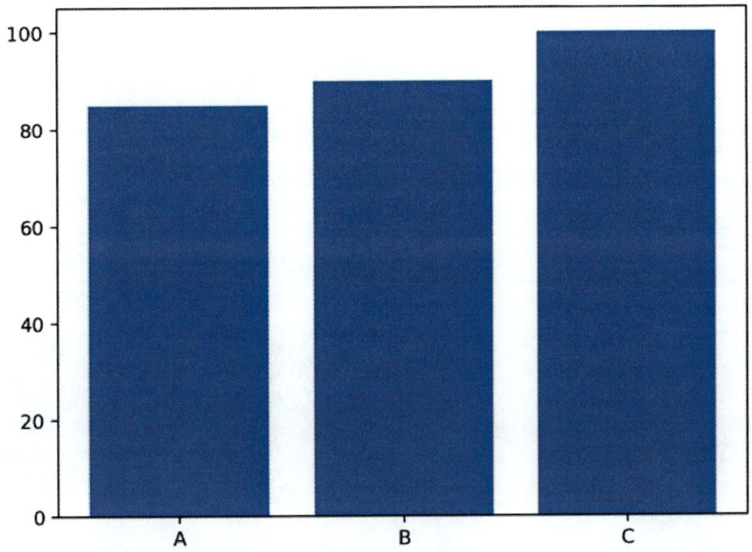

This is a very common lie that is used to exaggerate changes or differences that may be imperceptible at a normal scale.

Imports

```
import matplotlib.pyplot as plt
import seaborn as sns
import plotly.express as px
import plotly.graph_objects as go
import plotly.io as pio
pio.renderers.default = "browser"
mpg = sns.load_dataset('mpg')
```

Matplotlib

A Matplotlib bar chart is as easy as `plt.bar()` and is constructed by passing an `x` argument for labels/categories on the x axis and a `height` argument for the heights of the bars on the y axis. Let's take a look at the Ford Pinto:

```
pinto = mpg[mpg['name'] == 'ford pinto']
plt.bar(pinto['model_year'], pinto['mpg'])
plt.xlabel('Model Year')
plt.ylabel('MPG')
plt.title('Ford Pinto MPG vs Model Year')
plt.show()
```

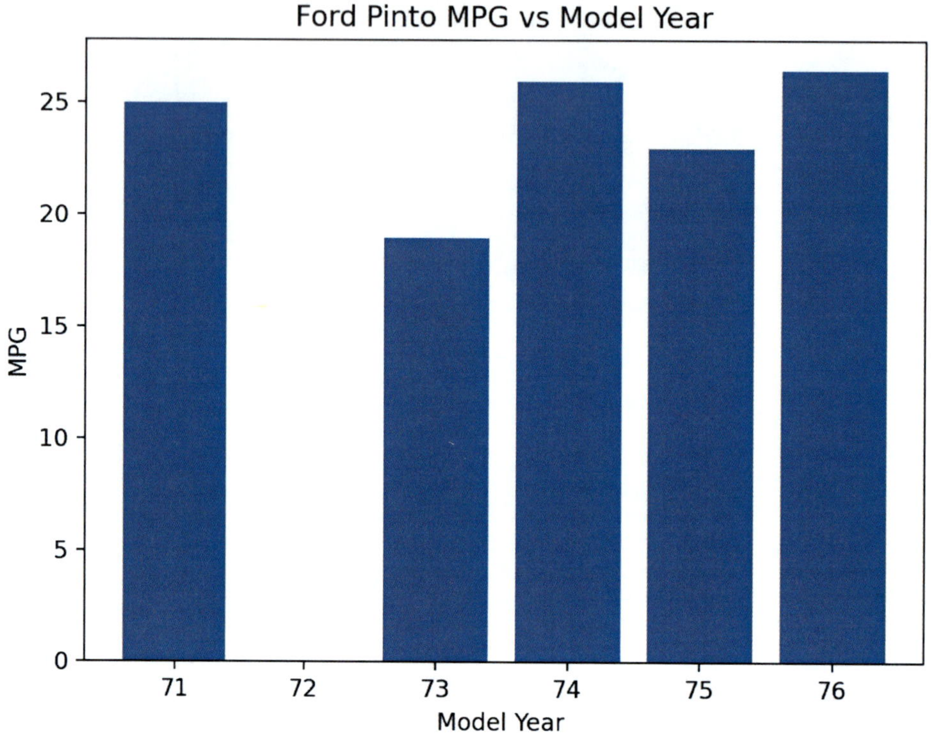

Since `model_year` represents time in years, it doesn't make sense to try to sort the values by MPG in ascending or descending order.

We can also make a horizontal bar chart. Typically, a horizontal bar chart is a better choice if you have long category names; let's create a horizontal bar chart with select 1976 cars and MPG. We will also sort from largest to smallest:

```
year1976 = mpg[mpg['model_year'] == 76]
year1976 = year1976.iloc[0:5]
year1976.sort_values(by='mpg', ascending=True, inplace=True)
plt.barh(year1976['name'], year1976['mpg'])
plt.xlabel('MPG')
plt.title('Select Model Year 1976 Cars vs MPG')
plt.show()
```

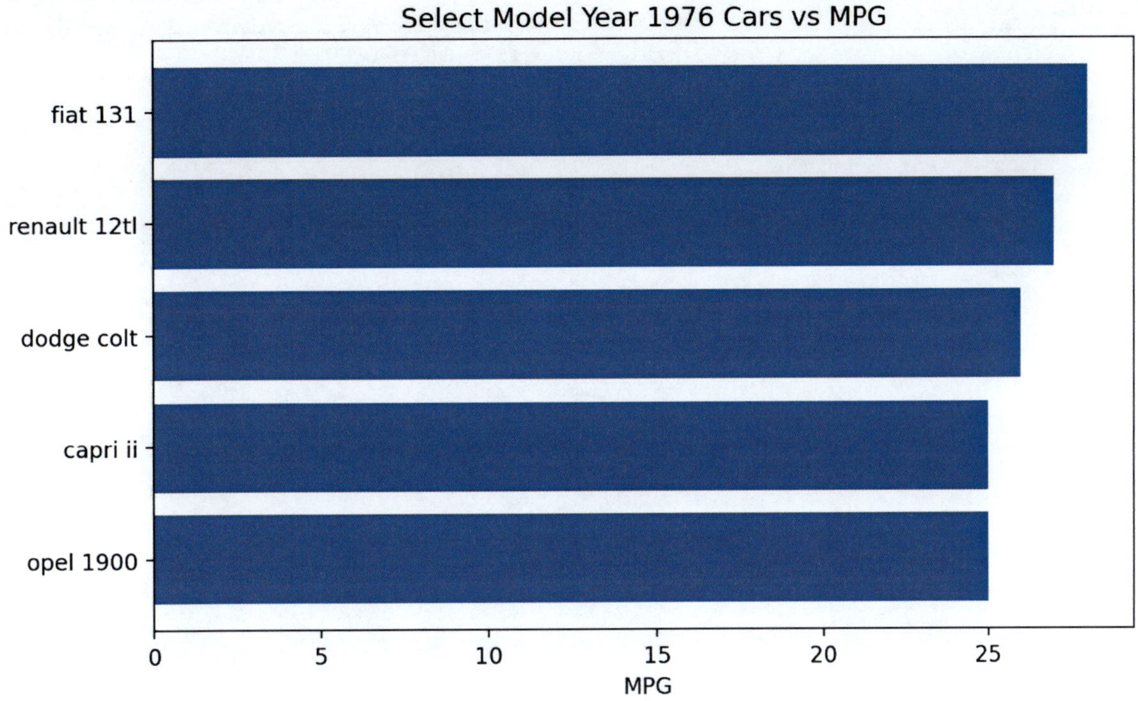

It is possible to add error bars to the tops of bar charts. This presents another opportunity for a caveat: error bars can hide information and can represent several different types of "error." For this example, we will assume a plus-or-minus 1 mpg error. We can customize the error bar color with `ecolor` and the length of the cap with the `error_kw` `dict`.

```
pinto = mpg[mpg['name'] == 'ford pinto']
errorbars = [1 for __ in range(len(pinto))]
plt.bar(pinto['model_year'], pinto['mpg'], yerr=errorbars,
        ecolor='r', error_kw={'capsize': 3.0})
plt.xlabel('Model Year')
plt.ylabel('MPG')
plt.title('Ford Pinto MPG vs Model Year')
plt.show()
```

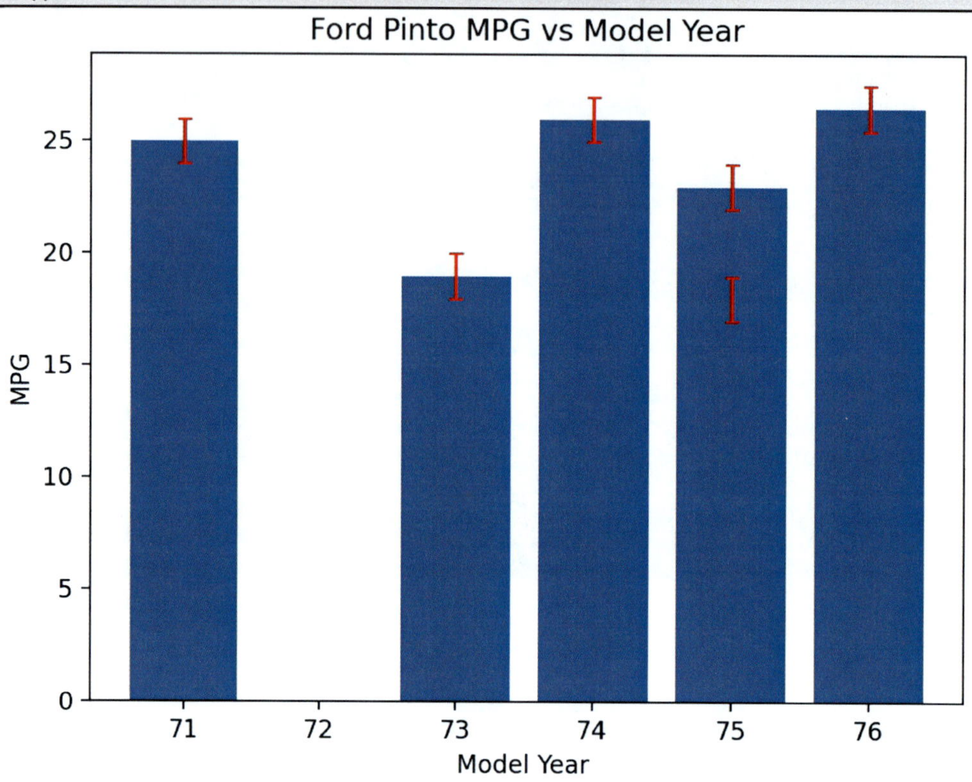

With these error bars, we discover that there are two Ford Pintos in 75: a 4 cylinder and a 6 cylinder variant. For any additional Pinto plots, we'll have to filter out that 6 cylinder car.

Once we have a bar chart, we can still plot other things on the figure. Let's group the dataset by model year and plot the average MPG as bars and as a line:

```
mpg_year = mpg.groupby('model_year')['mpg'].mean().reset_index()
plt.bar(mpg_year['model_year'], mpg_year['mpg'])
plt.xlabel('Model Year')
plt.ylabel('Average MPG')
plt.title('Average MPG vs Model Year')
plt.plot(mpg_year['model_year'], mpg_year['mpg'], 'r-')
plt.show()
```

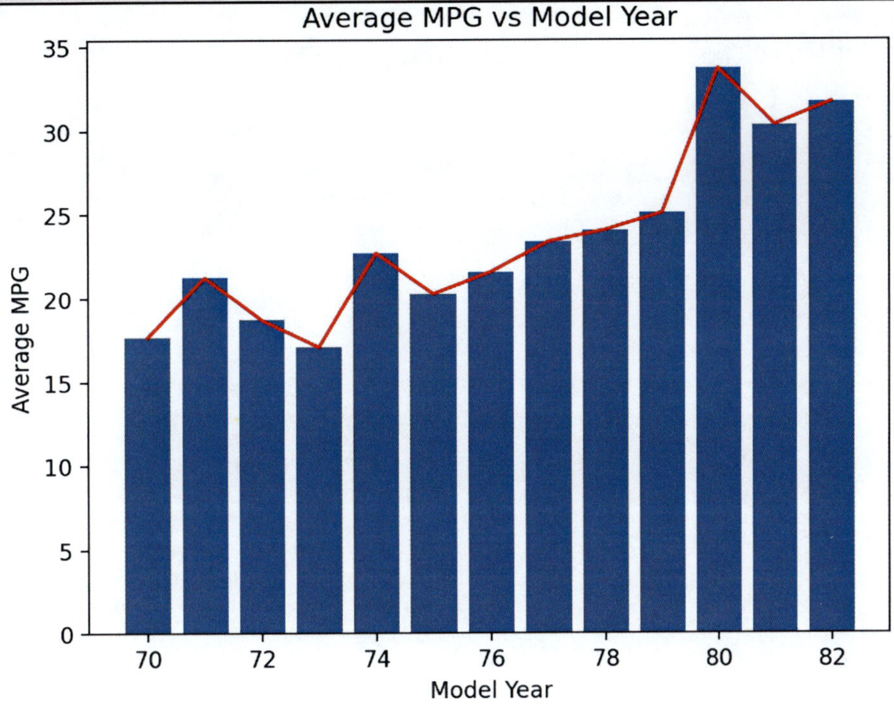

Let's move on to grouped bar charts. We have to manually assemble the groups, so it requires quite a bit of tweaking. We need to center a bar on the model year, then add a bar offset by either

-0.3 or +0.3 to keep the centering. Lastly, we need to set the `xticks` to only show the "centered" model years since we will be messing with the other model years in order to display the data correctly.

There are typically two different ways to plot with Matplotlib: using `plt` like we have been doing, and using the syntax `fig, ax = plt.subplots()`. Both methods display plots, and anything returned from `plt.bar()` is the same as `ax.bar()`. Calling `plt` closely mimics MATLAB-style syntax. Both methods accomplish the same chart types, though the syntax for adjusting axes is different for the two methods. It is good practice to be comfortable using either method to generate plots. Additionally, if you are using a unit of time as a plotted variable, it is not always necessary to label that axis. The next several examples do not label the x axis. Is it less clear what is being shown if there is no x axis label?

```
fig, ax = plt.subplots()
bar_width = 0.3
mpg_usa = mpg[mpg['origin'] ==
         'usa'].groupby('model_year')['mpg'].mean().reset_index()
mpg_usa['model_year'] = mpg_usa['model_year'] - bar_width
mpg_japan = mpg[mpg['origin'] ==
        'japan'].groupby('model_year')['mpg'].mean().reset_index()
mpg_europe = mpg[mpg['origin'] ==
       'europe'].groupby('model_year')['mpg'].mean().reset_index()
mpg_europe['model_year'] = mpg_europe['model_year'] + bar_width
ax.bar(mpg_usa['model_year'], mpg_usa['mpg'],
       label="USA", width=bar_width)
ax.bar(mpg_japan['model_year'], mpg_japan['mpg'],
       label="Japan", width=bar_width)
ax.bar(mpg_europe['model_year'], mpg_europe['mpg'],
       label="Europe", width=bar_width)
ax.set_ylabel("Average MPG")
ax.set_title("Average MPG by model year and origin")
ax.set_xticks(mpg_japan['model_year'])
ax.legend()
plt.show()
```

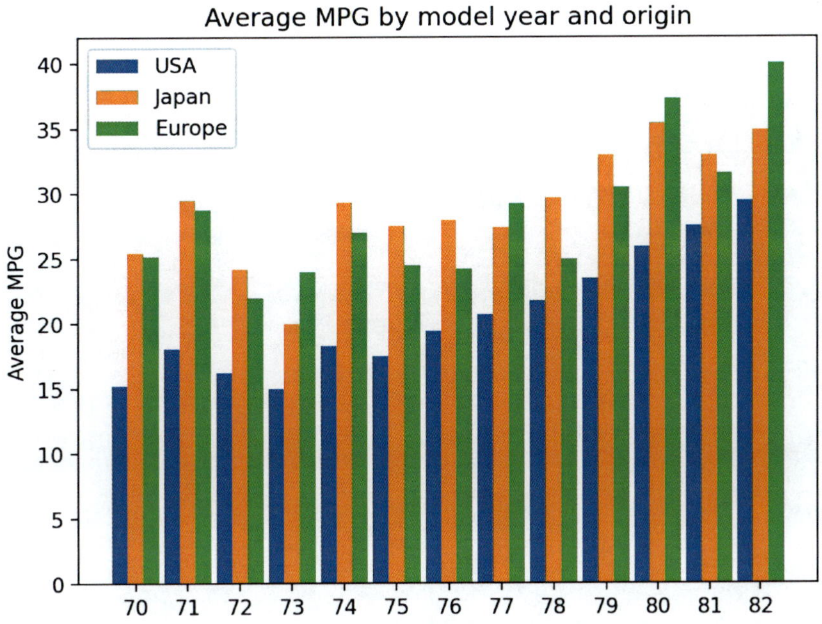

This visualization is incredibly busy, but it does show how to get grouped bar charts. There seems to be an upward trend over time, but it requires a lot of looking and focus to discern that message.

With a `v_autolabel` function, we can annotate the tops of each vertical bar with the value. Again, this is an awful visualization, but it proves the functionality. Since a bar chart is a lot of rectangles, we can get each rectangle, get its height, and place an annotation at an offset above the bar. Here is what the `v_autolabel` function does:

```
def v_autolabel(rects, axis):
        for rect in rects:
            height = rect.get_height()
            axis.annotate('{}'.format(int(round(height, 0))),
                          xy=(rect.get_x() + rect.get_width() / 2,
                              height),
                          xytext=(0, 3),
                          textcoords="offset points",
                          ha='center', va='bottom', size=7)
```

As long as we capture each bar plot (either `x = ax.bar(…)` or `x = plt.bar(…)`), we can use the `v_autolabel` function to automatically annotate each bar.

```
fig, ax = plt.subplots()
bar_width = 0.3
mpg_usa = mpg[mpg['origin'] ==
          'usa'].groupby('model_year')['mpg'].mean().reset_index()
mpg_usa['model_year'] = mpg_usa['model_year'] - bar_width
mpg_japan = mpg[mpg['origin'] ==

'japan'].groupby('model_year')['mpg'].mean().reset_index()
mpg_europe = mpg[mpg['origin'] ==
         'europe'].groupby('model_year')['mpg'].mean().reset_index()
mpg_europe['model_year'] = mpg_europe['model_year'] + bar_width
usa = ax.bar(mpg_usa['model_year'], mpg_usa['mpg'],
             label="USA", width=bar_width)
japan = ax.bar(mpg_japan['model_year'], mpg_japan['mpg'],
               label="Japan", width=bar_width)
europe = ax.bar(mpg_europe['model_year'], mpg_europe['mpg'],
                label="Europe", width=bar_width)
ax.set_ylabel("Average MPG")
ax.set_title("Average MPG by model year and origin")
ax.legend()
ax.set_xticks(mpg_japan['model_year'])
v_autolabel(usa, ax)
v_autolabel(japan, ax)
v_autolabel(europe, ax)
plt.show()
```

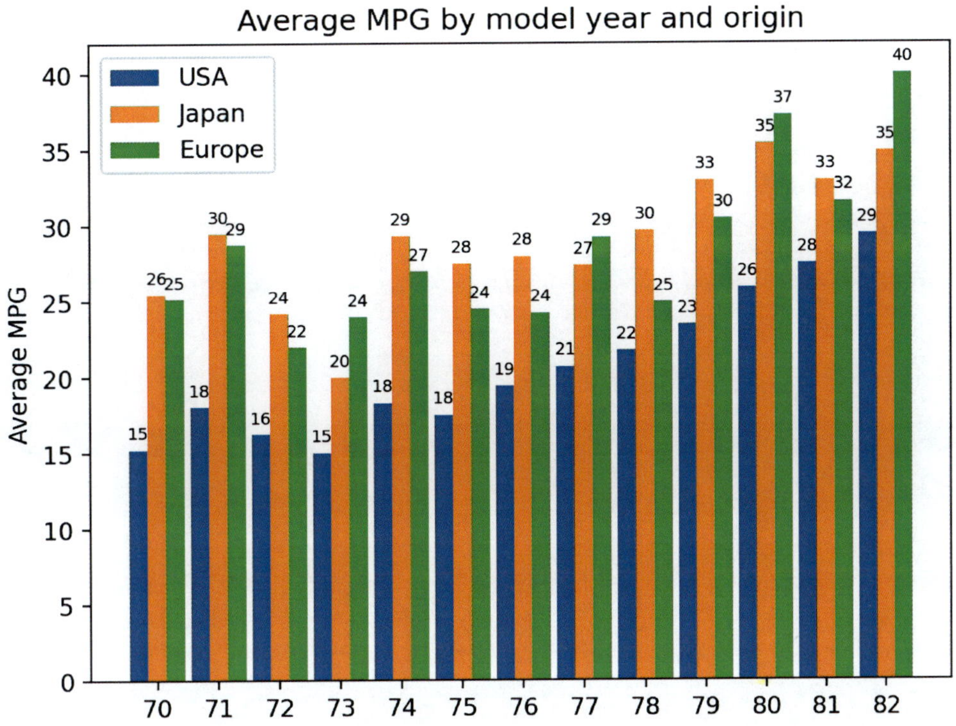

The annotations make a busy chart even busier, but it shows how we can annotate to emphasize information, should it be desired. To improve the chart, you should either narrow the model years, remove one of the origin categories, or do a combination of both.

For reference, this is what a horizontal bar chart autolabel function `h_autolabel` would look like:

```
def h_autolabel(rects, axis) -> None:
    for position, rect in enumerate(rects):
        x = rect.get_width()
        y = position
        axis.annotate('{}'.format(x),
                      xy=(x, y + 0.5),
                      xytext=(9, 0),
                      textcoords="offset points",
                      ha='center', va='bottom', size=7)
```

Lastly, we can create stacked bar charts with Matplotlib. We do this by passing a `bottom` argument to stack bars on top of established bars. Let's group `mpg` by `model_year` and `count()` how many cars there are by `origin`.

```
usa = mpg[mpg['origin'] ==
        'usa'].groupby('model_year')['name'].count().reset_index()
usa.rename(columns={'name': 'count'},
           inplace=True)
japan = mpg[mpg['origin'] ==
        'japan'].groupby('model_year')['name'].count().reset_index()
japan.rename(columns={'name': 'count'},
           inplace=True)
europe = mpg[mpg['origin'] ==
     'europe'].groupby('model_year')['name'].count().reset_index()
europe.rename(columns={'name': 'count'},
              inplace=True)
plt.bar(japan['model_year'], japan['count'], label="Japan")
plt.bar(europe['model_year'], europe['count'],
        bottom=japan['count'], label="Europe")
plt.bar(usa['model_year'], usa['count'],
        bottom=europe['count'], label="USA")
plt.ylabel("Number of Car Models Produced")
plt.xlabel('Model Year')
plt.title("Car Production")
plt.legend()
plt.gca().set_xticks(usa['model_year'])
plt.show()
```

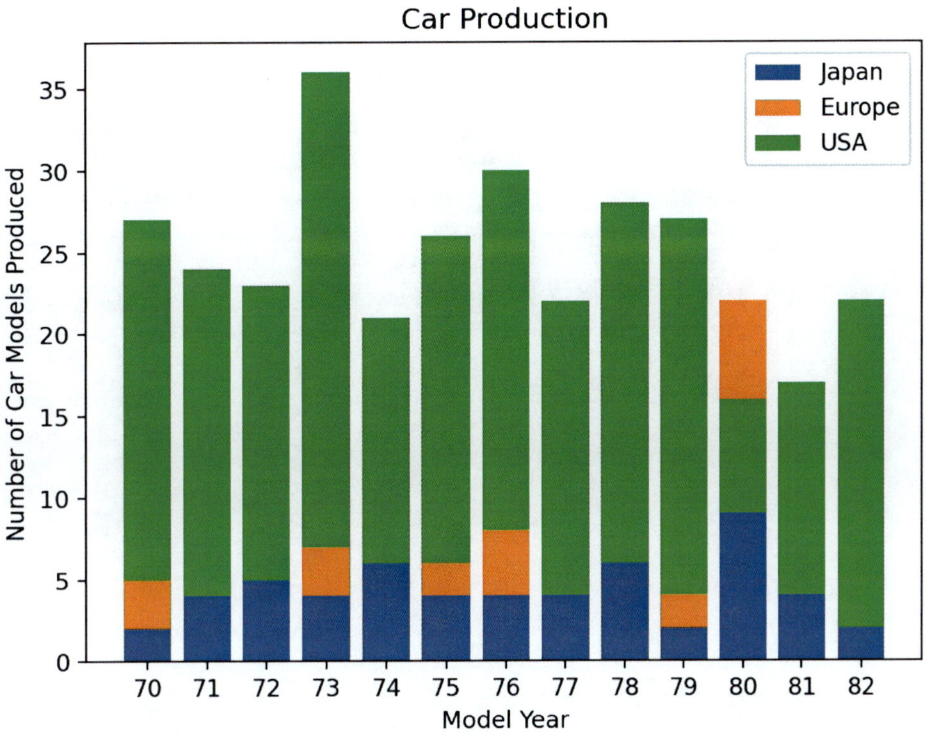

We run into issues if Europe is less than Japan because of how we have stacked the bars. We could write a more complicated plotting method, but let's see how Seaborn handles it.

Seaborn

To start, we'll return to our trusty Ford Pinto and use Seaborn's `barplot()`. Since the Pinto has two models, let's filter out anything that isn't 4 cylinders.

```
pinto = mpg[mpg['name'] == 'ford pinto']
pinto = pinto[pinto['cylinders'] == 4]
sns.barplot(data=pinto, x='model_year', y='mpg', color='b')
plt.title('Ford Pinto MPG vs Model Year')
plt.show()
```

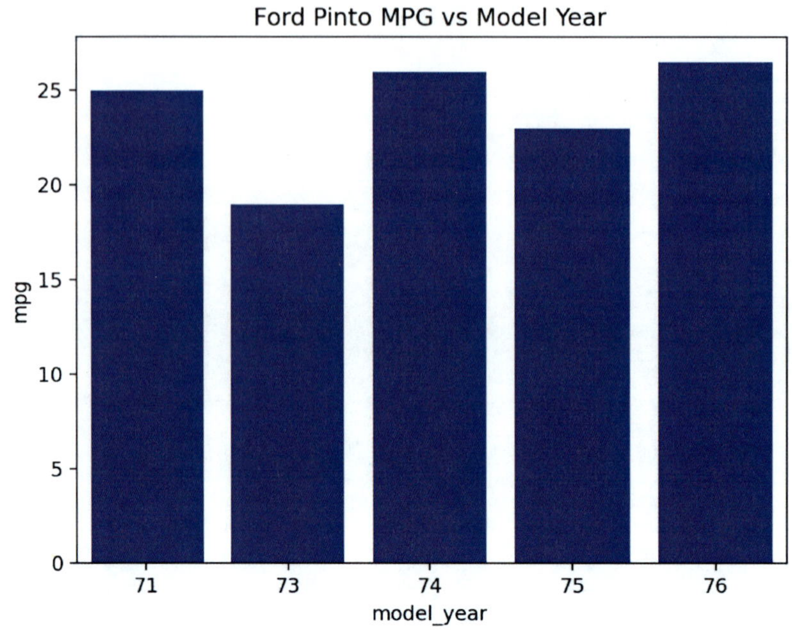

Creating a horizontal bar chart is as simple as passing `orient='h'` to `barplot()`. Let's return to our 1976 select cars:

```
year1976 = mpg[mpg['model_year'] == 76]
year1976 = year1976.iloc[0:5]
year1976.sort_values(by='mpg', ascending=False, inplace=True)
sns.barplot(data=year1976, x='mpg', y='name', orient='h',
            color='tab:blue')
plt.title('Select Model Year 1976 Cars vs MPG')
plt.show()
```

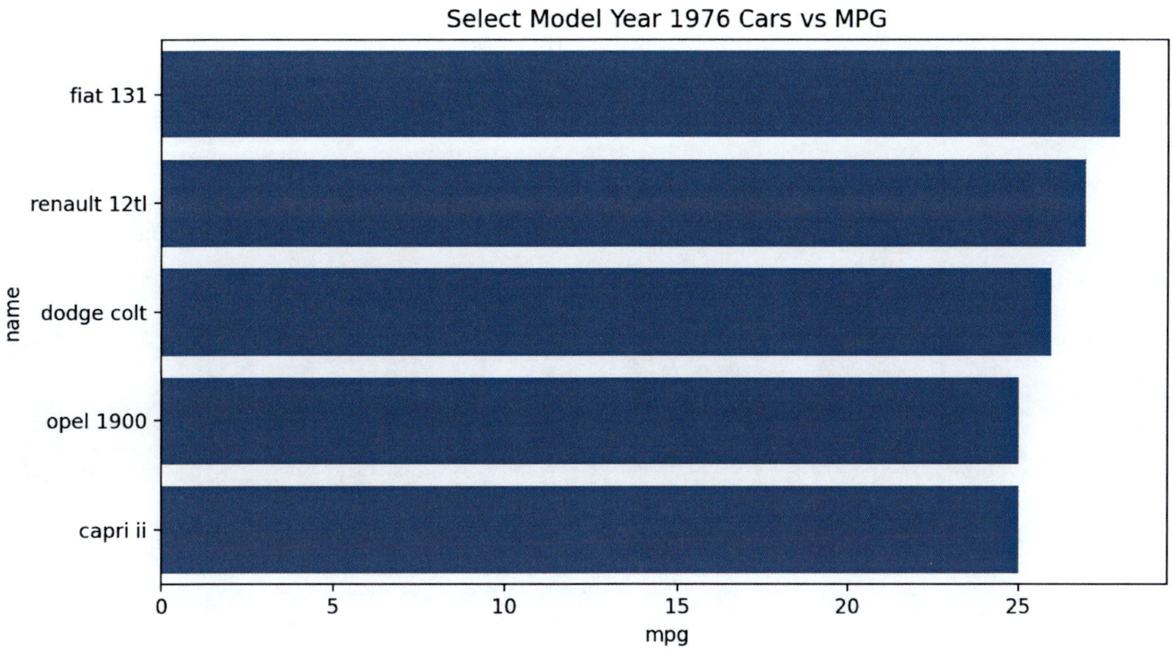

Remember all of that grouping code we had to write to align the bars on the model years? Seaborn takes care of that for us. All we need to do is pass the `hue="origin"` additional parameter to `barplot()`:

```
ax = sns.barplot(data=mpg, x='model_year', y='mpg', hue='origin',
                 errwidth=0)
ax.set(xlabel="Model Year", ylabel="MPG")
plt.title('Average MPG by model year and origin')
plt.show()
```

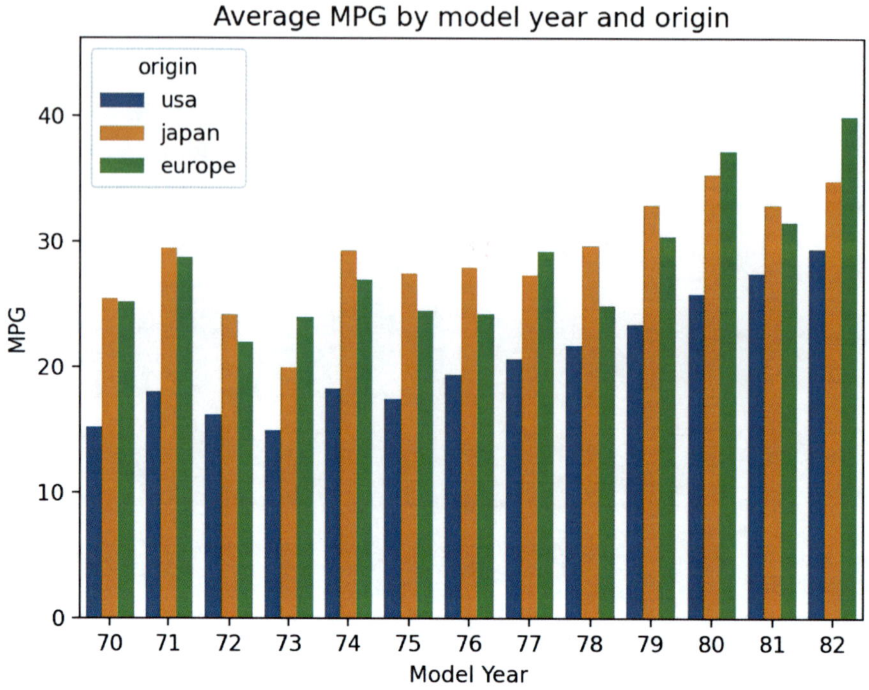

That is so much easier than messing with bar widths. Seaborn does not have a stacked bar chart method, but we can use some Pandas grouping and pivoting to get close:

```
temp_df = mpg.groupby(['model_year',
                  'origin'])[['name']].count().reset_index()
temp_df.set_index('model_year', inplace=True)
df = temp_df.pivot(columns='origin', values='name')
df.plot.bar(stacked=True)
plt.ylabel("Number of Car Models Produced")
plt.xlabel('Model Year')
plt.xticks(rotation=0)
plt.title("Car Production")
plt.show()
```

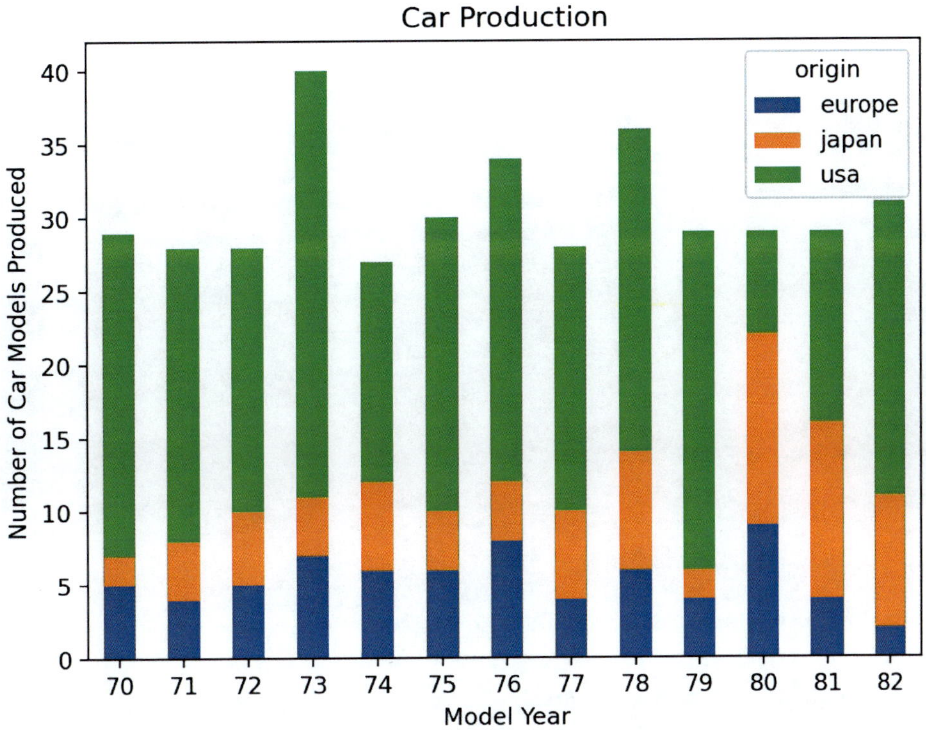

Next, on to Plotly for interactive bar charts.

Plotly

Perhaps unsurprisingly, Plotly Express `px.bar()` will create a bar chart. For the final time, let's check out the 4 cylinder Ford Pintos:

```
pinto = mpg[mpg['name'] == 'ford pinto']
pinto = pinto[pinto['cylinders'] == 4]
fig = px.bar(pinto, x='model_year', y='mpg')
fig.update_layout(title='Ford Pinto MPG vs Model Year',
                  xaxis_title="Model Year", yaxis_title="MPG")
fig.show()
```

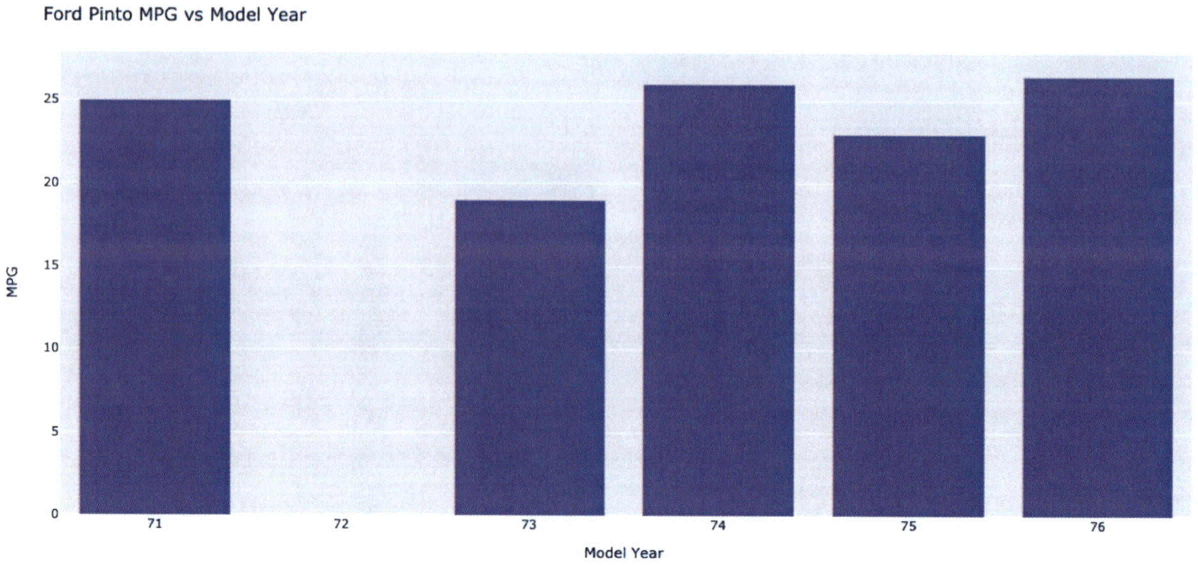

And, as a horizontal bar chart:

```
year1976 = mpg[mpg['model_year'] == 76]
year1976 = year1976.iloc[0:5]
year1976.sort_values(by='mpg', ascending=True, inplace=True)
fig = px.bar(year1976, x='mpg', y='name', orientation='h')
plt.show()
fig.update_layout(title='Select Model Year 1976 Cars vs MPG',
                  xaxis_title="MPG", yaxis_title="")
fig.show()
```

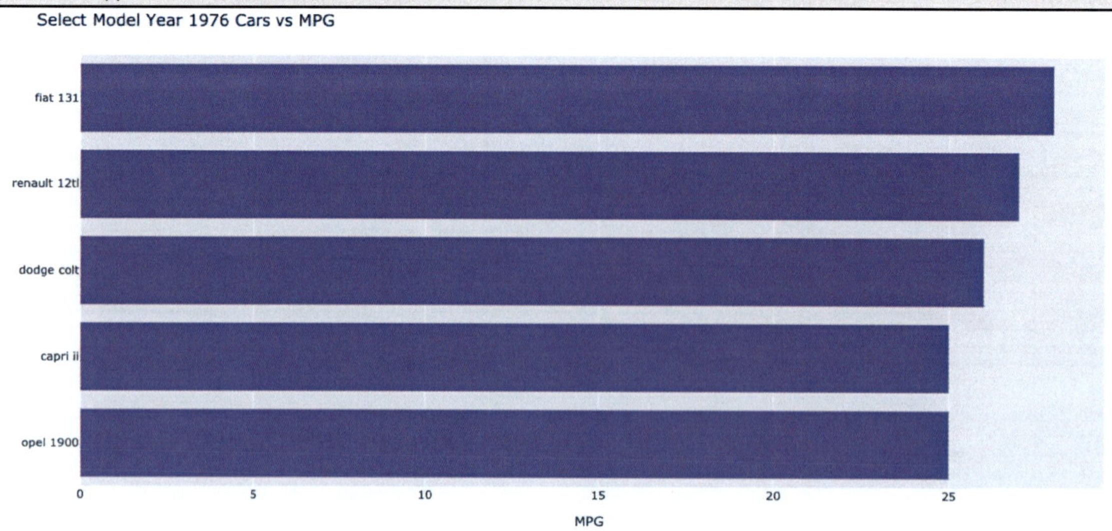

Plotly's grouping and stacking behavior is a little different:

```
fig = px.bar(mpg, x='model_year', y='mpg', color='origin')
fig.update_layout(barmode='group', title='MPG vs model year')
fig.show()
```

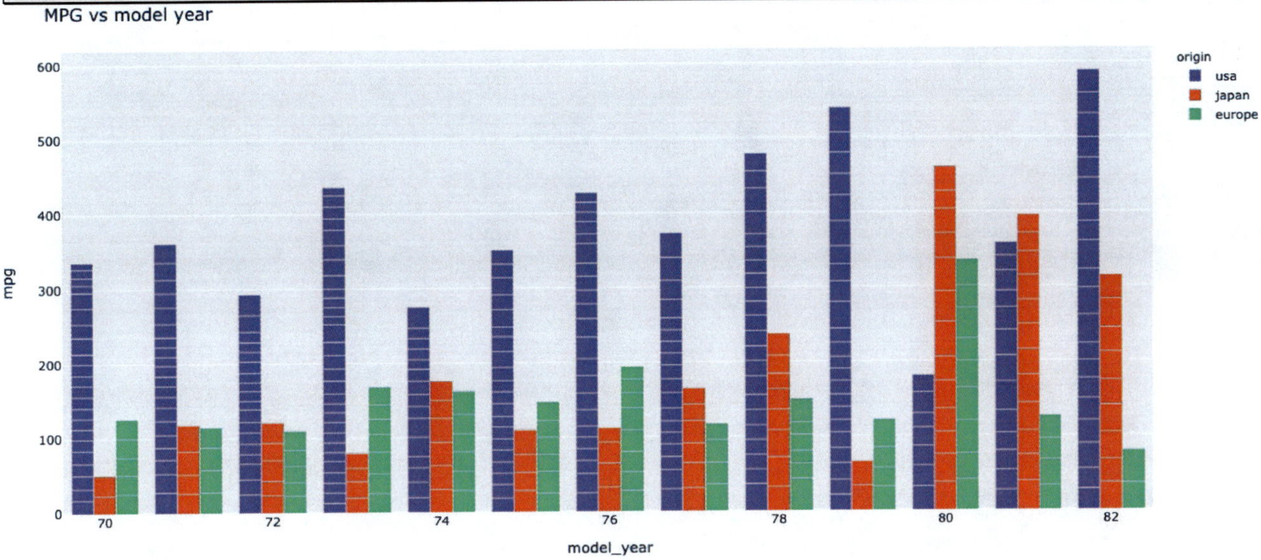

Even though the bars are grouped by origin in the *mpg* column, the data was not averaged and instead stacked on top of each other. No argument still results in stacking:

```
fig = px.bar(mpg, x='model_year', y='mpg', color='origin')
fig.show()
```

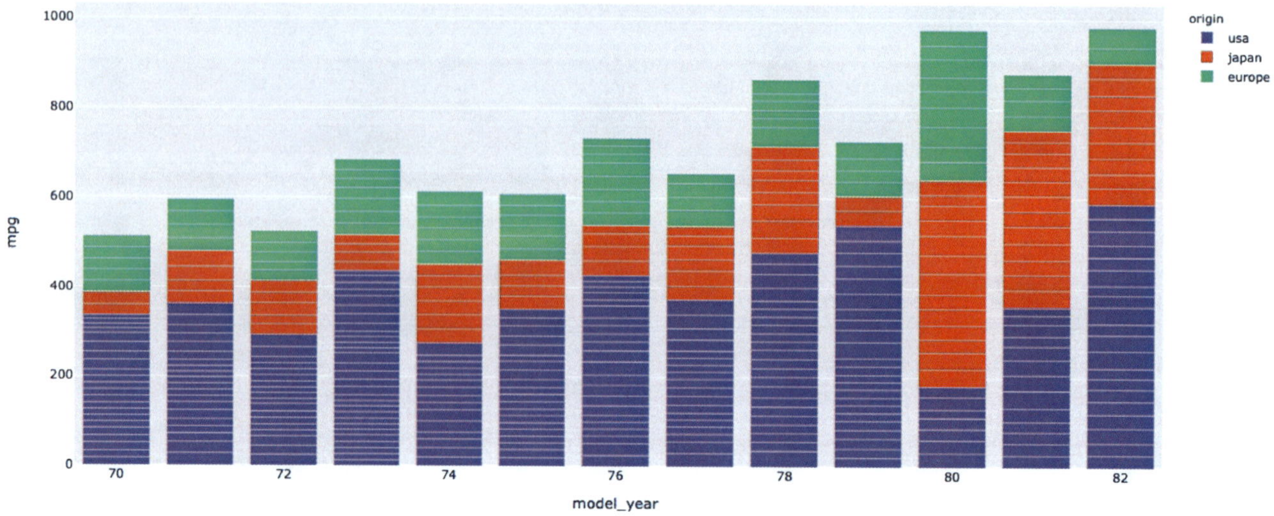

Be careful that you are stacking metrics you mean to stack; the stacked `mpg` column doesn't make any sense because `mpg` does not group and sum by `origin`. You would need to use Pandas' `groupby()` method for that aggregation.

Plotly allows labeling by giving a `text` argument and updating the trace with a `textposition`.

```
hornet = mpg[mpg['name'] == 'amc hornet']
fig = px.bar(hornet, x='model_year', y='mpg', text=hornet['mpg'])
fig.update_layout(title='AMC Hornet Model Year and MPG',
                  xaxis_title="Model Year", yaxis_title="MPG")
fig.update_traces(textposition='outside')
fig.show()
```

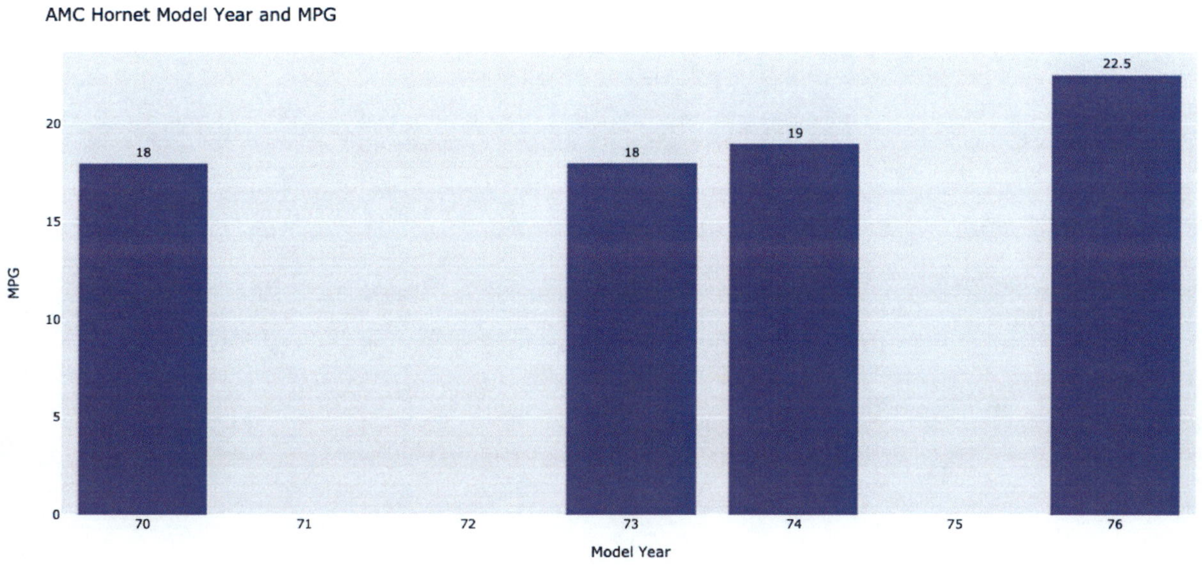

Graph Object bar charts can be accessed with *Bar()*; let's skip ahead to seeing stacked and grouped bar charts. First, stacked bar charts:

```
modelyear = mpg[mpg['model_year'] == 73]
data = modelyear.groupby('origin')['mpg'].count()
data = data.reset_index().rename(columns={'mpg': 'count'})
usa = data[data['origin'] == 'usa']
japan = data[data['origin'] == 'japan']
europe = data[data['origin'] == 'europe']
fig = go.Figure(data=[go.Bar(name='USA', x=[73],
                             y=usa['count'], width=0.1,
                      hovertemplate="%{y} cars produced in 19%{x}"),
                      go.Bar(name='Japan', x=[73],
                             y=japan['count'], width=0.1,
                      hovertemplate="%{y} cars produced in 19%{x}"),
                      go.Bar(name='Europe', x=[73],
                             y=europe['count'], width=0.1,
                 hovertemplate="%{y} cars produced in 19%{x}")])
# Change the bar mode
fig.update_layout(barmode='stack', title='Cars Produced in 1973')
fig.update_xaxes(title_text='Model Year', nticks=2)
fig.update_yaxes(title_text='Number of Cars Produced')
fig.show()
```

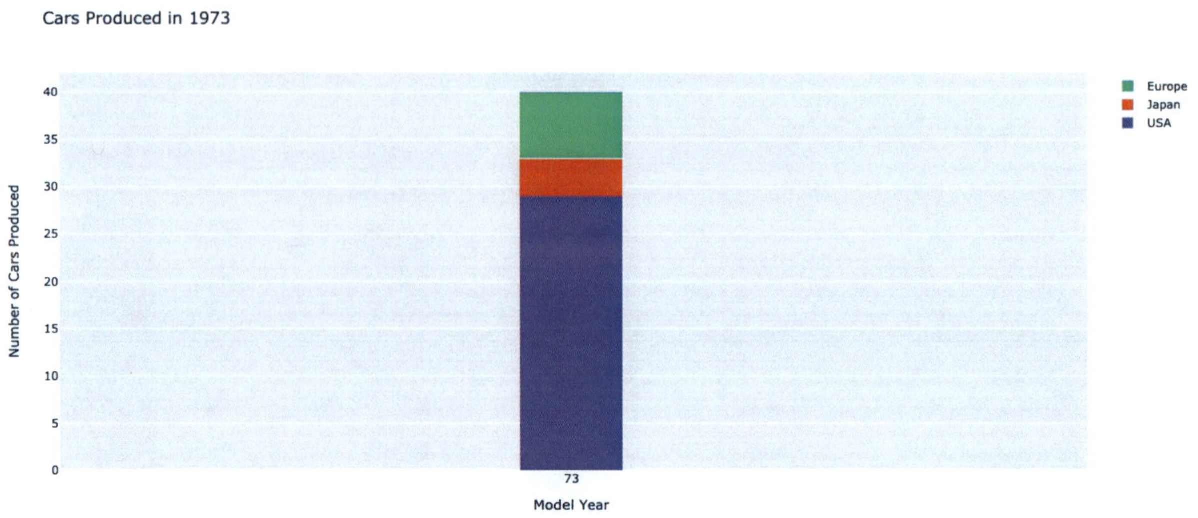

Next, grouped bar charts:

```
mpg_usa = mpg[mpg['origin'] ==
        'usa'].groupby('model_year')['mpg'].count().reset_index()
mpg_europe = mpg[mpg['origin'] ==
       'europe'].groupby('model_year')['mpg'].mean().reset_index()
fig = go.Figure(data=[go.Bar(name='Europe',
                             x=mpg_europe['model_year'],
                             y=mpg_europe['mpg']),
                      go.Bar(name='USA',
                             x=mpg_usa['model_year'],
                             y=mpg_usa['mpg'])])
# Change the bar mode
fig.update_layout(barmode='group', title="Car Production")
fig.update_xaxes(title_text='Model Year')
fig.update_yaxes(title_text='Number of Cars Produced')
fig.show()
```

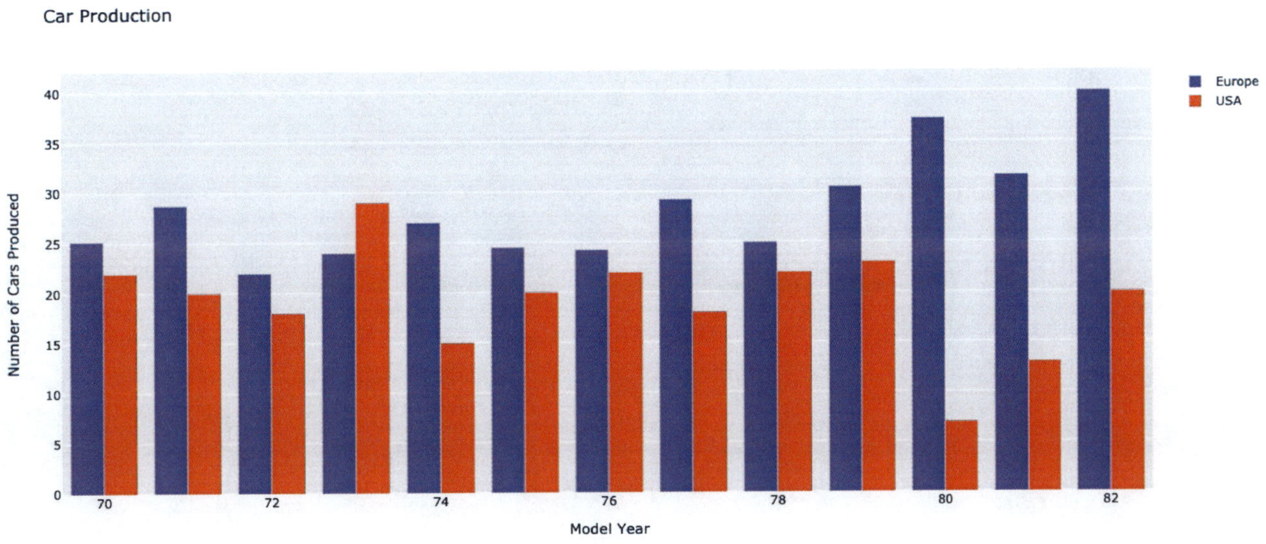

Graph Objects can require a lot of tweaking to get just right, so Plotly Express is usually recommended unless you absolutely need that level of detail and control.

Summary

Bar charts are used to plot one categorical variable and one numerical variable. With a stacked or grouped bar chart, they can be used to plot two numerical variables and one categorical variable (for example, Q1 and Q2 profit or loss for different business units). They can also be used in place of line plots with time on the x axis. There are a few rules of thumb for using bar charts:

- Don't truncate the numerical axis (y axis for a bar chart, x axis for a horizontal bar chart) because this can exaggerate the data visualization
- Resist the temptation to use cute images or patterns to replace solid rectangular bars
- Don't change the bar area; make the width uniform for all bars, and let the bar height tell the story

- Sort the bars from largest to smallest (or vice versa) if you have multiple categories
- Use color to emphasize certain bars to present your story

Examples for Each Library

```
import matplotlib.pyplot as plt
import seaborn as sns
import plotly.express as px
import plotly.graph_objects as go
import plotly.io as pio
pio.renderers.default = "browser"
mpg = sns.load_dataset('mpg')

# matplotlib basic bar chart
pinto = mpg[mpg['name'] == 'ford pinto']
plt.bar(pinto['model_year'], pinto['mpg'])
plt.xlabel('Model Year')
plt.ylabel('MPG')
plt.title('Ford Pinto MPG vs Model Year')
plt.show()

# matplotlib basic horizontal bar chart
year1976 = mpg[mpg['model_year'] == 76]
year1976 = year1976.iloc[0:5]
year1976.sort_values(by='mpg', ascending=True, inplace=True)
plt.barh(year1976['name'], year1976['mpg'])
plt.xlabel('MPG')
plt.title('Select Model Year 1976 Cars vs MPG')
plt.show()

# Matplotlib grouped bar chart with label at end
# if you want to avoid the default colors, you can pass your own
argument
def autolabel(rects):
    for rect in rects:
        height = rect.get_height()
        ax.annotate('{}'.format(int(round(height, 0))),
```

```
                    xy=(rect.get_x() + rect.get_width() / 2,
height),
                    xytext=(0, 3),
                    textcoords="offset points",
                    ha='center', va='bottom', size=7)
fig, ax = plt.subplots()
bar_width = 0.3
mpg_usa = mpg[mpg['origin'] ==
        'usa'].groupby('model_year')['mpg'].mean().reset_index()
mpg_usa['model_year'] = mpg_usa['model_year'] - bar_width
mpg_japan = mpg[mpg['origin'] ==
        'japan'].groupby('model_year')['mpg'].mean().reset_index()
mpg_europe = mpg[mpg['origin'] ==
        'europe'].groupby('model_year')['mpg'].mean().reset_index()
mpg_europe['model_year'] = mpg_europe['model_year'] + bar_width
usa = ax.bar(mpg_usa['model_year'], mpg_usa['mpg'],
             label="USA", width=bar_width)
japan = ax.bar(mpg_japan['model_year'], mpg_japan['mpg'],
               label="Japan", width=bar_width)
europe = ax.bar(mpg_europe['model_year'], mpg_europe['mpg'],
                label="Europe", width=bar_width)
ax.set_ylabel("Average MPG")
ax.set_title("Average MPG by model year and origin")
ax.legend()
ax.set_xticks(mpg_japan['model_year'])
autolabel(usa)
autolabel(japan)
autolabel(europe)
plt.show()

# Plotly Express bar chart with corrected data
pinto = mpg[mpg['name'] == 'ford pinto']
pinto = pinto[pinto['cylinders'] == 4]
fig = px.bar(pinto, x='model_year', y='mpg')
fig.update_layout(title='Ford Pinto MPG vs Model Year',
                  xaxis_title="Model Year",
                  yaxis_title="MPG")
fig.show()

# Plotly Express bar chart with direct labeling
```

```
hornet = mpg[mpg['name'] == 'amc hornet']
fig = px.bar(hornet, x='model_year', y='mpg', text=hornet['mpg'])
fig.update_layout(title='AMC Hornet Model Year and MPG',
                  xaxis_title="Model Year", yaxis_title="MPG")
fig.update_traces(textposition='outside')
fig.show()

# Advanced stacked bar chart
crashes = sns.load_dataset('car_crashes')
crashes = crashes.sort_values(by='total', ascending=True)
# needed to reduce overlap of text
plt.figure(figsize=(12.0, 8.0))
plt.subplot(1, 2, 1)
sns.set_color_codes('pastel')
sns.barplot(data=crashes, x='total', y='abbrev', color='b',
            label='Total')
sns.set_color_codes('dark')
sns.barplot(data=crashes, x='speeding', y='abbrev', color='b',
           label='Speeding-involved')
plt.legend()
plt.xlabel('Car crashes per 1 billion miles')
plt.ylabel('State')
plt.title('Speeding involvement in car crashes per billion miles')

plt.subplot(1, 2, 2)
sns.set_color_codes('pastel')
sns.barplot(data=crashes, x='total', y='abbrev', color='b',
            label='Total')
sns.set_color_codes('colorblind')
sns.barplot(data=crashes, x='alcohol', y='abbrev', color='b',
            label='Alcohol-involved')
plt.xlabel('Car crashes per 1 billion miles')
plt.ylabel('State')
plt.title('Alcohol involvement in car crashes per billion miles')
sns.despine(left=True, bottom=True)
plt.legend()
plt.savefig('crashes.png')
```

View this code on GitHub at https://github.com/alexkenan/pyviz/

Resources

[1] https://matplotlib.org/stable/api/_as_gen/matplotlib.pyplot.bar.html

[2] https://seaborn.pydata.org/generated/seaborn.barplot.html

[3] https://plotly.com/python/bar-charts/

Pie Charts

Introduction

Pie charts are part-to-whole visualizations that depict one categorical variable and one numerical variable; a pie chart takes a circle, slices it into pieces proportional to its subcategories, and relies on the different pie slices to tell the story. Pie charts are perhaps the most hated chart in data visualization history because of misuse, overuse, and abuse. Pies with more than about 5 slices can become very busy, and pies with slices of similar (but not the same) percentages can be distorted. Bar charts can almost always replace a pie chart; most data visualization experts recommend scrapping pie charts for bar charts. But, pie charts can still be useful.

So, in general, pie charts can be used, but they should only be used under certain circumstances: fewer than 6 slices and a big enough difference in proportions that it is easy to tell which slices has the largest percentage and which has the smallest. We will also explore treemaps at the end of the Plotly section; treemaps are another way to show a part-to-whole relationship.

We will use Plotly's 2010 alcohol consumption by country dataset and call it `alcohol`.

Column Name	**Datatype**	**Description**
location	`str`	Country
alcohol	`float`	Per capita alcohol consumption by some unit (Liters?)

The Lie

There are any number of visualizations that could go here to show pie chart lies. In general, pie charts lie when they are used with more than 5 slices, when their percentages don't sum to 100%, and if the slices are all approximately equal percentage. Consider this pie chart:

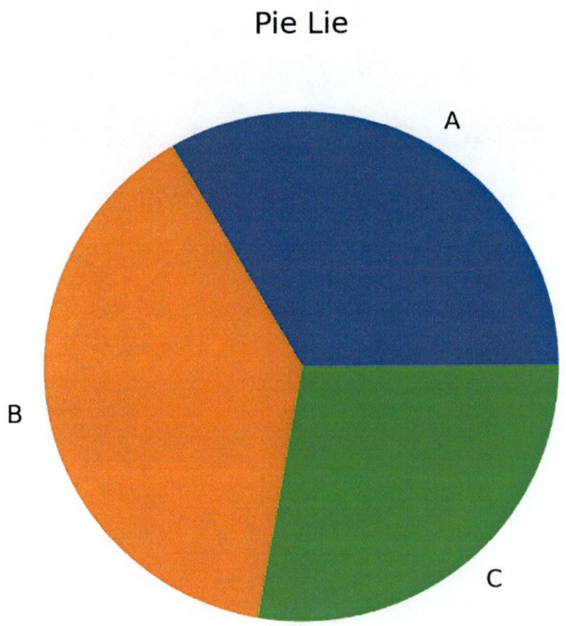

Which slice is largest? A is 30%, B is 35%, and C is 25%. If you study the visualization, C looks a little smaller, but A and B are too similar to make a good determination. This is why bar charts are suggested as a replacement for pie charts. Even though they can be pariahs, let's learn more about pie charts.

Imports

```
import pandas as pd
import matplotlib.pyplot as plt
import plotly.express as px
import plotly.graph_objects as go
import plotly.io as pio
pio.renderers.default = "browser"
alcohol = pd.read_csv('https://raw.githubusercontent.com/
                      alexkenan/pyviz/main/datasets/alcohol.csv')
plt.style.use('default')
```

Matplotlib

A basic pie chart can be created with `plt.pie()`. It accepts values to plot and labels to assign to each piece of the pie.

```
plt.pie(alcohol['alcohol'], labels=alcohol['location'])
plt.title('Alcohol Consumption by Country')
plt.show()
```

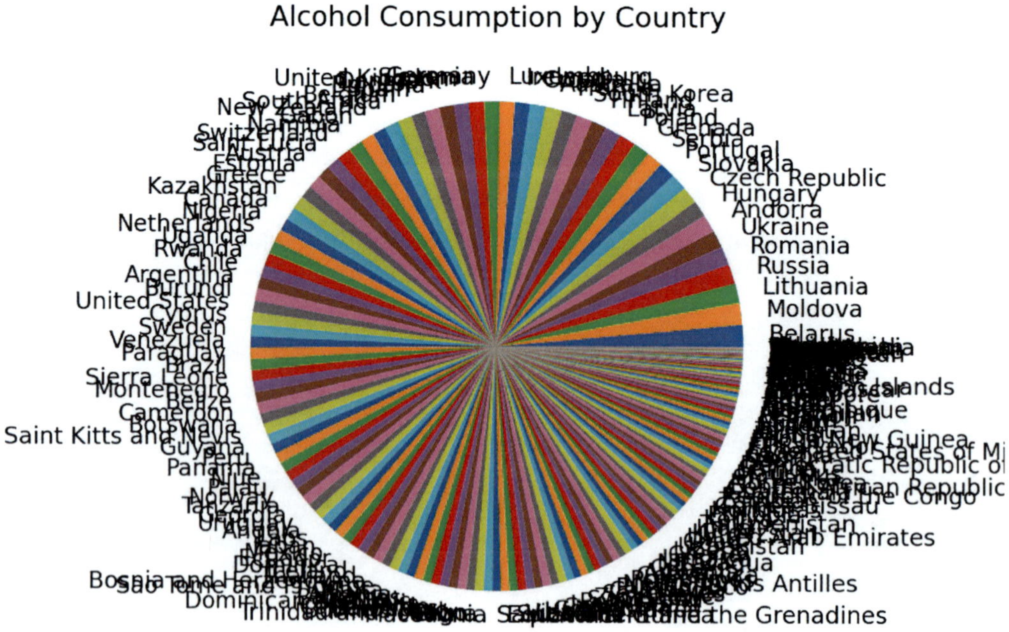

Well, that certainly is beautiful, isn't it? This example is taken to an extreme, but it shows why a pie with too many slices becomes unreadable: it's hard to pick out a single country, and all of the labels overlap. Since showing all of the countries is an absolute mess, we will use a selection of four countries for the remainder of this chapter: Belarus, France, Japan, and Honduras.

We could just find out each country's consumption and create our own `list`, but let's use Pandas Boolean indexing and the logical OR operator `|` (this is the vertical pipe "|" above the Enter/Return key) to whittle the `alcohol` DataFrame into a `countries` DataFrame. The parentheses are necessary to force Pandas to accept all conditions (Belarus OR France OR Japan OR Honduras).

```
countries = alcohol[(alcohol['location'] == 'Belarus')
                    | (alcohol['location'] == 'France')
                    | (alcohol['location'] == 'Japan')
                    | (alcohol['location'] == 'Honduras')]
```

Let's take a look at including the consumption percentage on the chart. This percentage will be the percentage of each country out of the four countries, not the percentage out of the entire alcohol dataset, because pie charts must sum to 100%. We have to pass the old string format to `autopct`; formatting to 20.5%, for example, is `{:.1%}` in the new string format and `%1.1f%%` in the old string format.

```
plt.pie(countries['alcohol'], labels=countries['location'],
        autopct='%1.1f%%')
plt.title('Alcohol Consumption for Select Countries')
plt.show()
```

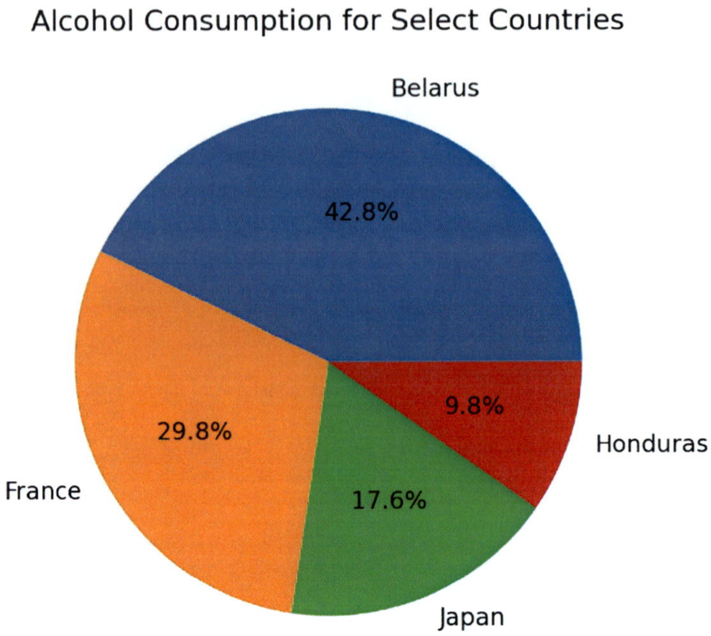

It is also possible to create an "exploded" pie chart with one or more slices offset from the center of the pie. This technique is generally considered to be chart junky and to detract from the story, but one exploded slice can sometimes highlight a label well. We need to pass a `list`-like object to the `explode` parameter of the offset to use for each label. In this case, we will offset only Japan, so our `offset` is `[0, 0, 0.1, 0]`.

```
offset = [0, 0, 0.1, 0]
plt.pie(countries['alcohol'], explode=offset,
        labels=countries['location'],
        autopct='%1.1f%%')
plt.title('Alcohol Consumption for Select Countries')
plt.show()
```

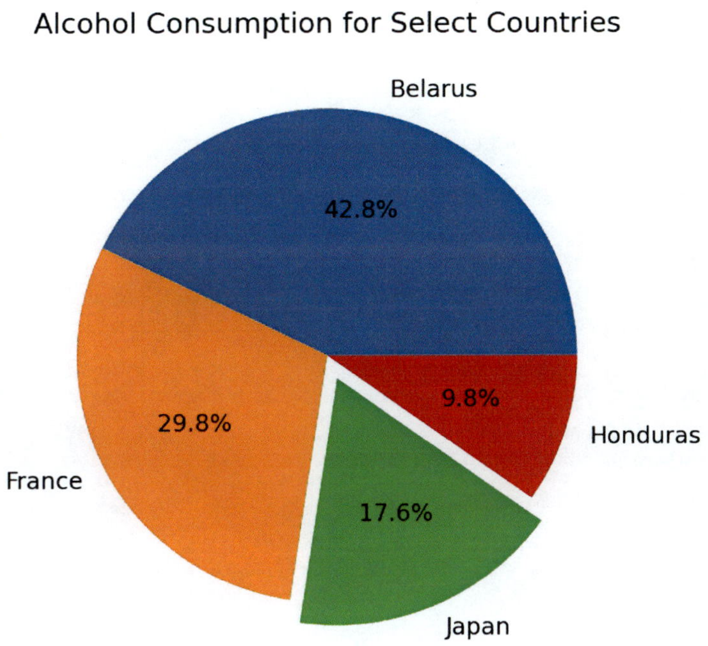

This is the only potentially bad habit you will learn in this book. Exploded pie charts are generally not an effective message; if you have gotten to the point where you are considering an exploded pie chart, you should consider an alternative visualization like a bar chart.

It is also possible to create a donut chart, which is a pie chart with a hole cut out of the middle. It looks like this:

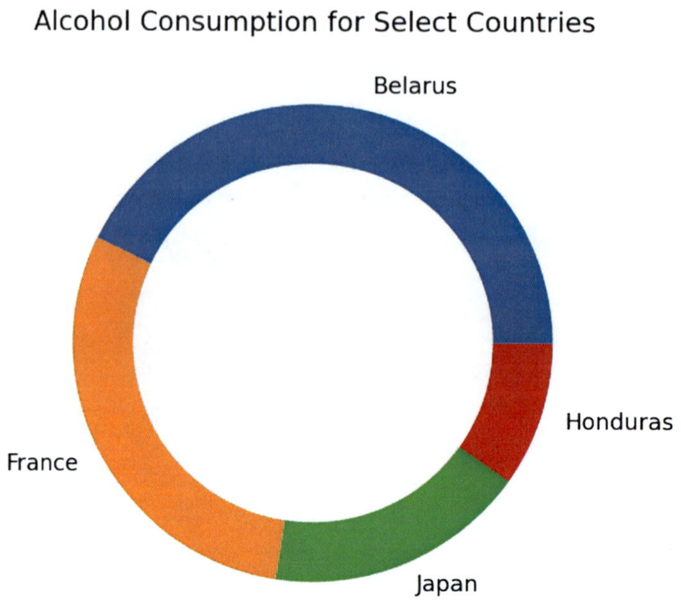

Donut charts are pie charts made even worse. Donut charts are empty calories and should not be used because a donut chart requires the reader to interpret how arc length relates to area. They have become trendy in technology dashboard settings, but please resist the urge to use them.

Seaborn

Seaborn does not have any functions for creating pie charts; this should tell you all you need to know about Seaborn's opinion of pie charts.

Plotly

Plotly Express has a `pie()` function for creating pie charts, and it is remarkably similar to Matplotlib's `pie()` function:

```
fig = px.pie(countries, values='alcohol', names='location',
             title="Alcohol Consumption by Select Countries")
fig.show()
```

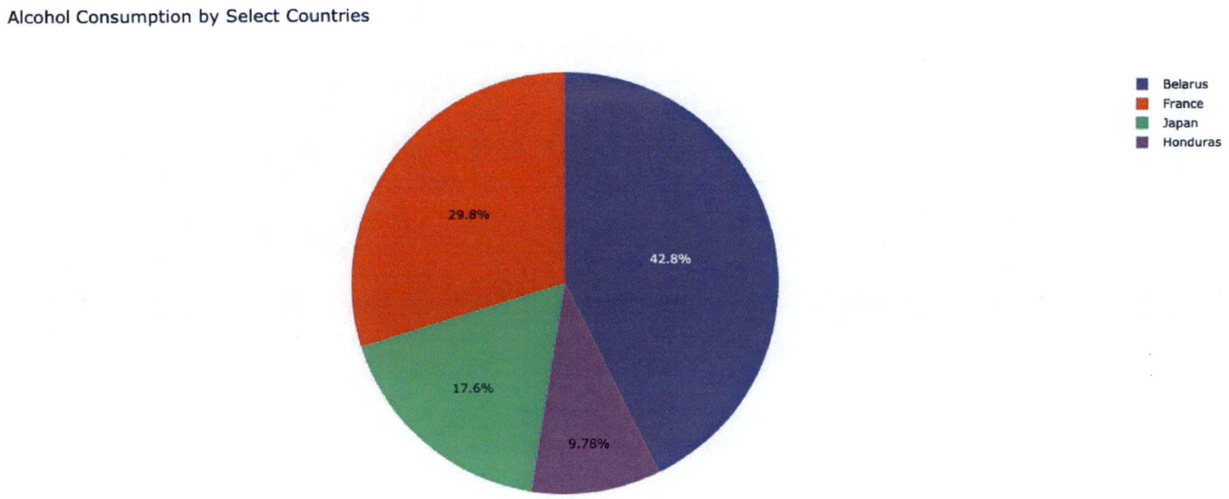

We can customize the label information to include the country, and we could add hover information if our DataFrame had more than two columns:

```
fig = px.pie(countries, values='alcohol', names='location',
             title="Alcohol Consumption by Select Countries")
fig.update_traces(textposition='inside', textinfo='percent+label')
fig.update_layout(showlegend=False)
fig.show()
```

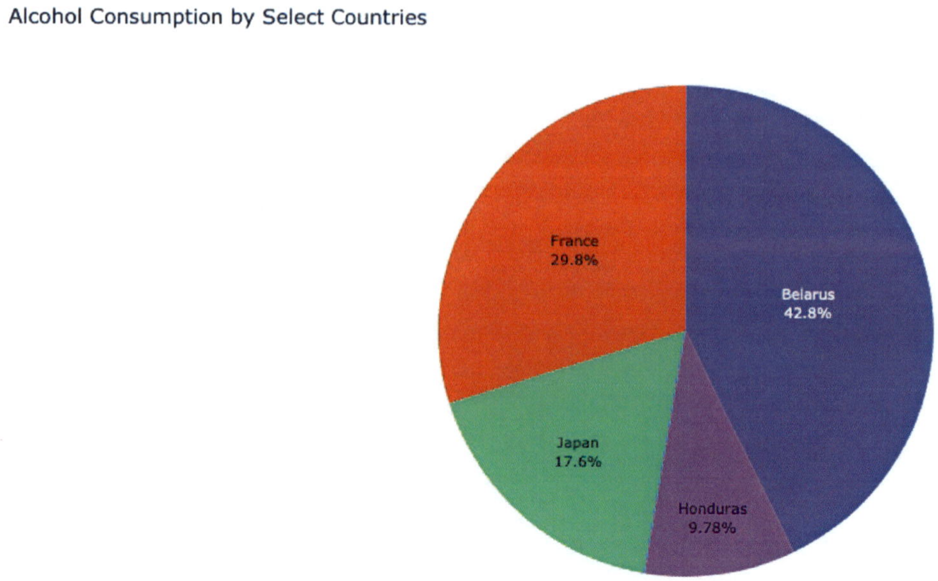

If Plotly Express doesn't have enough for your pie chart needs, you can always go directly to the Graph Objects source:

```
fig = go.Figure(data=[go.Pie(labels=countries['location'],
                             values=countries['alcohol'])])
fig.update_layout(title="Alcohol Consumption by Select Countries")
fig.show()
```

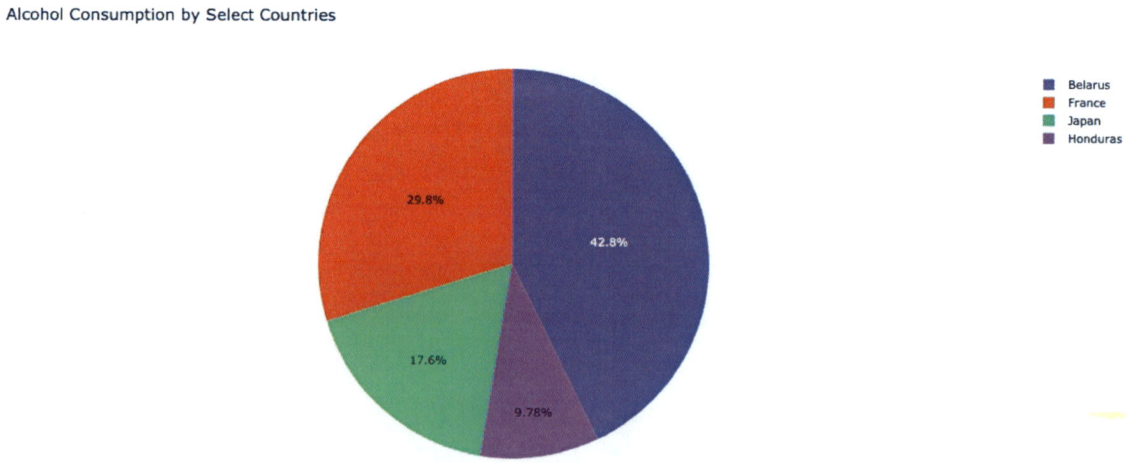

Since pie charts are often criticized, it's a good idea to discuss another visualization method for displaying part-to-whole relationships: the treemap. This type of chart is typically used to show hierarchical relationships (for example, World → North America → Canada), but it can be used for a part-to-whole comparison with one parent. There are a few different helper libraries for generating a treemap to make one with Matplotlib, but Plotly has a `Treemap()` function that we can use. There is also a Graph Objects `Treemap()`, but we will only show Plotly Express treemaps. Let's look at our selection of countries first:

```
fig = px.treemap(countries, names='location', values='alcohol',
                 parents=["" for _ in countries['location']])
fig.update_layout(title="Alcohol Consumption by Select Countries")
fig.show()
```

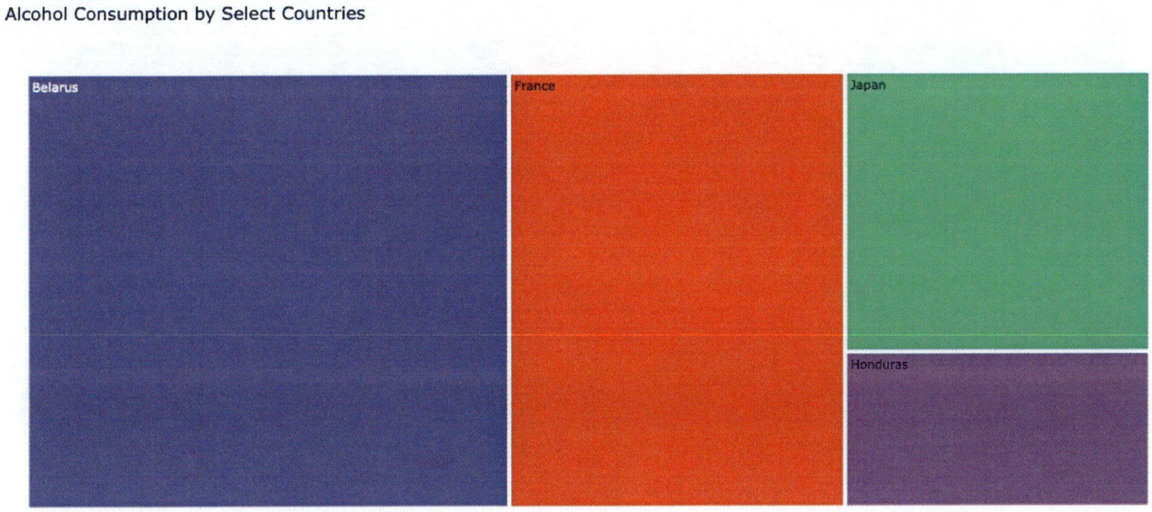

Since we don't want to show any parents (which would be a rectangle encompassing all of our shapes), we pass the list comprehension `["" for _ in countries['location']]` of empty `strs`.

As a final nod to the beginning of this chapter, we can create a treemap for the entire `alcohol` dataset.

```
fig = px.treemap(alcohol, names='location', values='alcohol',
                 parents=["World" for _ in alcohol['location']])
fig.update_layout(title='Alcohol Consumption by Country')
fig.show()
```

Alcohol Consumption by Country

This visualization is still busy, but it at least better conveys a message than the original pie chart did.

Summary

Pie charts are a touchy subject. Some books on data visualization have a one-page pie chart chapter that looks something like this: "Pie Charts: Don't." Pie charts are frowned upon partially because they are often the first type of data visualization that is learned, and therefore, they are misused and misunderstood. If you are going to use a pie chart, keep the following rules in mind:

1) Pie charts should have about 5 slices or fewer. Anything more, and the pie chart becomes hard to read

2) Don't make a pie chart even worse by using a donut chart

3) Consider using a bar chart since (savvy data visualization) people have such a visceral disdain for pie charts

Treemaps and Sankey diagrams are alternative part-to-whole visualizations that convey the same message without the bad reputation of a pie chart.

Examples for Each Library

```
import pandas as pd
import matplotlib.pyplot as plt
import plotly.express as px
import plotly.graph_objects as go
import plotly.io as pio
pio.renderers.default = "browser"
alcohol = pd.read_csv('https://raw.githubusercontent.com/
                      alexkenan/pyviz/main/datasets/alcohol.csv')
countries = alcohol[(alcohol['location'] == 'Belarus')
                        | (alcohol['location'] == 'France')
                        | (alcohol['location'] == 'Japan')
                        | (alcohol['location'] == 'Honduras')]
plt.style.use('default')

# Matplotlib selection of countries with pct labels
plt.pie(countries['alcohol'], labels=countries['location'],
        autopct='%1.1f%%')
plt.title('Alcohol Consumption for Select Countries')
plt.show()

# Plotly Express pie customization
fig = px.pie(countries, values='alcohol', names='location',
             title="Alcohol Consumption by Select Countries")
fig.update_traces(textposition='inside', textinfo='percent+label')
fig.show()

# Plotly Graph Objects
fig = go.Figure(data=[go.Pie(labels=countries['location'],
```

```
                              values=countries['alcohol'])])
fig.update_layout(title="Alcohol Consumption by Select Countries")
fig.show()

# PX treemap for narrowed df
fig = px.treemap(countries, names='location', values='alcohol',
                 parents=["" for _ in countries['location']])
fig.update_layout(title="Alcohol Consumption by Select Countries")
fig.show()

# PX treemap for alcohol df
fig = px.treemap(alcohol, names='location', values='alcohol',
                 parents=["World" for _ in alcohol['location']])
fig.update_layout(title='Alcohol Consumption by Country')
fig.show()
```

View this code on GitHub at https://github.com/alexkenan/pyviz/

Resources

[1] https://matplotlib.org/stable/api/_as_gen/matplotlib.pyplot.pie.html

[2] https://plotly.com/python/pie-charts/

[3] https://plotly.com/python/treemaps/

[4] https://plotly.com/python/sankey-diagram/

Seaborn and Plotly Extras

Introduction

Seaborn offers some additional data visualizations: some are not part of the standard charts, and some are novel ways to display two types of standard charts on one figure. This chapter is a bonus section that outlines a few of these visualizations. We will use the `tips` dataset from earlier since it has so many different datatypes. This chapter will not necessarily create beautiful, effective data visualizations, but it will show you how to make novel visualizations of the data. Remember: a data visualization should lead to intuitive understanding from your reader, and it should not be a dump of all of the data that you have.

Imports

```
import matplotlib.pyplot as plt
import seaborn as sns
tips = sns.load_dataset('tips')
```

Seaborn

The first novel method uses a 2D density plot to plot two numerical variables against each other. This visualization is closely related to a heatmap, which we will discuss in a later chapter.

```
sns.displot(tips, x='total_bill', y="tip")
plt.xlabel('Total Bill')
plt.ylabel('Tip')
plt.suptitle('Tips Total Bill 2D Density Plot)
plt.show()
```

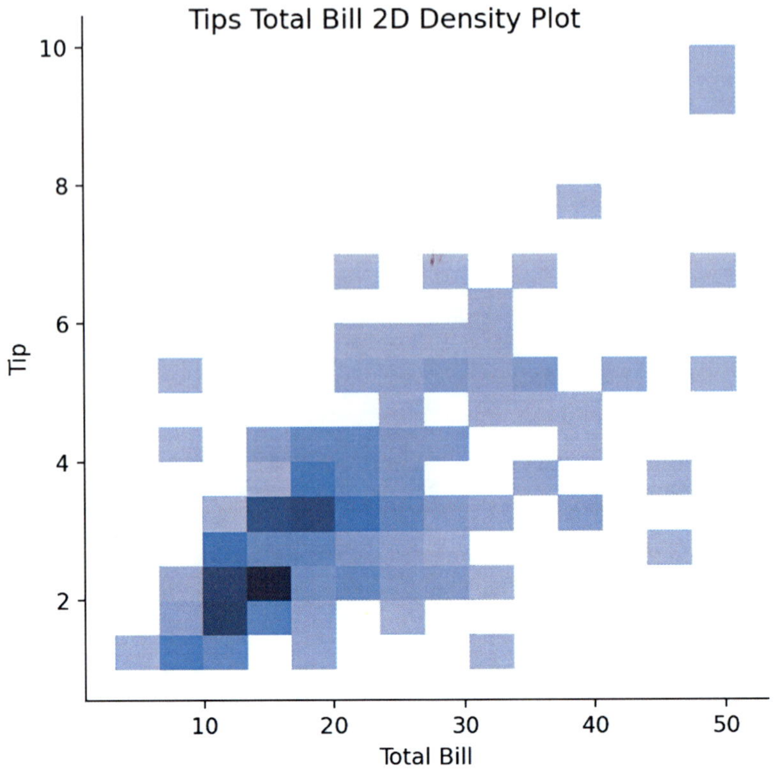

In this case, we have to use `plt.suptitle()` instead of `plt.title()` because `plt.title()` sends the title text off of the figure area. Using the convention that a darker hue means a larger amount, it is easy for a reader to tell that the most frequently occurring combination of total bill and tip is around $15 and $2.25, respectively.

Seaborn also allows for contour plotting, which overlays two-dimensional contours on the plot. This method uses a Kernel Density Estimate (KDE) function which Seaborn calls under the hood:

```
sns.displot(tips, x='total_bill', y='tip', kind="kde")
plt.suptitle('Seaborn Tips Contour Plot')
plt.show()
```

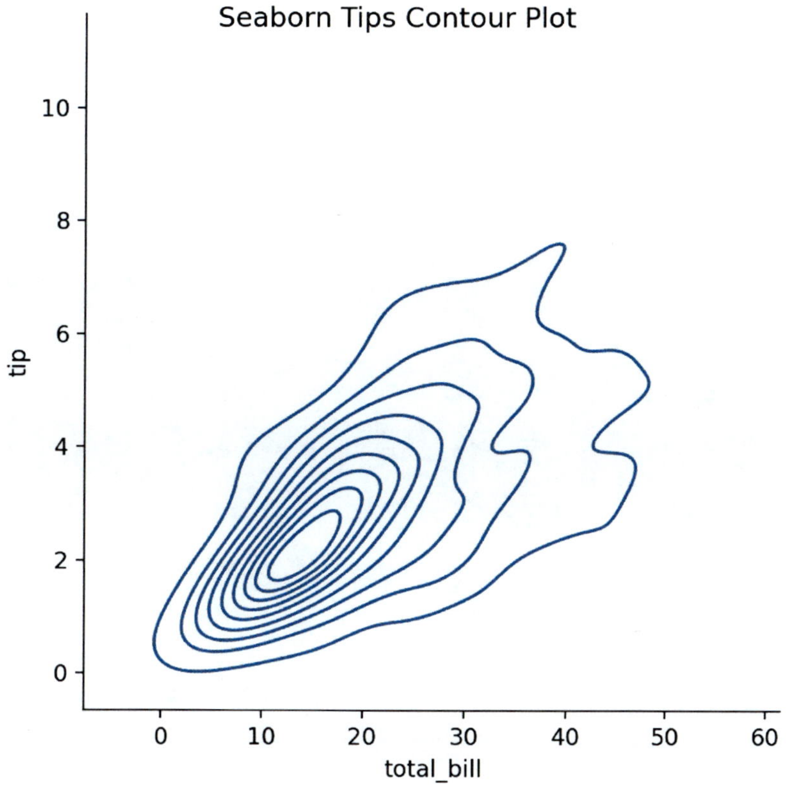

It is also possible to add "rugs" which show the marginal data distribution:

```
sns.displot(tips, x='total_bill', y='tip', kind="kde", rug=True)
plt.suptitle('Seaborn Tips Contour Plot')
plt.show()
```

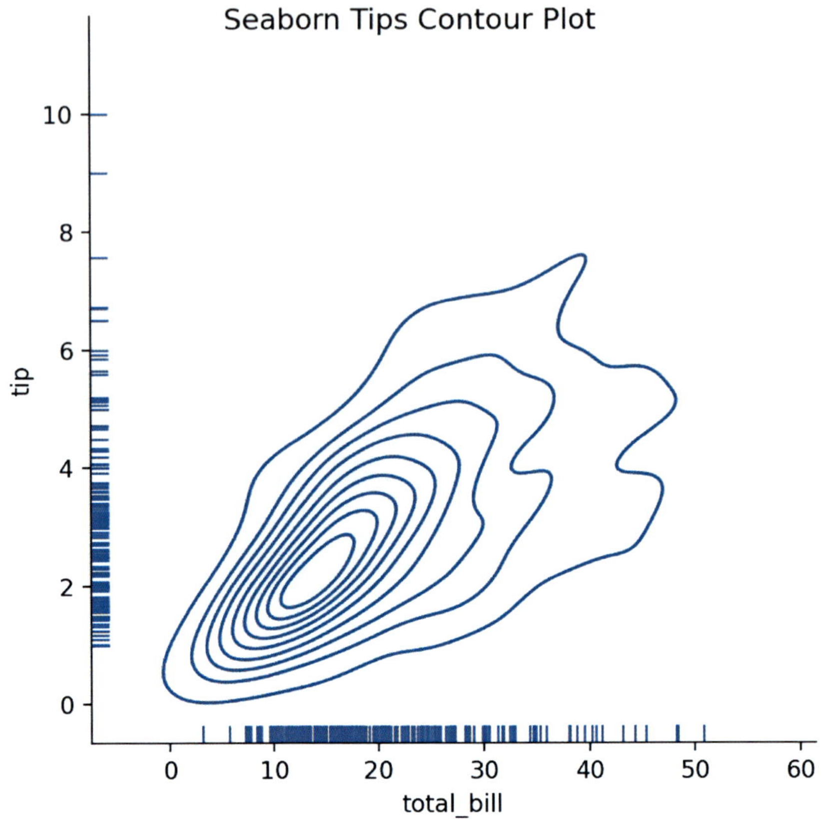

You can pass an optional *hue* parameter to add color, but in this case, it makes a busy chart even busier.

Seaborn also offers the ability to pair multiple plots together into joint plots. A popular data visualization choice is to pair a scatter plot with histograms in the x and y margins to show distributions of those variables. In our case, we can show the scatter plot of *tip* vs *total_bill* with marginal distributions of each axis:

```
sns.jointplot(data=tips, x='total_bill', y='tip', alpha=0.75)
plt.suptitle('Seaborn Tips Jointplot')
plt.show()
```

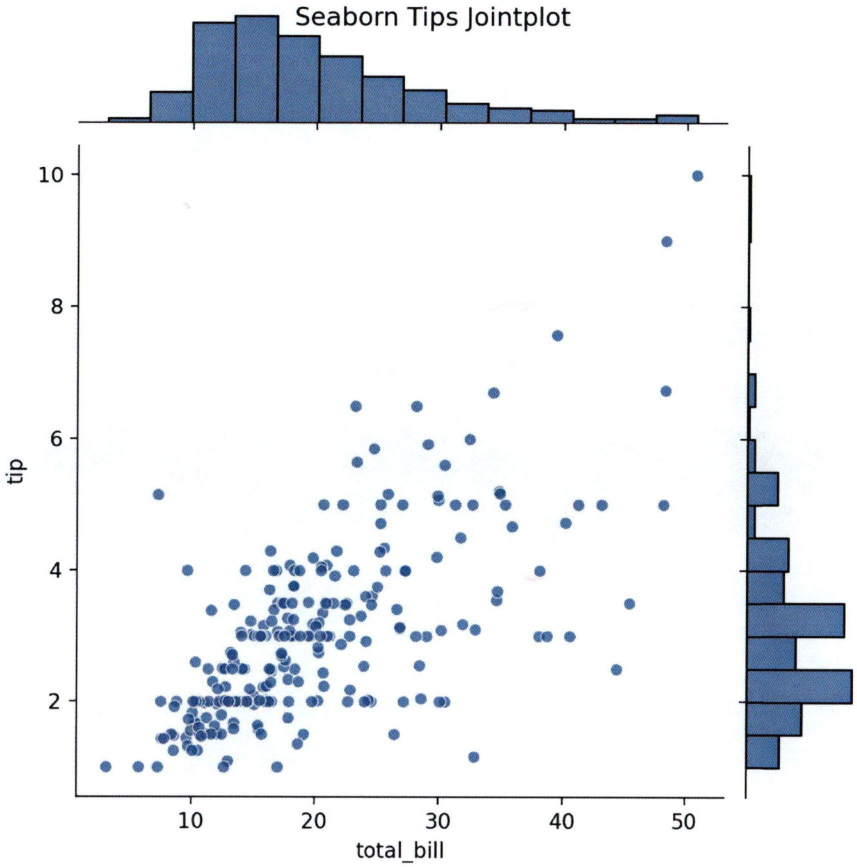

With a joint plot, we can improve upon the 2D density plot.

Instead of using squares, another common data visualization is to use hexagons with color to represent density. Hexagons pack together nicely, and it gives a more presentable look over plain squares:

```
sns.jointplot(data=tips, x='total_bill', y='tip', kind='hex')
plt.suptitle('     Seaborn Tips Hex Jointplot')
plt.show()
```

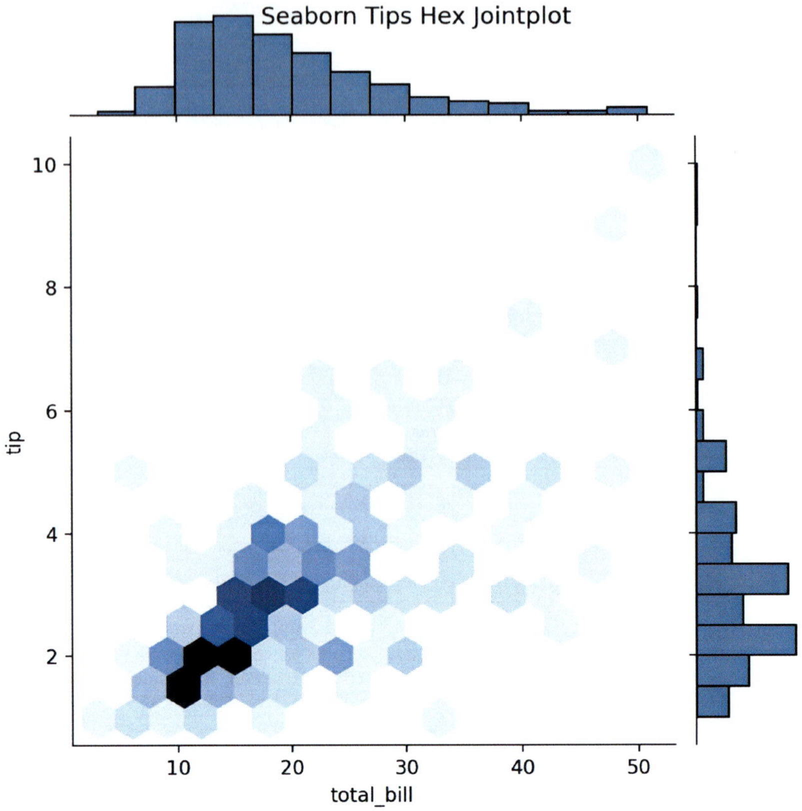

The `total_bill` distribution interferes with the `plt.suptitle()` text, so we add a few spaces to create enough space.

Lastly, Seaborn offers pair plot functionality. Pair plots take each numerical variable and plot pairwise scatter plots for all columns in the dataset. These plots can be quite large, so it is usually a good idea to save them as an image file rather than display them.

```
pairplot = sns.pairplot(tips)
#plt.show()
pairplot.savefig("tips_pairplot.png")
```

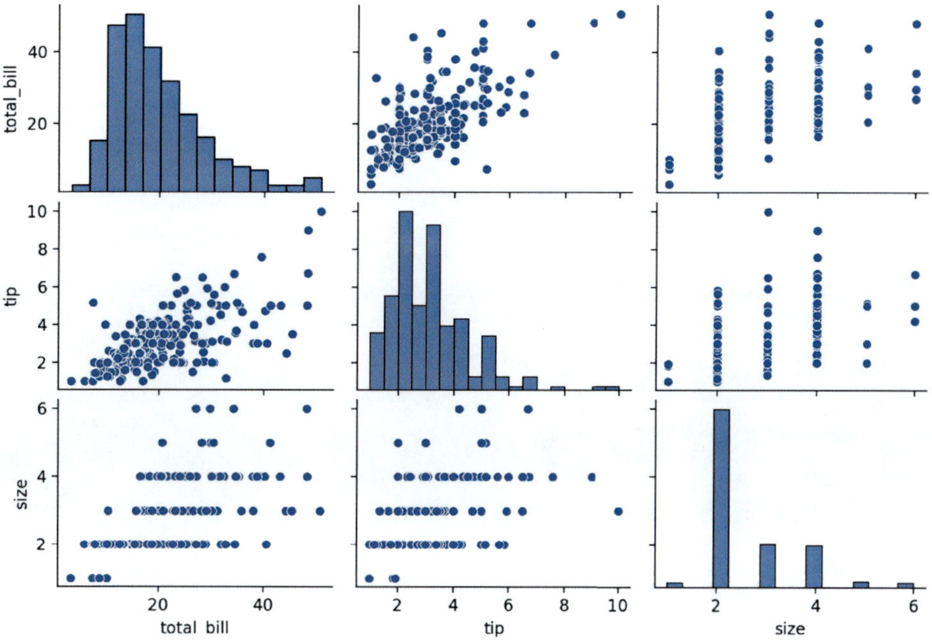

For datasets with many columns of numerical data, the figure can be almost impossible to show with `plt.show()`. This visualization is a good tool to use for exploratory data analysis to gain understanding of the data that you have.

Summary

Seaborn offers some capabilities to wrap around Matplotlib for additional data visualization. These additional visualizations have a time and a place, but they can be used very effectively to communicate your story. Just because you can "make something look cool" does not make it an effective visualization; always remember that you should convey the message with the simplest visualization and with the least ink.

Examples for Each Library

```
import matplotlib.pyplot as plt
import seaborn as sns
tips = sns.load_dataset('tips')
# Seaborn 2D density plot
sns.displot(tips, x='total_bill', y="tip")
plt.xlabel('Total Bill')
plt.ylabel('Tip')
plt.suptitle('Tips Total Bill 2D Density Plot')
plt.show()
# Seaborn contour with rug
sns.displot(tips, x='total_bill', y='tip', kind="kde", rug=True)
plt.suptitle('Seaborn Tips Contour Plot')
plt.show()
# Seaborn bivariate jointplot
sns.jointplot(data=tips, x='total_bill', y='tip', alpha=0.75)
plt.suptitle('Seaborn Tips Jointplot')
plt.show()
# Seaborn hex bivariate jointplot
sns.jointplot(data=tips, x='total_bill', y='tip', kind='hex')
plt.suptitle('     Seaborn Tips Hex Jointplot')
plt.show()
# Seaborn pairplot
pairplot = sns.pairplot(tips)
pairplot.savefig("tips_pairplot.png")
# or, to show the pairplot:
# plt.show()
```

View this code on GitHub at https://github.com/alexkenan/pyviz/

Resources

[1] https://seaborn.pydata.org/generated/seaborn.displot.html

[2] https://seaborn.pydata.org/generated/seaborn.jointplot.html

[3] https://seaborn.pydata.org/generated/seaborn.pairplot.html

Choropleths

Introduction

A choropleth (pronounced koro-pleth, not kloro-pleth) is a type of map that colors different geographic areas (ZIP codes, states, countries, or something else) by a numerical variable or a categorical variable. Choropleths are a great way to show how something varies across regions. Aggregating by region creates an easy visualization that usually does not require advanced statistical analysis. This type of data visualization has a more narrow use-case than visualizations that we have previously discussed, but choropleths are often misused with shading, so it is prudent to discuss them here.

We will be using the `states` dataset that contains each US state's population in 2014.

Column Name	**Datatype**	**Description**
Rank	`int`	Ranking of each state's agricultural exports. Not used in this chapter
State	`str`	The full state name
Postal	`str`	2 letter abbreviation for the state
Population	`float`	Population of that state in 2014

Imports

```
import plotly.express as px
import plotly.graph_objects as go
import pandas as pd
import plotly.io as pio
pio.renderers.default = "browser"
df = pd.read_csv('https://raw.githubusercontent.com/
                alexkenan/pyviz/main/datasets/states.csv')
```

It is possible to create choropleths in Matplotlib via a geographic library like GeoPandas; however, a brief Google search shows that users often have trouble installing GeoPandas with `pip install geopandas`. Because GeoPandas depends on some third-party libraries, pip sometimes fails to complete the download. For this reason, we will only explore choropleths in Plotly which can handle geographic data natively.

Plotly

Plotly Express has a ready-made `choropleth()` function that accepts geographic data and a numerical variable to plot on the geography. Plotly has two built-in geometries: US state names and country names. US state names must be passed as two-letter abbreviations, and country names must be passed as 3-letter ISO country codes. Since we are dealing with US states, we will pass the US state abbreviation to the `locations` keyword for proper parsing.

We can also take advantage of default mapping by passing a `locationmode` and a `scope`. These parameters set up the projection to be US-focused, and they create a three-window view to show Alaska and Hawaii. Plotly does not recognize Puerto Rico as a state, so even if you undo the `scope`, Puerto Rico is still not filled in.

With those explanations out of the way, we can create our choropleth:

```
fig = px.choropleth(df, locations='Postal',
                    locationmode="USA-states",
                    scope="usa",
                    color='Population',
                    color_continuous_scale='Blues')
fig.update_layout(title='US State Populations in 2014')
fig.show()
```

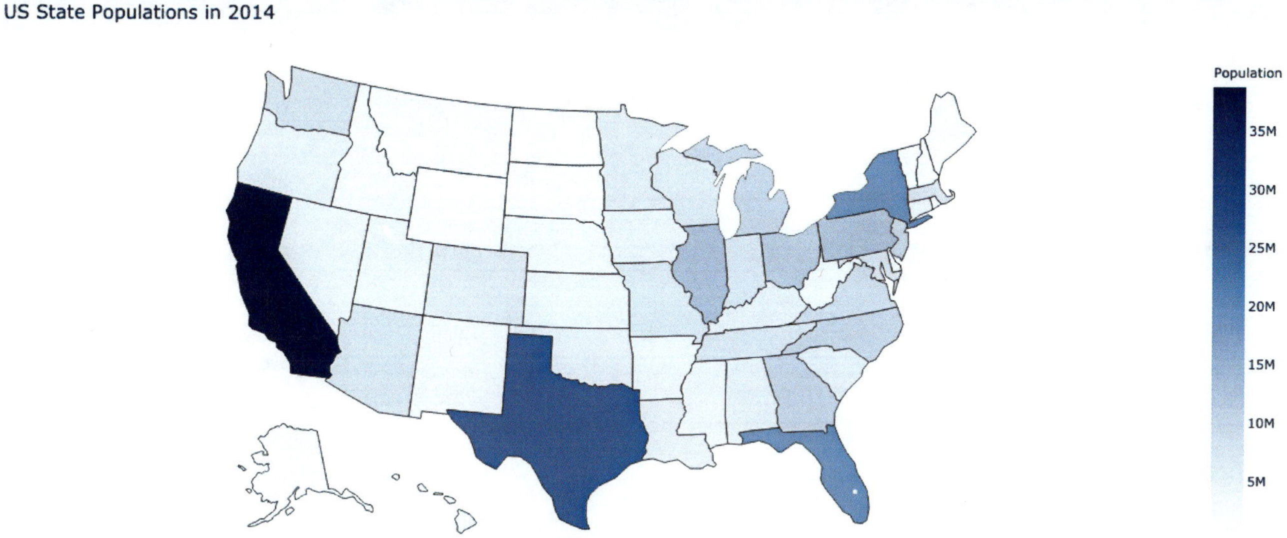

Using a continuous color scale like `Blues`, `Blacks`, or `Reds` is an intuitive use of color: the darker shading represents more population, and the lighter shading represents less population. It can be incredibly tempting to use a cute bivariate color or otherwise match colors to make the choropleth look "good." A bivariate color scale has two colors and fills in areas from most to least. For example, "Viridis" is a popular colorscale choice:

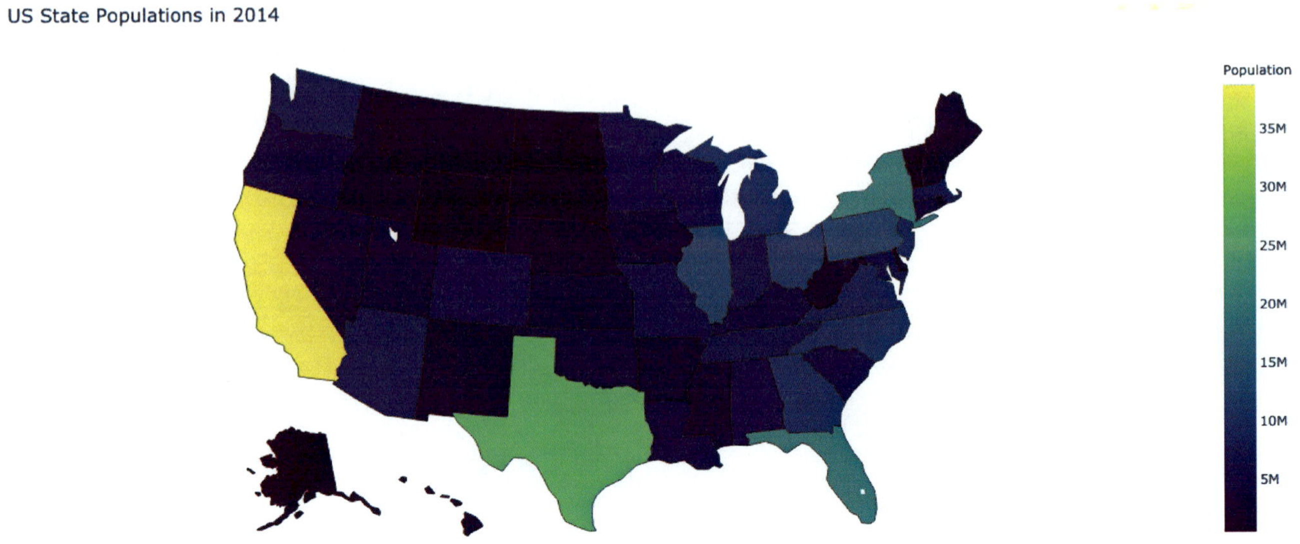

In this case, California stands out, but the rest of the colorscale is not intuitive. What does green represent? What does dark blue represent? What do teal and turquoise represent? If you are plotting a numerical variable, use color palettes with care. For example, a common color scale is the red/black diverging bivariate color palette for plotting profit and loss by state. There are some use cases for bivariate color scales, but in general, a single-color continuous color scale is going to be the best way to represent your numerical data.

Plotly Graph Objects gives us some more customization options. We have to explicitly pass columns of the DataFrame, and the `color` argument becomes the `z` argument. Let's create a new column in the DataFrame called `Readable` which creates custom hover text for the state, its abbreviation, and its population, rounded to 1 decimal place.

```python
def readable_pop(row):
    if row['Population'] >= 1E6:
        return '{} ({})<br>Population {:.1f}M'.format(row['State'],
                                    row['Postal'], row['Population']/1E6)
    else:
        return '{} ({})<br>Population {:.1f}K'.format(row['State'],
                                        row['Postal'], row['Population']/1E3)
```

We need to `apply` it across the DataFrame rows:

```python
df['Readable'] = df.apply(readable_pop, axis=1)
```

And, finally, we can create our choropleth:

```python
fig = go.Figure(data=go.Choropleth(locations=df['Postal'],
                                    locationmode="USA-states",
                                    z=df['Population'],
                                    colorscale='Blues',
                                    text=df['Readable'],
                                    hovertemplate='%{text}',
                                    name=""))
fig.update_layout(geo_scope='usa',
                  title="US State Populations in 2014")
fig.show()
```

US State Populations in 2014

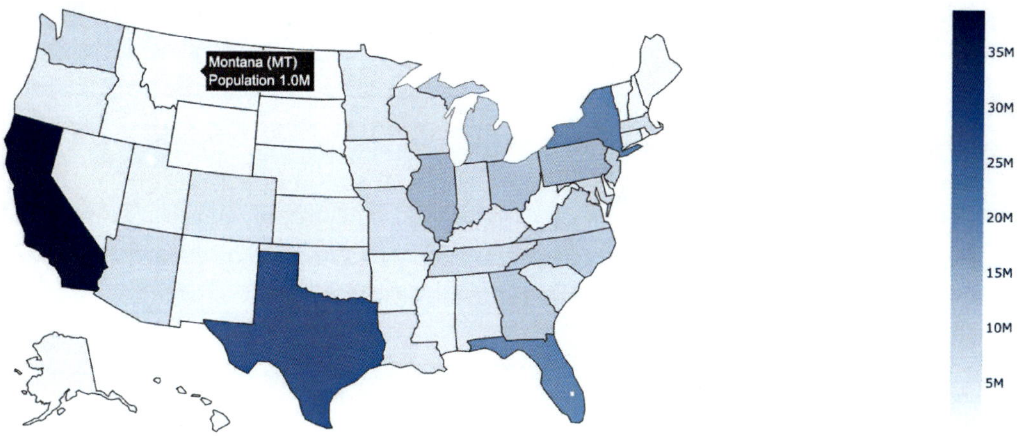

The map does not look any different between Plotly Express and Plotly Graph Objects, but the ability to customize nearly every parameter is important should you need that granular functionality.

Summary

Choropleths overlay either a numerical or a categorical variable on top of geographic information. The temptation to use "fun" color scales is high, but make sure you use an intuitive color scale to make your visualization easy to understand. A color legend is usually a good choice, and make sure that your geographic regions make sense and do not skew your data. For example, if California had a population of 250 million people, it would appear as a dark blue on the map, and every other state would be washed out to a similar light blue color due to the population difference. Also, make sure you pronounce "choropleth" correctly!

Now that we have covered the basic types of data visualization, we will move on to more advanced visualizations with datasets found in the wild.

Examples for Each Library

```
import plotly.express as px
import plotly.graph_objects as go
import pandas as pd
import plotly.io as pio
pio.renderers.default = "browser"
df = pd.read_csv('https://raw.githubusercontent.com/
                alexkenan/pyviz/main/datasets/states.csv')

# Plotly choropleth of state populations
fig = px.choropleth(df, locations='Postal',
                    locationmode="USA-states",
```

```
                    scope="usa",
                    color='Population',
                    color_continuous_scale='Blues')
fig.update_layout(title='US State Populations in 2014')
fig.show()


# Plotly GO US map with populations
df = pd.read_csv('https://raw.githubusercontent.com/plotly/
             datasets/master/2014_usa_states.csv')

def readable_pop(row):
    if row['Population'] >= 1E6:
        return '{} ({})<br>Population {:.1f}M'.format(row['State'],
                     row['Postal'], row['Population']/1E6)
    else:
        return '{} ({})<br>Population {:.1f}K'.format(row['State'],
                     row['Postal'], row['Population']/1E3)


df['Readable'] = df.apply(readable_pop, axis=1)
fig = go.Figure(data=go.Choropleth(locations=df['Postal'],
                                   locationmode="USA-states",
                                   z=df['Population'],
                                   colorscale='Blues',
                                   text=df['Readable'],
                                   hovertemplate='%{text}',
                                   name=""))
fig.update_layout(geo_scope='usa', title="US State Populations in
2014")
fig.show()
```

View this code on GitHub at https://github.com/alexkenan/pyviz/

Resources

[1] https://plotly.com/python/choropleth-maps/

Heatmaps

Introduction

A heatmap can be thought of as a combination of a choropleth and a scatter plot/density map. It is used to provide a graphical representation of data, often in a density form to show distribution. The use of color in a heatmap is very important: generally, a single color with intensity like `Blues`, `Greys`, or `Reds` is a good choice. A colorbar is a legend that shows the range of colors and maps them to numerical values. It is usually prudent to include a colorbar for your heatmaps.

In the trivia game show Jeopardy!, there are Daily Double events "randomly" hidden behind some tiles; any contestants who find these tiles have the opportunity to wager a double-or-nothing bet to increase their earnings. But, are these Daily Double events truly randomly hidden? We will use all three visualization libraries to generate heatmaps to answer this question.

We will use a dataset that contains the percentage that the Daily Double has been at each grid location. This dataset has been cobbled together from multiple sources around GitHub that collect Jeopardy! information. The Jeopardy! board is 6 columns by 5 rows, and our new coordinate system needs an explanation:

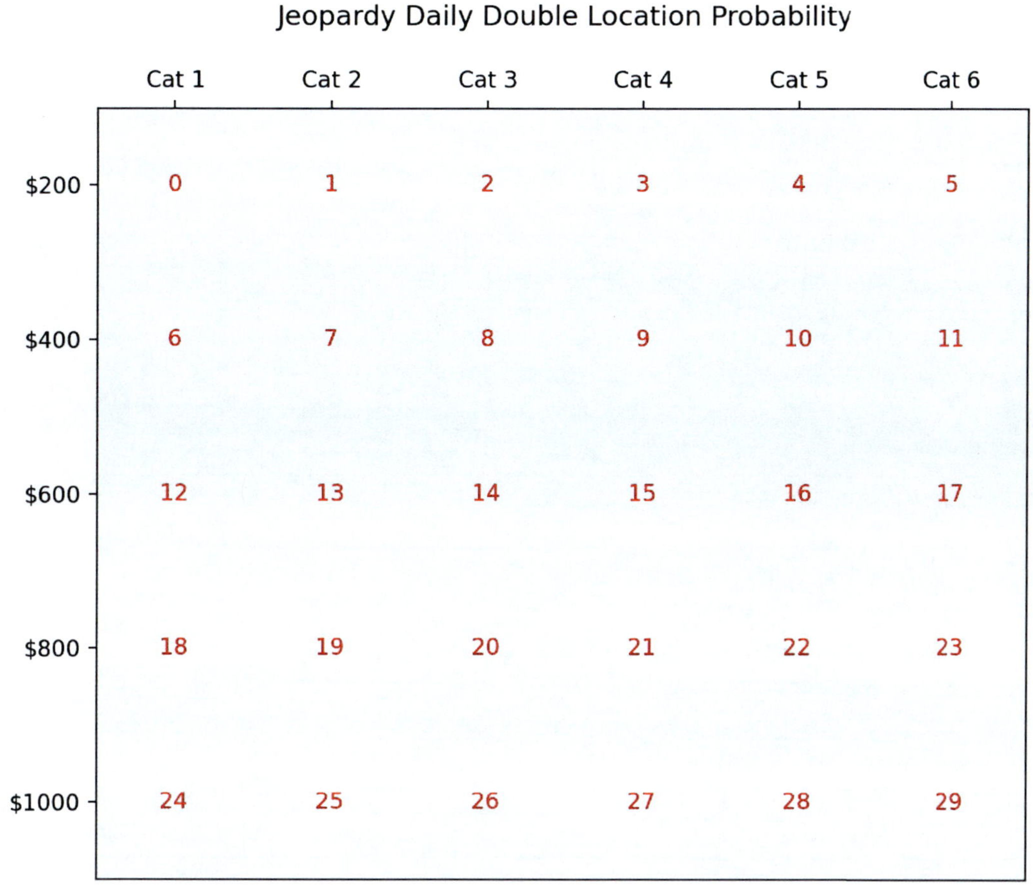

The Category 1 (Cat 1), $200 tile is at location 0, and the location increments by 1; this is how our dataset refers to locations. The dataset is a nested dictionary (`dict`), so let's take a look at what is inside:

Column Name	**Datatype**	**Description**
locations	`dict`	`dict` with keys of locations as `str` and values of historical percentage as `float`
total	`int`	Total number of observations

We could get the number of times that the Daily Double has been at each location by multiplying the percentage by the total number of observations.

There is an "error" in our dataset: the keys of the locations `dict` are `str`, not `int`. Since we can't always control how we get our data, we will have to account for this issue when we load the dataset.

Imports

```
import json
import pandas as pd
import matplotlib.pyplot as plt
import matplotlib.ticker as ticker
import seaborn as sns
import plotly.express as px
import plotly.graph_objects as go
import numpy as np
import plotly.io as pio
pio.renderers.default = "browser"
```

We need the JSON module to help manage our dataset, and we will use Numpy to help make the heatmap array.

Matplotlib

We need to address the `str` and `int` issue for the keys of `Locations`. So, we need a function `jeopardy()` that will accept the `path` of the `dict`, use the `pd.Load_json()` function to load the data, and finally, go through each key and cast it to an `int`.

```
def jeopardy(path: str) -> dict:
    imported_dict = pd.load_json(path)
    new_dict = {"locations": {}}

    for key in imported_dict['locations'].keys():
        newkey = int(key)
        new_dict["locations"][newkey] =
                        imported_dict['locations'][key]

    return new_dict
```

Now, we can build our `location_array` with a few lines. We will need to carefully build this array to mimic the same coordinate system and structure as our heatmap, with 0 corresponding to the top left, and 29 corresponding to the bottom right.

```
all_info = jeopardy('https://raw.githubusercontent.com/
                    alexkenan/pyviz/main/datasets/jeopardy_dd.json')
daily = all_info["locations"]
location_array = np.array(
  [[daily[0], daily[1], daily[2], daily[3],daily[4], daily[5]],
   [daily[6], daily[7], daily[8], daily[9], daily[10], daily[11]],
   [daily[12], daily[13], daily[14], daily[15], daily[16],
daily[17]],
   [daily[18], daily[19], daily[20], daily[21], daily[22],
daily[23]],
   [daily[24], daily[25], daily[26], daily[27], daily[28],
daily[29]]]
    )
```

Now that the information has been correctly imported, we need to get Matplotlib ready.

We can create heatmaps with Matplotlib's `imshow()` function, which converts 2D data into an image. The one required parameter is an array-like object (`locations_array`), and we will pass a `cmap` argument to choose a ColorMap. Matplotlib defaults to Viridis, and as we discussed in the Choropleth chapter, this is almost always a poor choice. Since we will need to use an `ax` object to handle the colorbar legend, we'll use the `fig, ax = plt.subplots()` notation. Let's see what the first attempt looks like:

```
fig, ax = plt.subplots()
im = ax.imshow(location_array, cmap='Blues')
fig.tight_layout()
fig.set_size_inches((8, 6))
plt.show()
```

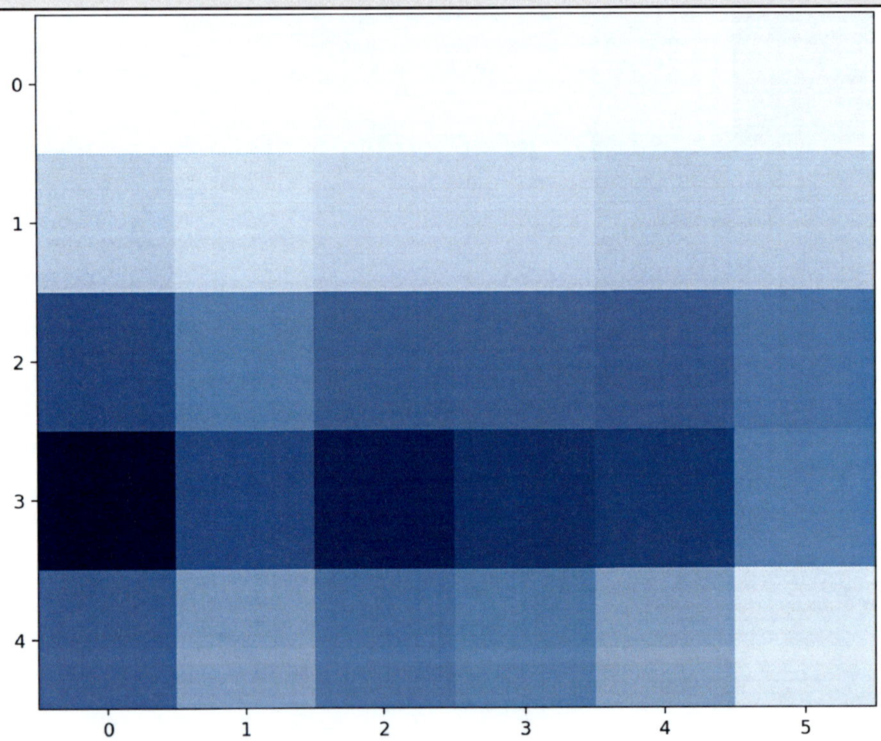

It's a heatmap! Now we need to tweak the formatting. From the colorscale, it looks like the higher-value rows have a greater likelihood of having a Daily Double.

Fortunately, we can override the default axis tick labels, and we can move the x ticks to the top. First, we define what we want the ticks to be, and then we set and place them:

```python
y = ['$200', '$400', '$600', '$800', '$1000']
x = ['Cat 1', 'Cat 2', 'Cat 3', 'Cat 4', 'Cat 5', 'Cat 6']

# We want to show all ticks...
ax.set_xticks(np.arange(len(x)))
ax.set_yticks(np.arange(len(y)))
# ... and label them with the respective list entries
ax.set_xticklabels(x)
ax.xaxis.tick_top()
ax.set_yticklabels(y)
```

Here is the program so far (without the import statements at the beginning of the chapter):

```python
y = ['$200', '$400', '$600', '$800', '$1000']
x = ['Cat 1', 'Cat 2', 'Cat 3', 'Cat 4', 'Cat 5', 'Cat 6']

fig, ax = plt.subplots()
im = ax.imshow(location_array, cmap='Blues')

ax.set_xticks(np.arange(len(x)))
ax.set_yticks(np.arange(len(y)))
ax.set_xticklabels(x)
ax.xaxis.tick_top()
ax.set_yticklabels(y)
fig.tight_layout()
fig.set_size_inches((8, 6))
plt.show()
```

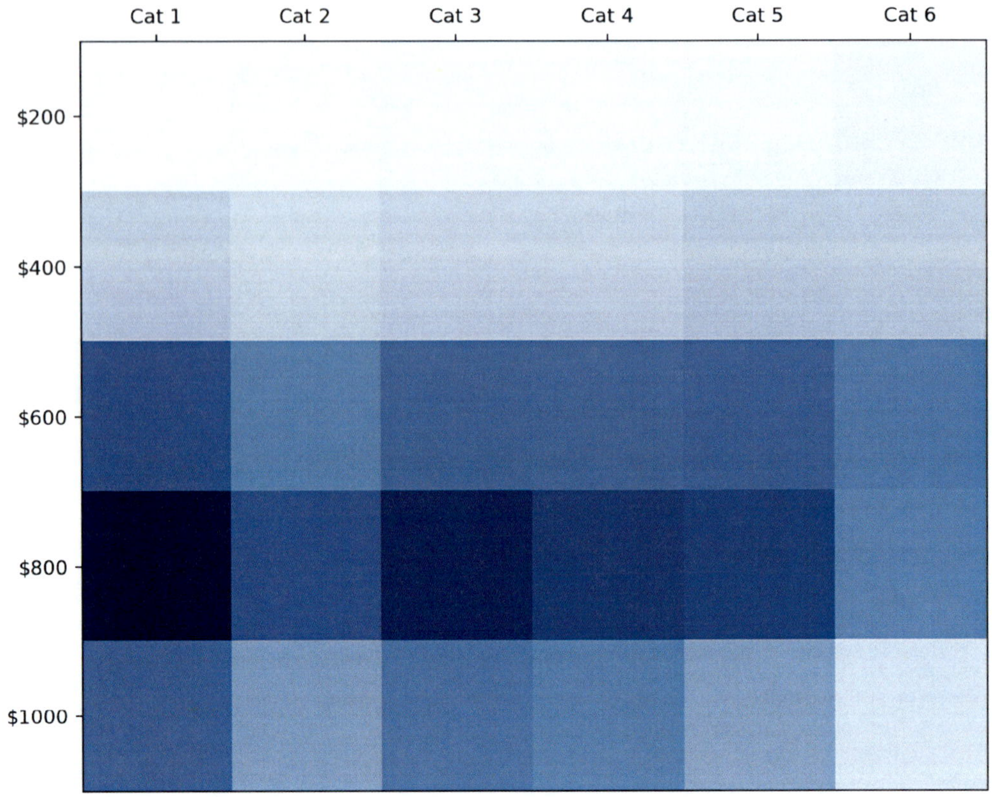

The new ticks clearly show that the $800 row is the most likely Daily Double row, and the Category 1 and Category 3 columns are the most likely within that row. We have two more things to do: add text annotations and make a colorbar.

Let's tackle the text annotations first. Since we have a pre-defined coordinate system, we can use two `for` loops to get each x and y location and stamp the percentage onto that location. The only tricky part is that we will need to use black text for the light backgrounds and white text for the dark backgrounds. So, we can use a simple `if` statement to select the text color, and we will use the value `3.50` to segment into black or white text.

```
for i in range(len(y)):
    for j in range(len(x)):
        if location_array[i, j]*100 >= 3.50:
            text_color = "w"
        else:
            text_color = "k"

        ax.text(j, i, '{:.2f}%'.format(location_array[i, j]*100),
                ha="center", va="center", color=text_color)
```

Lastly, we need to create the colorbar. We will use `ax.figure.colorbar()` and pass `location_array`, the axis `ax`, and some formatting parameters. The colorbar defaults to using the raw decimal values for the legend; however, we can create a formatting function to turn these values into actual percentages (e.g., transform `0.07` into `7%`). Let's make the custom formatter first:

```
def fmt(input_num, *args):
    return '{:.0%}'.format(input_num)
```

Easy enough! The formatter is passed two arguments, but we only care about the number `input_num`.

With the formatter function written, we can create the colorbar, set its title, and take care of some overall plot formatting:

```
cbar = ax.figure.colorbar(im, ax=ax, shrink=0.85, pad=0.09,
                          format=ticker.FuncFormatter(fmt))
cbar.ax.set_title("Probability (%)")

ax.set_title("Jeopardy Daily Double Location Probability\n")
fig.tight_layout()
fig.set_size_inches((8, 6))
```

Here is the finished Matplotlib portion:

```
all_info = jeopardy('https://raw.githubusercontent.com/
                    alexkenan/pyviz/main/datasets/jeopardy_dd.json')
daily = all_info["locations"]
location_array = np.array(
  [[daily[0], daily[1], daily[2], daily[3],daily[4], daily[5]],
   [daily[6], daily[7], daily[8], daily[9], daily[10], daily[11]],
   [daily[12], daily[13], daily[14], daily[15], daily[16],
daily[17]],
   [daily[18], daily[19], daily[20], daily[21], daily[22],
daily[23]],
   [daily[24], daily[25], daily[26], daily[27], daily[28],
daily[29]]]
    )

def fmt(input_num, *args):
    return '{:.0%}'.format(input_num)


y = ['$200', '$400', '$600', '$800', '$1000']
x = ['Cat 1', 'Cat 2', 'Cat 3', 'Cat 4', 'Cat 5', 'Cat 6']

fig, ax = plt.subplots()
im = ax.imshow(location_array, cmap='Blues')

ax.set_xticks(np.arange(len(x)))
ax.set_yticks(np.arange(len(y)))
ax.set_xticklabels(x)
ax.xaxis.tick_top()
ax.set_yticklabels(y)

for i in range(len(y)):
    for j in range(len(x)):
        if location_array[i, j]*100 >= 3.50:
            text_color = "w"
        else:
            text_color = "k"
```

```
        ax.text(j, i, '{:.2f}%'.format(location_array[i, j]*100),
                ha="center", va="center", color=text_color)

cbar = ax.figure.colorbar(im, ax=ax,
                          format=ticker.FuncFormatter(fmt),
                          shrink=0.85, pad=0.09)
cbar.ax.set_title("Probability (%)")

ax.set_title("Jeopardy Daily Double Location Probability\n")
fig.tight_layout()
fig.set_size_inches((8, 6))
plt.show()
```

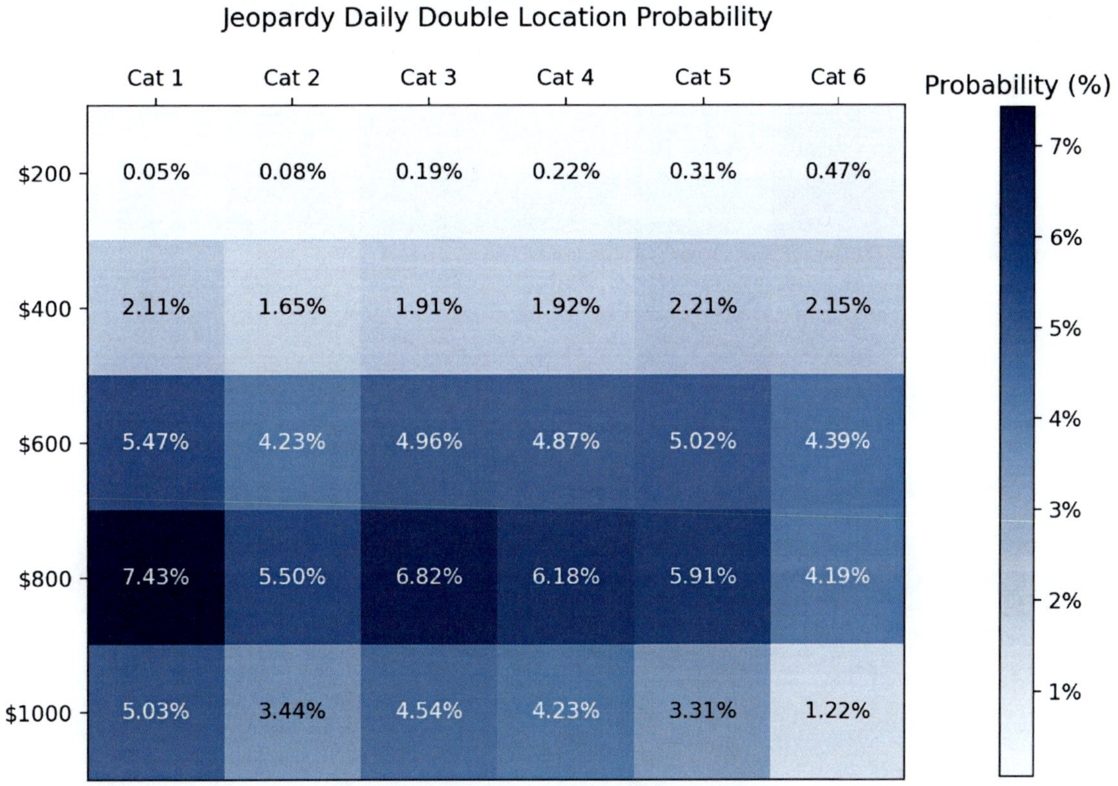

Two decimal places is probably an excessive amount of precision, but the colorscale, colorbar, and annotations help guide the reader through the story that higher value rows have a better chance of having a Daily Double.

Seaborn

Perhaps unsurprisingly, Seaborn's `heatmap()` contains a lot of helper functions that let us quickly create a very similar heatmap. It accepts the same arguments as Matplotlib's `imshow()`, and it takes a few more customization parameters that quickly accomplish the same customization that we did with Matplotlib. Let's see the basic heatmap:

```
fig, ax = plt.subplots(figsize=(8, 6))
sns.heatmap(location_array, cmap="Blues")
ax.set_title("Jeopardy Daily Double Location Probability")
fig.tight_layout()
fig.set_size_inches((8, 6))
plt.show()
```

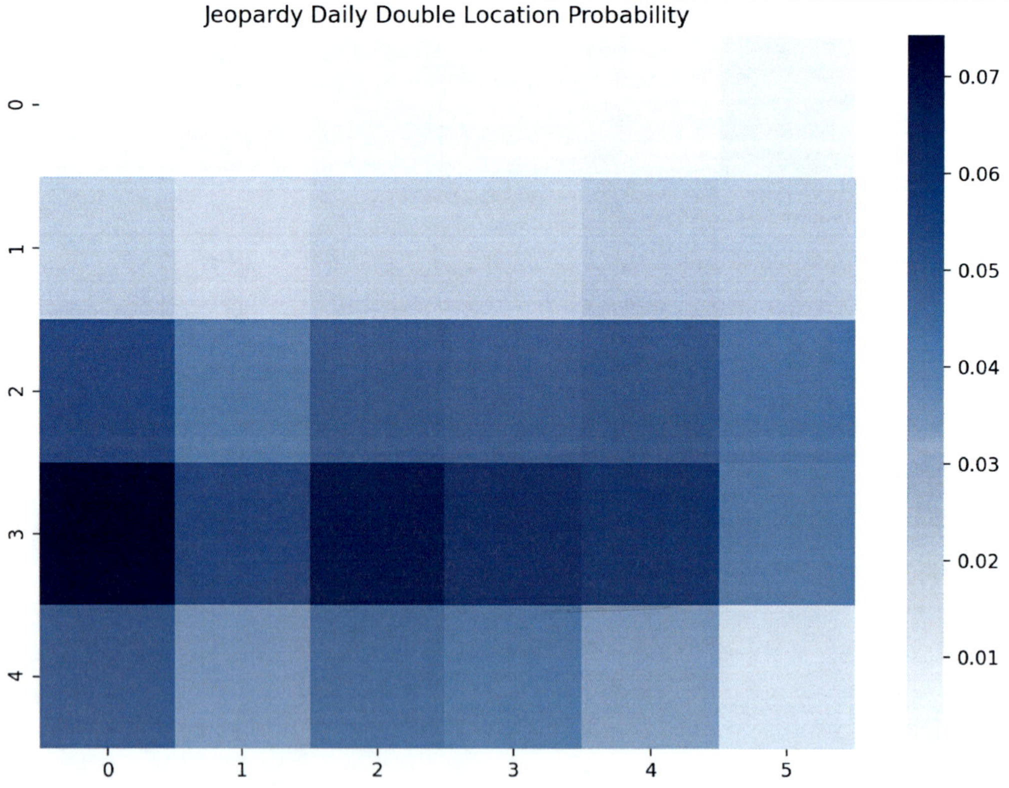

There is a colorbar included by default, and the axes tick labels are the same 0-4 or 0-5 that we saw initially with Matplotlib. We can add `yticklabels` and `xticklabels` arguments to have Seaborn do the work for us:

```
sns.heatmap(location_array, cmap="Blues",
            yticklabels=['$200', '$400', '$600', '$800', '$1000'],
            xticklabels=['Cat 1', 'Cat 2', 'Cat 3',
                         'Cat 4', 'Cat 5', 'Cat 6'])
```

This is what the labels look like:

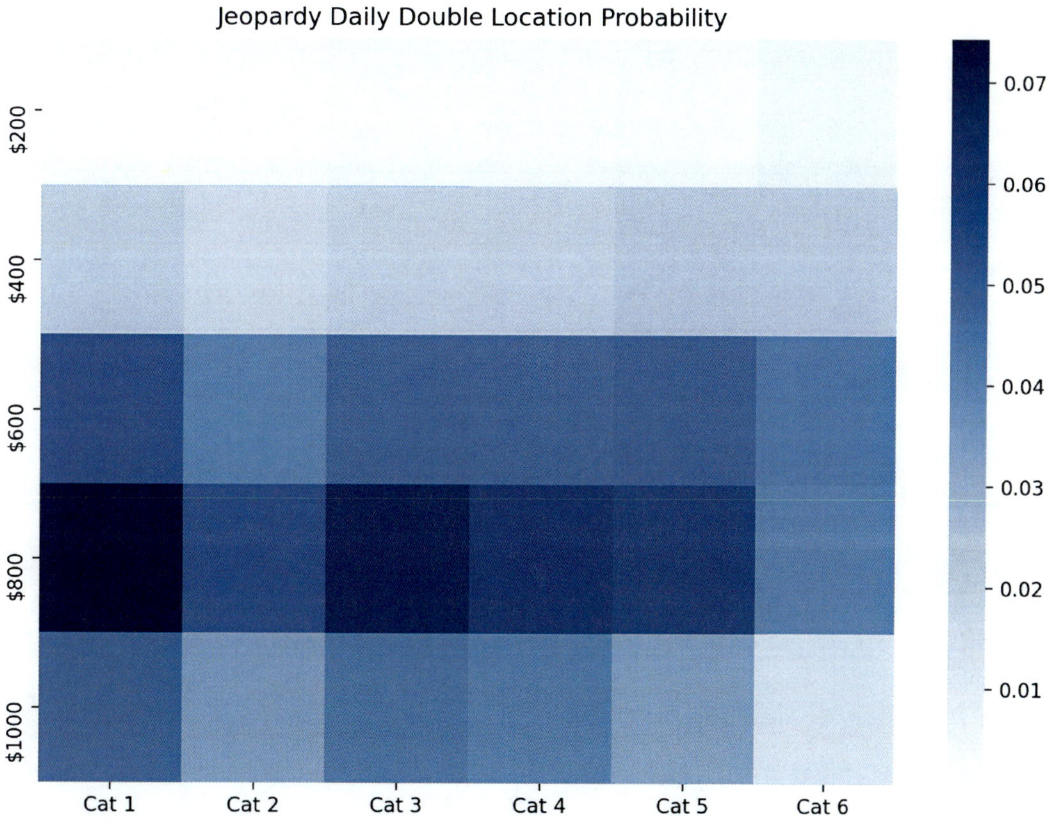

We can rotate the y labels and move the x ticks and labels with two commands:

```
ax.xaxis.tick_top()
plt.setp(ax.get_yticklabels(), rotation=0)
```

We can enable text annotations and colorbar arguments by passing parameters directly to `heatmap()`: `annot=True` turns on annotations, and `fmt=".2%"` gives the same `7.62%` format that we used previously. For the colorbar, `cbar=True` enables the colorbar, and then we can pass arguments to `cbar_kw`:

```
cbar_kws={'format': ticker.FuncFormatter(fmt),
          'label': 'Probability (%)'}
```

Here is what we have so far:

```
def fmt(input_num, *args):
    return '{:.0%}'.format(input_num)

all_info = jeopardy('https://raw.githubusercontent.com/
                     alexkenan/pyviz/main/datasets/jeopardy_dd.json')
daily = all_info["locations"]
location_array = np.array(
  [[daily[0], daily[1], daily[2], daily[3],daily[4], daily[5]],
   [daily[6], daily[7], daily[8], daily[9], daily[10], daily[11]],
   [daily[12], daily[13], daily[14], daily[15], daily[16],
daily[17]],
   [daily[18], daily[19], daily[20], daily[21], daily[22],
daily[23]],
   [daily[24], daily[25], daily[26], daily[27], daily[28],
daily[29]]]
    )

# Seaborn
fig, ax = plt.subplots(figsize=(8, 6))
sns.heatmap(location_array, cmap="Blues", annot=True, fmt=".2%",
            yticklabels=['$200', '$400', '$600',
```

```
                  '$800', '$1000'],
        xticklabels=['Cat 1', 'Cat 2', 'Cat 3',
                     'Cat 4', 'Cat 5', 'Cat 6'],
        cbar=True,
        cbar_kws={'format': ticker.FuncFormatter(fmt),
                  'label': 'Probability (%)'})
ax.xaxis.tick_top()
ax.set_title("Jeopardy Daily Double Location Probability")
# Rotate the tick labels and set their alignment.
plt.setp(ax.get_yticklabels(), rotation=0)
fig.tight_layout()
fig.set_size_inches((8, 6))
plt.show()
```

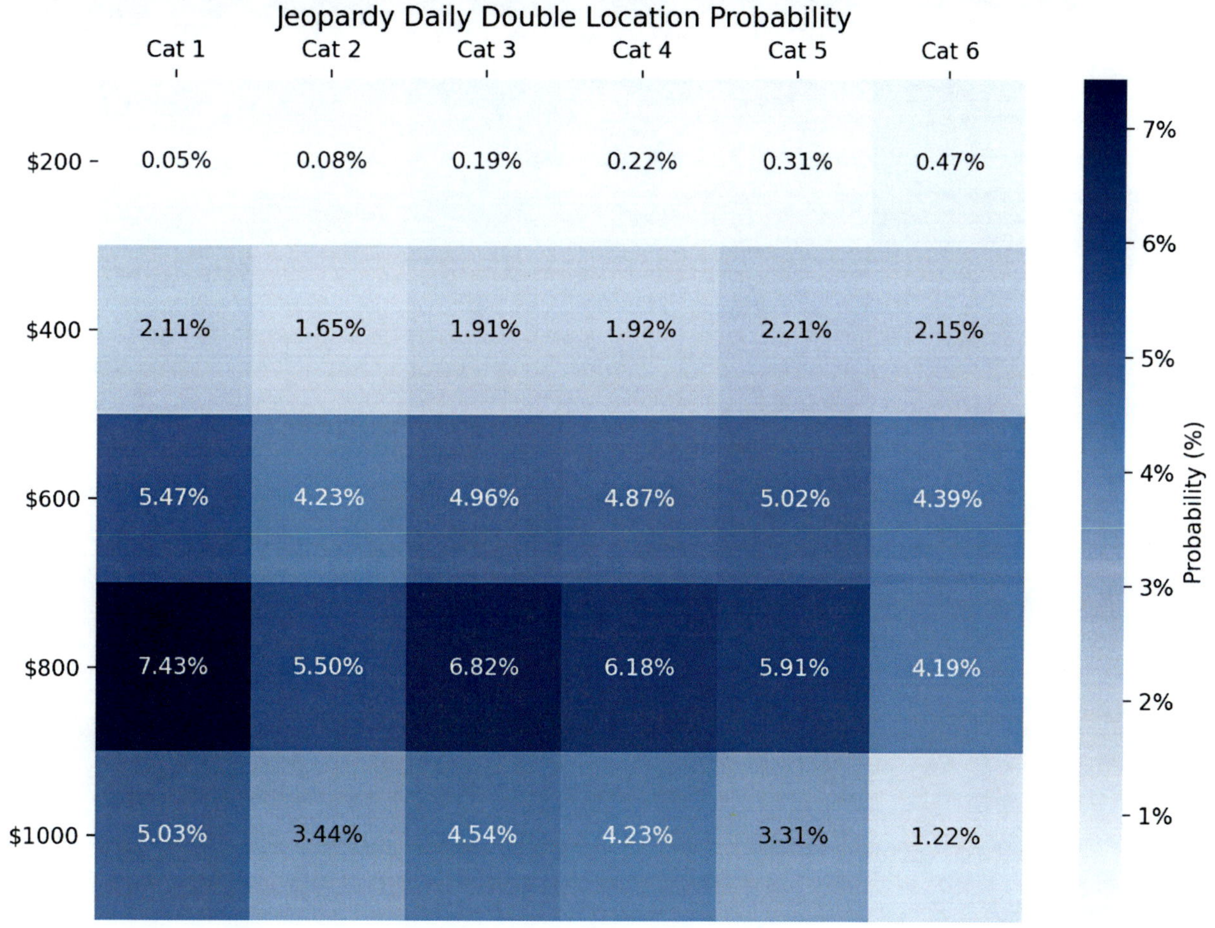

We could also experiment with a horizontal colorbar with an additional `cbar_kw` parameter `'orientation': 'horizontal'`:

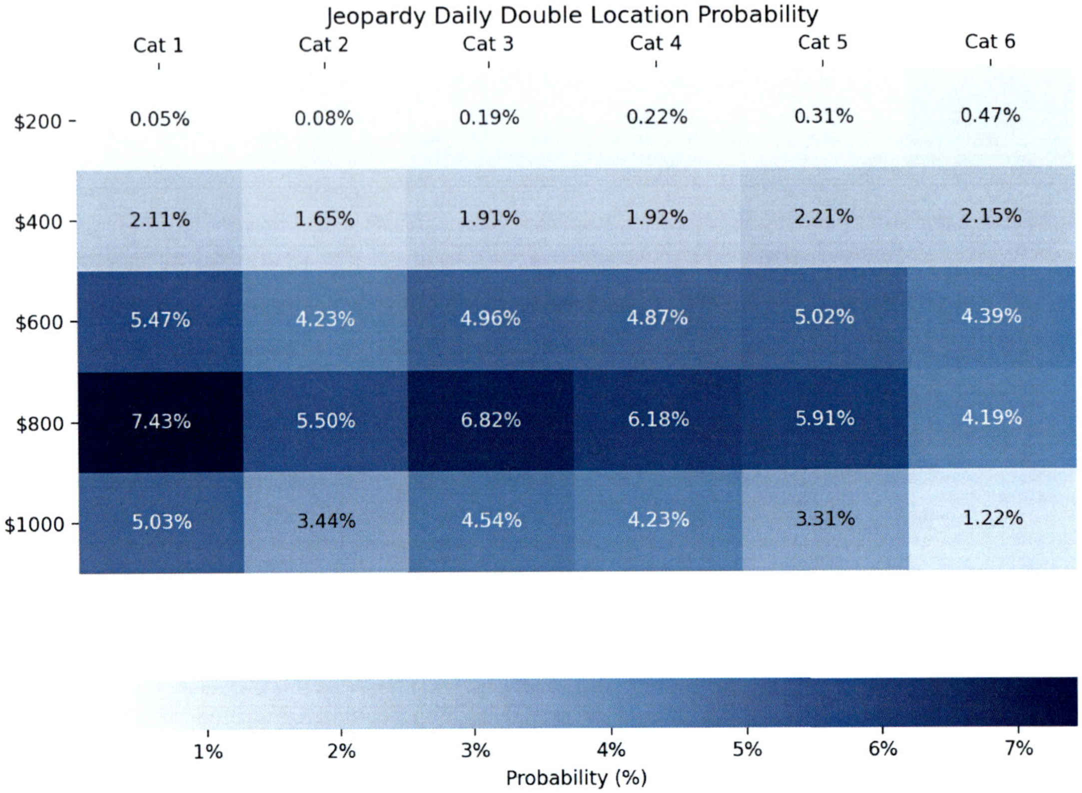

The vertical colorbar looks better, so let's stick with that and try no colorbar title:

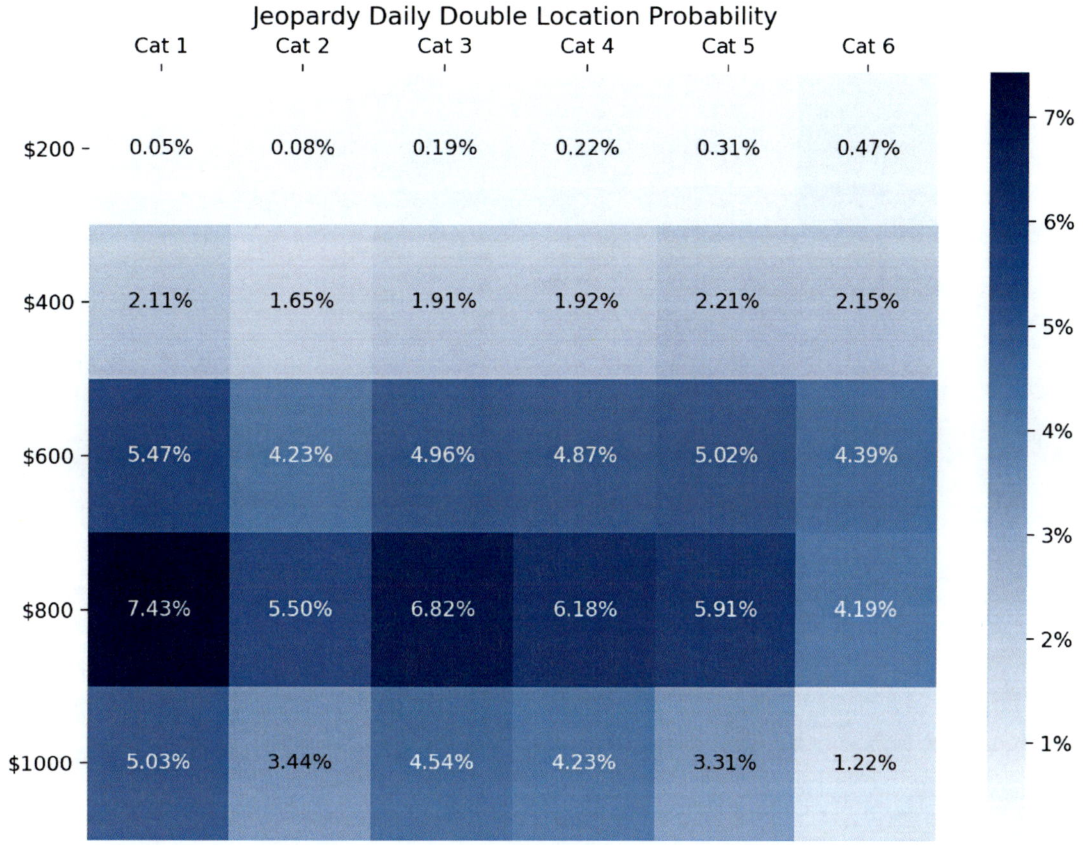

Plotly

Plotly Express also uses an `imshow()` function to create heatmaps. To expedite the formatting, let's go ahead and multiply `location_array` by 100 when creating the heatmap.

```
fig = px.imshow(location_array*100,
                labels={'x': '', 'y': '',
                        'color': '<b>Probability (%)</b>'},
                x=x, color_continuous_scale='blues')
fig.update_layout(title="<b>Jeopardy Daily Double Location
                        Probability</b>")

fig.show()
```

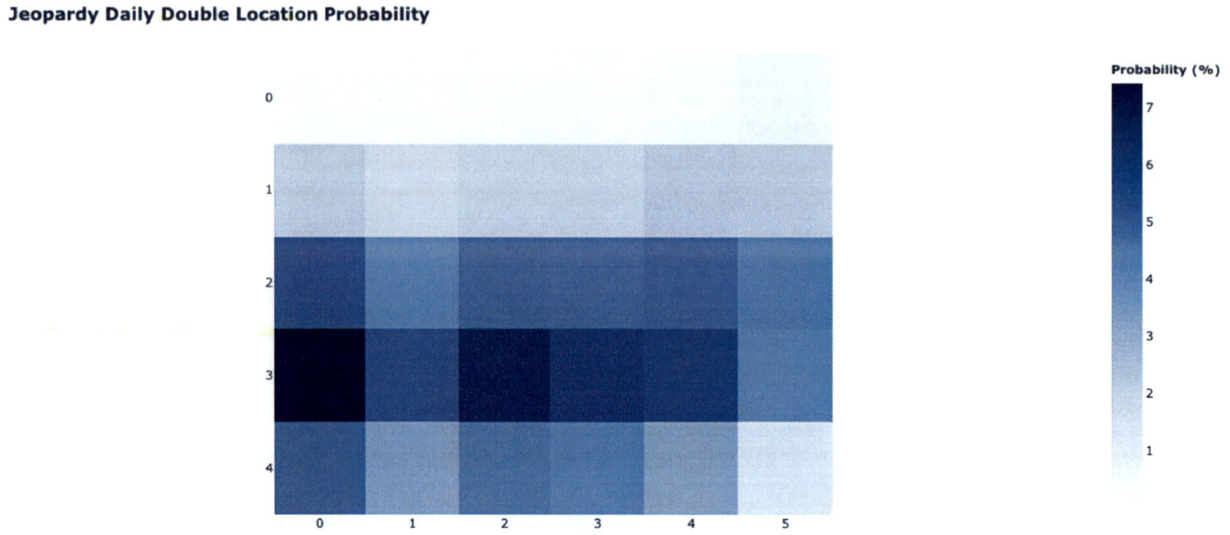

The x tick labels are consistent, but the y tick labels are counting from 4-0 instead of 0-4. We can still fix that by adjusting the tick labels, but we will need to be mindful of the rearranged order. We can move the x ticks to the top, as well, and we can add some hover info:

```
x = ['<b>Cat 1</b>', '<b>Cat 2</b>', '<b>Cat 3</b>', '<b>Cat 4</b>',
     '<b>Cat 5</b>', '<b>Cat 6</b>']
y = ['<b>$200</b> ', '<b>$400</b> ', '<b>$600</b> ', '<b>$800</b> ',
     '<b>$1000</b> ']
fig = px.imshow(location_array*100,
               labels={'x': '', 'y': '',
                       'color': '<b>Probability (%)</b>'}, x=x,
               color_continuous_scale='blues')
fig.update_xaxes(side="top")
fig.update_layout(title="<b>Jeopardy Daily Double Location
                          Probability</b>",
                 yaxis={'tickmode': 'array',
                        'tickvals': [0, 1, 2, 3, 4], 'ticktext':
y})
fig.update_traces(hovertemplate="Probability: %{z:.2f}%", name="")
fig.show()
```

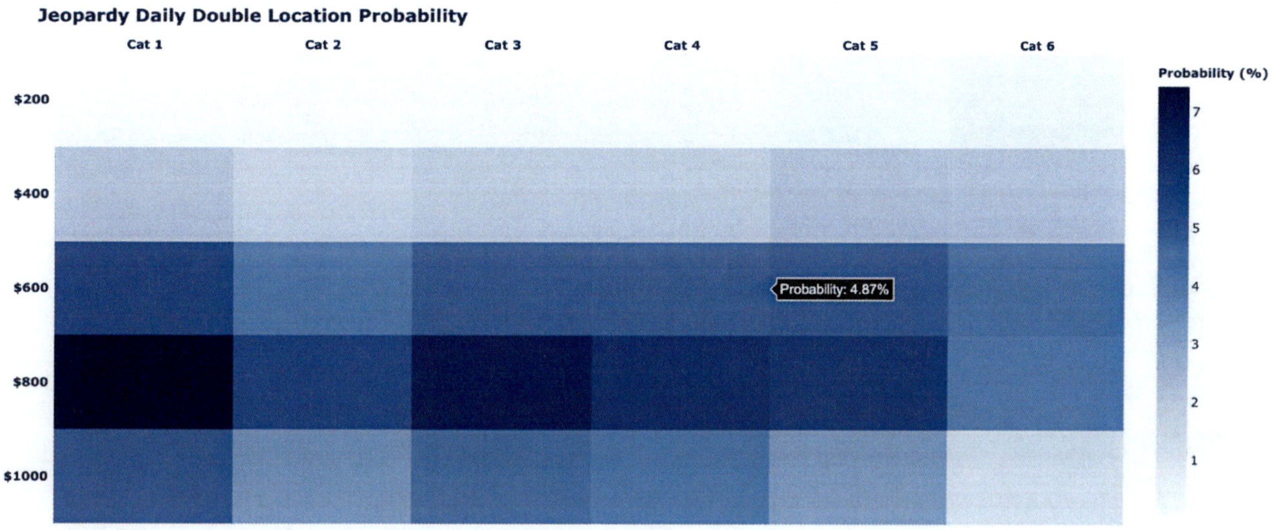

Lastly, we add text annotations in a similar manner to how we did in Matplotlib.

```
for i in range(len(y)):
    for j in range(len(x)):
        if location_array[i, j]*100 >= 3.50:
            text_color = 'white'
        else:
            text_color = 'black'

        fig.add_annotation(x=j, y=i,
                text='{:.2f}%'.format(location_array[i, j]*100),
                           showarrow=False, align="center",
                           font={'color': text_color})
```

Here is the full code:

```
all_info = jeopardy('https://raw.githubusercontent.com/
                    alexkenan/pyviz/main/datasets/jeopardy_dd.json')
daily = all_info["locations"]
location_array = np.array(
  [[daily[0], daily[1], daily[2], daily[3],daily[4], daily[5]],
   [daily[6], daily[7], daily[8], daily[9], daily[10], daily[11]],
   [daily[12], daily[13], daily[14], daily[15], daily[16],
daily[17]],
   [daily[18], daily[19], daily[20], daily[21], daily[22],
daily[23]],
   [daily[24], daily[25], daily[26], daily[27], daily[28],
daily[29]]])
x = ['<b>Cat 1</b>', '<b>Cat 2</b>', '<b>Cat 3</b>',
     '<b>Cat 4</b>', '<b>Cat 5</b>', '<b>Cat 6</b>']
y = ['<b>$200</b> ', '<b>$400</b> ', '<b>$600</b> ',
     '<b>$800</b> ', <b>$1000</b> ']
fig = px.imshow(location_array*100,
                labels={'x': '', 'y': '',
                'color': '<b>Probability (%)</b>'}, x=x,
                color_continuous_scale='blues')
fig.update_xaxes(side="top")
for i in range(len(y)):
    for j in range(len(x)):
        if location_array[i, j]*100 >= 3.50:
            text_color = 'white'
        else:
            text_color = 'black'

        fig.add_annotation(x=j, y=i,
          text='{:.2f}%'.format(location_array[i, j]*100),
                    showarrow=False, align="center",
                    font={'color': text_color})

fig.update_layout(title="<b>Jeopardy Daily Double Location
                    Probability</b>",
           yaxis={'tickmode': 'array',
                  'tickvals': [0, 1, 2, 3, 4],
```

```
                        'ticktext': y})
fig.update_traces(hovertemplate="Probability: %{z:.2f}%", name="")
fig.show()
```

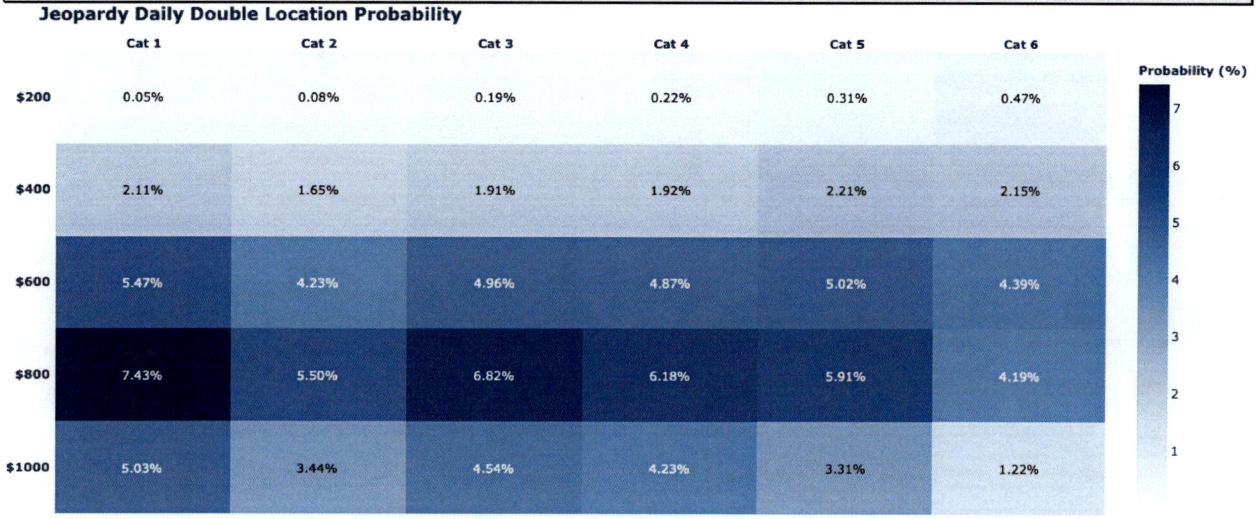

The Plotly Graph Objects code looks very similar to the Plotly Express code. We use `go.Heatmap()`, and we can manually set the colorbar labels 1 through 7. It is also important to note that the `go.Heatmap()` function plots the coordinates in reverse, so we need to reverse our `location_array` before we pass it to the heatmap function.

```
x = ['<b>Cat 1</b>', '<b>Cat 2</b>', '<b>Cat 3</b>',
     '<b>Cat 4</b>', '<b>Cat 5</b>', '<b>Cat 6</b>']
y = ['<b>$200</b> ', '<b>$400</b> ', '<b>$600</b> ',
     '<b>$800</b> ', '<b>$1000</b> ']
location_array = np.array(list(reversed(location_array)))
fig = go.Figure(go.Heatmap(z=location_array*100, x=x,
                           colorscale='Blues',
                           hovertemplate='Probability: %{z:.2f}%',
                           colorbar={'title': '<b>Probability</b>',
                                     'tickvals': [1, 2, 3, 4, 5,
                                                  6, 7],
                                     'ticktext': ['1%', '2%', '3%',
                                                  '4%', '5%', '6%',
                                                  '7%']},
```

```
                        name=""))
fig.update_xaxes(side="top")
for i in range(len(y)):
    for j in range(len(x)):
        if location_array[i, j]*100 >= 3.50:
            text_color = 'white'
        else:
            text_color = 'black'

        fig.add_annotation(x=j, y=i,
                  text='{:.2f}%'.format(location_array[i, j]*100),
                           showarrow=False, align="center",
                           font={'color': text_color})

fig.update_layout(title="<b>Jeopardy Daily Double Location
                  Probability</b>",
                  yaxis={'tickmode': 'array',
                         'tickvals': [4, 3, 2, 1, 0],
                         'ticktext': y})
fig.show()
```

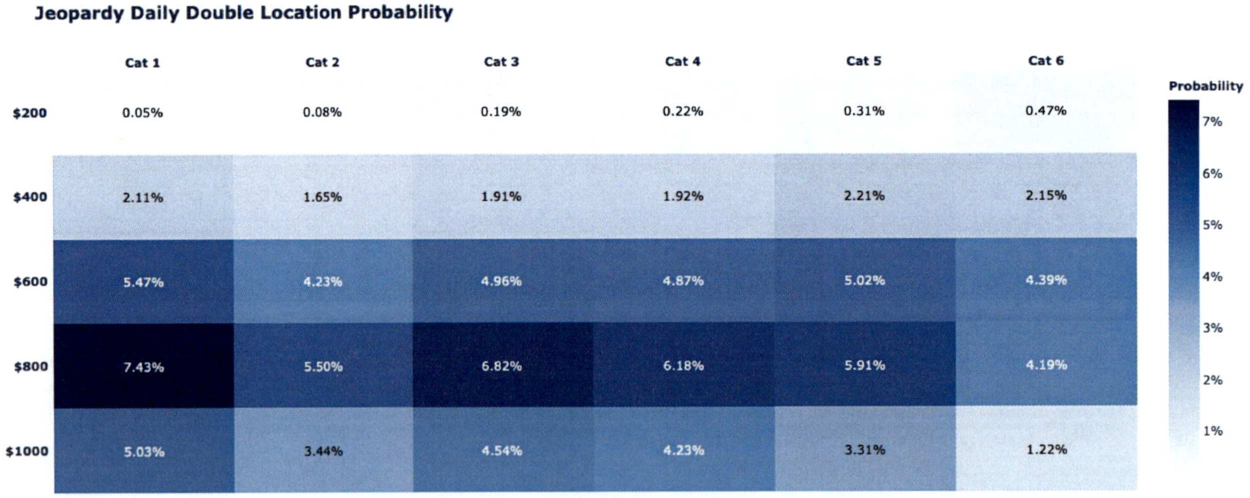

Summary

Heatmaps are a good way to qualitatively show frequency and distribution for numerical variables and categorical variables. We overlaid the percentage to add a quantitative spin, but with our colorscale selection, it should have been intuitive to any reader that the darker blue was more likely to occur than the lighter blue.

Some data processing may be required to make an effective heat map. For example, if one percentage had been 50%, it would have caused one tile to be dark blue, and the rest of the tiles to be very similar shades of light blue. Colorscale selection is incredibly important; don't use Viridis!

Examples for Each Library

```
import json
import pandas as pd
import matplotlib.pyplot as plt
import matplotlib.ticker as ticker
import seaborn as sns
import plotly.express as px
import plotly.graph_objects as go
import numpy as np
import plotly.io as pio
pio.renderers.default = "browser"

def jeopardy(path: str) -> dict:
    imported_dict = pd.load_json(path)
    new_dict = {"locations": {}}

    for key in imported_dict['locations'].keys():
        newkey = int(key)
        new_dict["locations"][newkey] =
                  imported_dict['locations'][key]

    return new_dict
```

```
def fmt(input_num, *args):
    return '{:.0%}'.format(input_num)


all_info = jeopardy('https://raw.githubusercontent.com/
                    alexkenan/pyviz/main/datasets/jeopardy_dd.json')
daily = all_info["locations"]
location_array = np.array(
  [[daily[0], daily[1], daily[2], daily[3],daily[4], daily[5]],
   [daily[6], daily[7], daily[8], daily[9], daily[10], daily[11]],
   [daily[12], daily[13], daily[14], daily[15], daily[16],
daily[17]],
   [daily[18], daily[19], daily[20], daily[21], daily[22],
daily[23]],
   [daily[24], daily[25], daily[26], daily[27], daily[28],
daily[29]]]
    )

# Matplotlib
y = ['$200', '$400', '$600', '$800', '$1000']
x = ['Cat 1', 'Cat 2', 'Cat 3',
     'Cat 4', 'Cat 5', 'Cat 6']

fig, ax = plt.subplots()
im = ax.imshow(location_array, cmap='Blues')

ax.set_xticks(np.arange(len(x)))
ax.set_yticks(np.arange(len(y)))
ax.set_xticklabels(x)
ax.xaxis.tick_top()
ax.set_yticklabels(y)

for i in range(len(y)):
    for j in range(len(x)):
        if location_array[i, j]*100 >= 3.50:
            text_color = "w"
        else:
            text_color = "k"
```

```
        ax.text(j, i, '{:.2f}%'.format(location_array[i, j]*100),
                ha="center", va="center", color=text_color)

cbar = ax.figure.colorbar(im, ax=ax,
                          format=ticker.FuncFormatter(fmt),
                          shrink=0.85, pad=0.09)
cbar.ax.set_title("Probability (%)")

ax.set_title("Jeopardy Daily Double Location Probability\n")
fig.tight_layout()
fig.set_size_inches((8, 6))
plt.show()

# Seaborn
fig, ax = plt.subplots(figsize=(8, 6))
sns.heatmap(location_array, cmap="Blues",
            annot=True, fmt=".2%",
            yticklabels=['$200', '$400', '$600',
                         '$800', '$1000'],
            xticklabels=['Cat 1', 'Cat 2', 'Cat 3',
                         'Cat 4', 'Cat 5', 'Cat 6'], cbar=True,
            cbar_kws={'format': ticker.FuncFormatter(fmt),
                      'label': ''})
ax.xaxis.tick_top()
ax.set_title("Jeopardy Daily Double Location Probability")
# Rotate the tick labels and set their alignment.
plt.setp(ax.get_yticklabels(), rotation=0)
fig.tight_layout()
fig.set_size_inches((8, 6))
plt.show()

# Plotly Express
x = ['<b>Cat 1</b>', '<b>Cat 2</b>', '<b>Cat 3</b>',
     '<b>Cat 4</b>', '<b>Cat 5</b>', '<b>Cat 6</b>']
y = ['<b>$200</b> ', '<b>$400</b> ', '<b>$600</b> ',
     '<b>$800</b> ',  '<b>$1000</b> ']
fig = px.imshow(location_array*100,
                labels={'x': '', 'y': '',
                        'color': '<b>Probability (%)</b>'}, x=x,
                color_continuous_scale='blues')
```

```
fig.update_xaxes(side="top")
for i in range(len(y)):
    for j in range(len(x)):
        if location_array[i, j]*100 >= 3.50:
            text_color = 'white'
        else:
            text_color = 'black'

        fig.add_annotation(x=j, y=i,
                text='{:.2f}%'.format(location_array[i, j]*100),
                           showarrow=False, align="center",
                           font={'color': text_color})

fig.update_layout(title="<b>Jeopardy Daily Double Location
                           Probability</b>",
                  yaxis={'tickmode': 'array',
                         'tickvals': [0, 1, 2, 3, 4],
                         'ticktext': y})
fig.update_traces(hovertemplate="Probability: %{z:.2f}%", name="")
fig.show()

# Plotly Graph Objects
x = ['<b>Cat 1</b>', '<b>Cat 2</b>', '<b>Cat 3</b>',
     '<b>Cat 4</b>', '<b>Cat 5</b>', '<b>Cat 6</b>']
y = ['<b>$200</b> ', '<b>$400</b> ', '<b>$600</b> ',
     '<b>$800</b> ', '<b>$1000</b> ']
location_array = np.array(list(reversed(location_array)))
fig = go.Figure(go.Heatmap(z=location_array*100,
                           x=x,
                           colorscale='Blues',
                           hovertemplate='Probability: %{z:.2f}%',
                           colorbar={'title': '<b>Probability</b>',
                                     'tickvals': [1, 2, 3, 4, 5,
                                                  6, 7],
                                     'ticktext': ['1%', '2%', '3%',
                                                  '4%', '5%', '6%',
                                                  '7%']},
                           name=""))
fig.update_xaxes(side="top")
for i in range(len(y)):
```

```
    for j in range(len(x)):
        if location_array[i, j]*100 >= 3.50:
            text_color = 'white'
        else:
            text_color = 'black'

        fig.add_annotation(x=j, y=i,
                     text='{:.2f}%'.format(location_array[i, j]*100),
                          showarrow=False, align="center",
                          font={'color': text_color})

fig.update_layout(title="<b>Jeopardy Daily Double Location
                         Probability</b>",
                  yaxis={'tickmode': 'array',
                         'tickvals': [4, 3, 2, 1, 0],
                         'ticktext': y})
fig.show()
```

View this code on GitHub at https://github.com/alexkenan/pyviz/

Resources

[1] https://matplotlib.org/stable/api/_as_gen/matplotlib.pyplot.imshow.html

[2] https://seaborn.pydata.org/generated/seaborn.heatmap.html

[3] https://plotly.com/python/heatmaps/

Advanced Line Charts

Introduction

In this chapter, we will learn how to use a line chart to show changes in rank, order, or opinion over time. These changes in rank can be shown in a variety of ways with a bump chart, a slope chart, or a lollipop chart. The basic line chart has time on the x axis and a quantity on the y axis. In our case, we will show "time" on the x axis and rank on the y axis, where "time" can be any type of time. Normally, it is a faux-pas to invert the y axis; however, since tables, results, and other rankings are typically shown with first place at the top, we need to invert the y axis to maintain an intuitive chart.

A bump chart shows how a ranking changes over time for all observations. It is usually used to show performance over time of an individual or a league. A slope chart is a simplified bump chart that shows only a few observations. A lollipop chart is a combination of a bar chart and a line chart, and it shows two observations at one instance in time. There does not seem to be a clear consensus on the nomenclature differences between a lollipop chart, a Cleveland Dotplot, or a dumbbell chart. In this chapter, all three names refer to the same data visualization of two dots connected by a line.

To learn about these charts, we will use data from the 2018-2019 English Premier League season; we will show how each team's standing changed over all 38 matchweeks for the bump chart, show how each team's standing changed from matchweek 19 (the half-way point) to matchweek 38 (the end of the season) for the slope chart, and use predictions from The Guardian newspaper to see how each team performed relative to The Guardian's prediction for the lollipop chart.

This data is in two csv files that can be found at the GitHub site: `prem.csv` and `predictions.csv`. This is what `prem.csv` looks like:

Column Name	Datatype	Description
Matchweek	`int`	The matchweek (basically a week of the season) in which the observation occurred
Team	`str`	The team's name
Rank	`int`	The ranking of that team for that matchweek

And this is what `predictions.csv` looks like:

Column Name	Datatype	Description
Team	`str`	The team's name
Actual	`int`	The actual ranking of the team at the end of the season
Predicted	`int`	The predicted ranking of the team at the end of the season

For all of these data visualizations, we will be using a combination of scatter plots and line plots; therefore, we won't use Seaborn because using it would just mean re-using Matplotlib functions.

Imports

```
import matplotlib.pyplot as plt
from matplotlib.ticker import FuncFormatter
import plotly.express as px
import plotly.graph_objects as go
import pandas as pd
import numpy as np
import plotly.io as pio
pio.renderers.default = "browser"

df = pd.read_csv('https://raw.githubusercontent.com/
                 alexkenan/pyviz/main/datasets/prem.csv',
                 names=['Matchweek', 'Team', 'Rank'], header=0)
preds = pd.read_csv('https://raw.githubusercontent.com/
                    alexkenan/pyviz/main/datasets/predictions.csv',
                    names=['Team', 'Actual', 'Predicted'], header=0)
plt.style.use('default')
```

Matplotlib

Let's start off with one team: Manchester United. For Matplotlib, a bump chart is a line chart and a scatter plot in the same canvas, so we need to plot the positions as circles and connect them with a solid line. Lastly, we need to invert the y axis, force the y axis to display integers, and adjust both axes limits:

```
manu = df[df['Team'] == 'Manchester United']
plt.plot(manu['Matchweek'], manu['Rank'], 'r-')
plt.plot(manu['Matchweek'], manu['Rank'], 'ro')
plt.xlim(0, 40)
plt.ylim(0.5, 21)
plt.yticks(np.arange(0.0, 21.0, 1.0))
plt.gca().invert_yaxis()
plt.gca().get_yaxis().set_major_formatter(
```

```
            FuncFormatter(lambda x, p: format(int(x), ',')))
plt.xlabel('Matchweek')
plt.title('Premier League 2018-2019 Season Bump Chart')
plt.show()
```

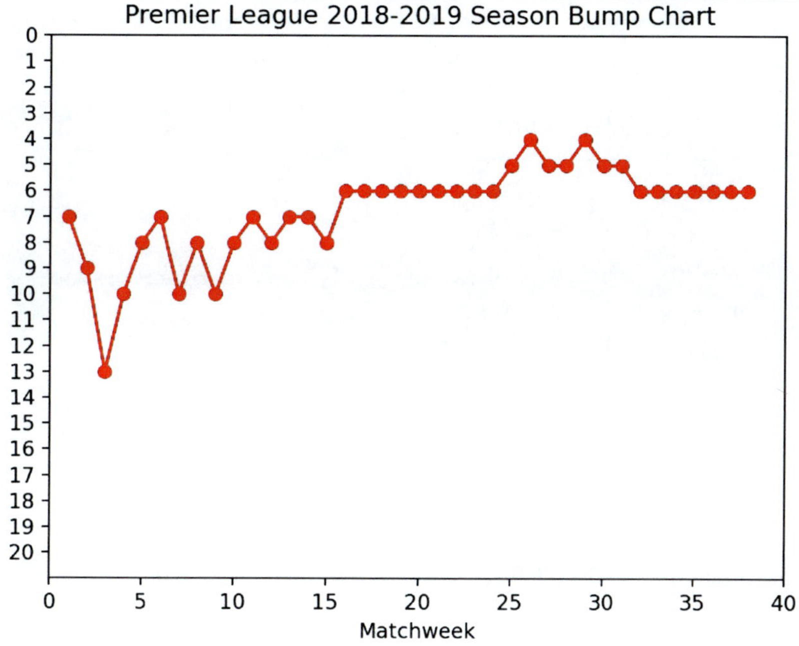

We will need to make sure that 0 is not showing on the y axis, but this chart shows that our scatter plot and line plot work together. Now, we can use a `for` loop to create a bump line for each team on the same canvas. We will run into team color issues, though, so let's fix that.

James Curley at the University of Texas has a GitHub repository of English soccer data; there is a specific folder that contains team primary and secondary color information [1]. We can use some of this data to create team colors for each bump line. Some color adjustment was necessary so that there weren't four of the same blue hues next to each other. Here is an `add_team_color()` function that we can apply down `df1` to add a team color column:

```python
def add_team_color(df1) -> str:
    name = df1['Team']
    colors = {'Bournemouth': '#cc2900',
              'Crystal Palace': "#0000FF",
              'Liverpool': '#CD0206',
              'Chelsea': '#0000CC',
              'Manchester City': '#99CCFF',
              'Watford': '#cccc00',
              'Manchester United': '#FF0000',
              'Tottenham Hotspur': '#FFFFFF',
              'Everton': '#0000CC',
              'Wolverhampton Wanderers': '#EFBE29',
              'Burnley': '#99172B',
              'Southampton': '#FF0000',
              'Leicester City': '#6666ff',
              'Newcastle United': '#000000',
              'Arsenal': '#ff3333',
              'Brighton and Hove Albion': '#47a5ff',
              'Cardiff City': '#0039e6',
              'Fulham': '#FFFFFF',
              'Huddersfield Town': '#0099FF',
              'West Ham United': '#99182B'
              }

    if name in colors.keys():
        return colors[name]
    else:
        return '#000000'
```

Then, applying these colors to `df` is a simple one-liner:

```python
df['Color'] = df.apply(add_team_color, axis=1)
```

The last order of business is annotating the team names after matchweek 38. We will just get the last ranking as the y value, set an x value of 40 or so, and annotate the plot with the team name in the team color. Here is what our improved bump chart looks like:

```
df['Color'] = df.apply(add_team_color, axis=1)
for team in df['Team'].unique():
    info = df[df['Team'] == team]
    linecolor = info['Color'].unique()[0]
    plt.plot(info['Matchweek'], info['Rank'],
             color=linecolor, linestyle='-')
    plt.plot(info['Matchweek'], info['Rank'],
             color=linecolor, marker='o')
    plt.annotate(text=team,
                 xy=(40, info['Rank'].tail(1) + 0.15),
                 fontsize=7, color=linecolor)
plt.yticks(np.arange(0, 21, 1))
plt.xticks(np.arange(0, 39, 2))
plt.xlim(0.33, 52)
plt.ylim(0.33, 20.66)
plt.gca().invert_yaxis()
plt.gca().get_yaxis().set_major_formatter(
        FuncFormatter(lambda x, p: format(int(x), ',')))
plt.gcf().set_size_inches((9, 6))
plt.xlabel('Matchweek')
plt.title('Premier League 2018-2019 Season Bump Chart')
plt.show()
```

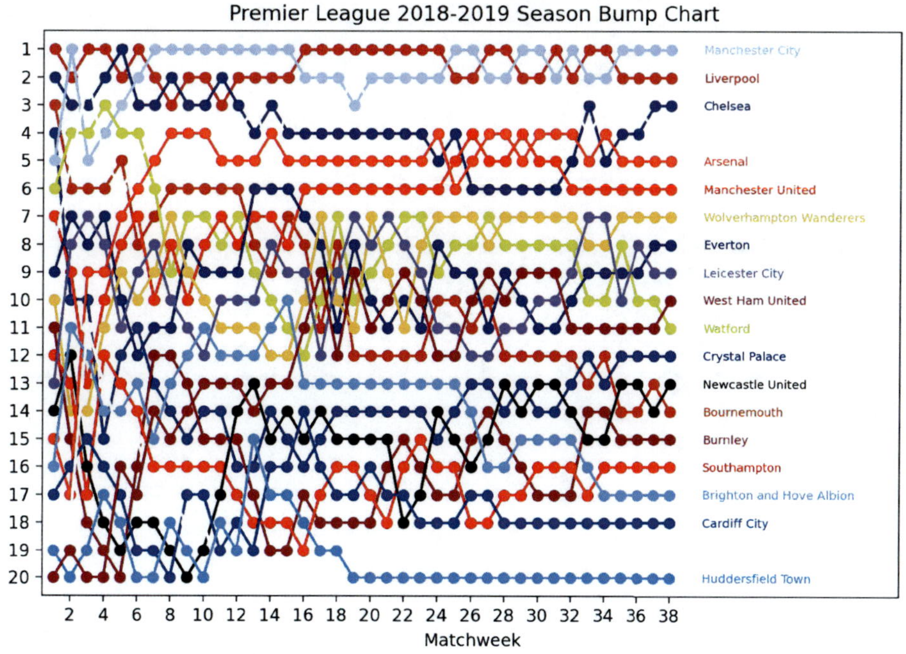

It looks a little busy, but you can trace the course of Liverpool's title chase throughout the season. We have one last problem, though: white is the primary color of both Tottenham and Fulham, and the background color for the entire figure is white.

We can make the canvas background gray to reduce some of the eye strain and to make the white primary team colors visible:

```
plt.gca().set_facecolor('#e6e6e6')
```

That is the only change we need to make to the last blob of code. The resulting chart looks like this:

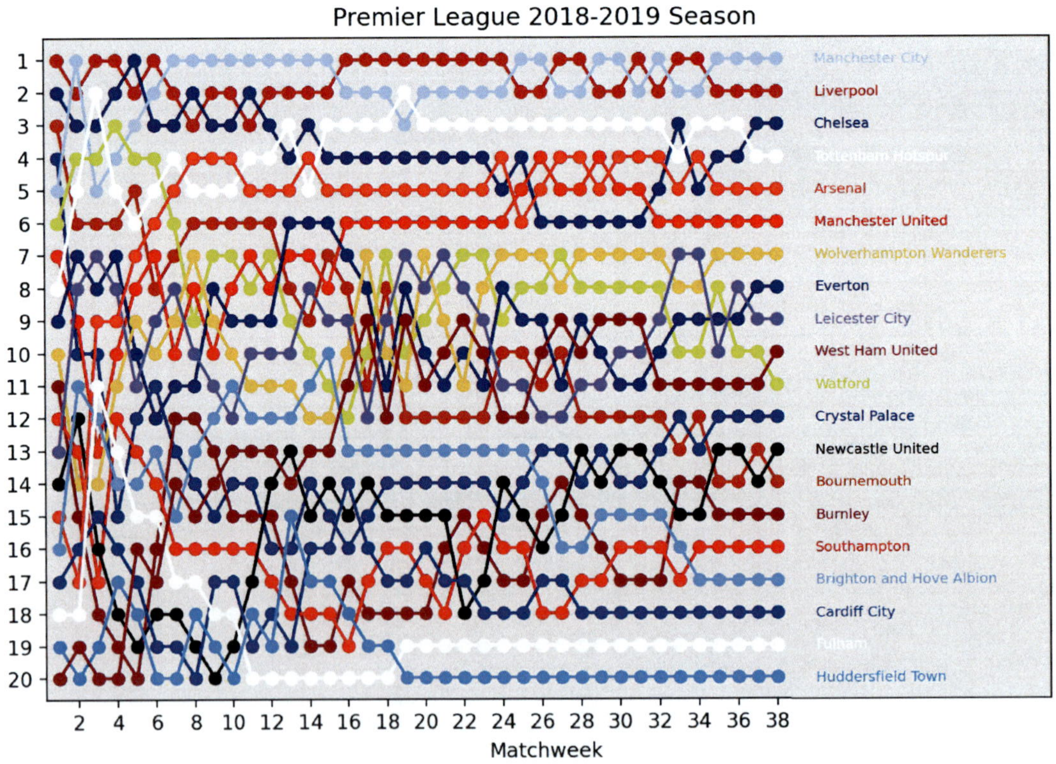

Now that we have a completed bump chart, the slope chart is even easier. All we need to do is trim down the data to just be matchweeks 19 and 38. We can also adjust the x ticks so that only 19 and 38 are visible on the x axis.

```
plt.style.use('default')
mw19 = df[df['Matchweek'] == 19]
mw38 = df[df['Matchweek'] == 38]
slope_data = mw19.append(mw38, ignore_index=True)

for team in slope_data['Team'].unique():
    temp_df = slope_data[slope_data['Team'] == team].reset_index()
    linecolor = temp_df['Color'][0]
    plt.plot(temp_df['Matchweek'], temp_df['Rank'],
             color=linecolor, linestyle='-')
    plt.plot(temp_df['Matchweek'], temp_df['Rank'],
             color=linecolor, marker='o')
    plt.annotate(text=team,
                 xy=(40, temp_df['Rank'].tail(1) + 0.15),
                 fontsize=7, color=linecolor)
plt.xlim(17, 50)
plt.ylim(0.33, 21)
plt.yticks(range(1, 21, 1))
plt.xticks([19, 38])
plt.gca().invert_yaxis()
plt.gca().get_yaxis().set_major_formatter(
          FuncFormatter(lambda x, p: format(int(x), ',')))
plt.xlabel('Matchweek')
plt.title('Premier League 2018-2019 Season')
plt.gca().set_facecolor('#e6e6e6')
plt.show()
```

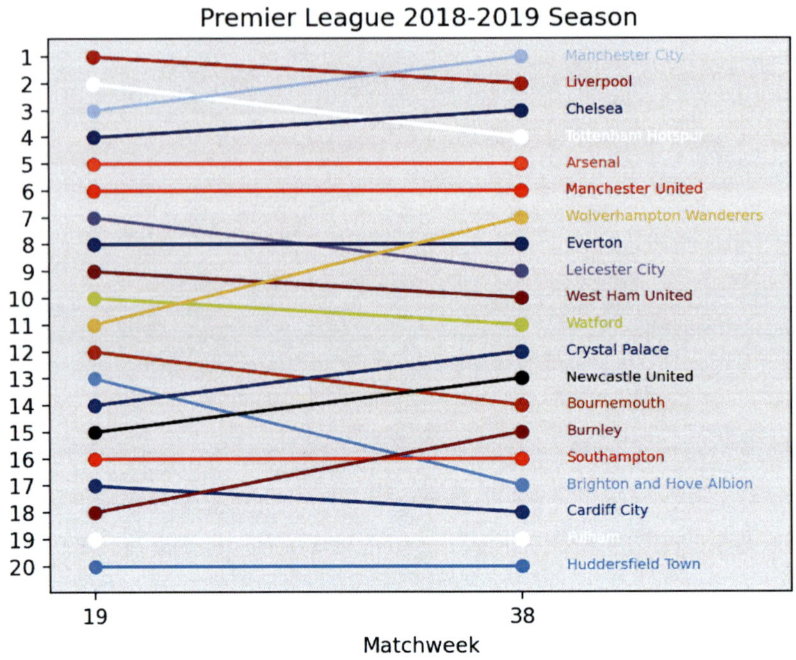

We can see that, to within a couple of places, the half-way point is a pretty good predictor of what the end of the season rankings will look like.

Lastly, let's create a lollipop chart with The Guardian's predictions. We need to define "actual performance" as the team's position after Matchweek 38 and "predicted performance" as The Guardian's prediction for that team. How we create this chart is a little confusing: we will use the same inverted y axis, and we will use the actual performance as both the x and y coordinates. If the actual performance is the same as the predicted performance, we will plot one blue circle at the point (actual, actual). For example, Tottenham was predicted to finish 4th and finished 4th, so its coordinate is (4, 4). If the actual performance is different from the predicted performance, we will plot the predicted performance as the x coordinate and the actual as the y coordinate (predicted, actual), and we will plot the actual performance as (actual, actual). For example, Chelsea was predicted to finish in 6th and actually finished in 3rd. There will be a blue dot at (3, 3) and an orange dot at (6, 3).

We will also create a `toplot` coordinate so that we can plot the team name to the right of the right-most dot. So that we don't have a legend that takes up half of the plot, we won't label any of the teams, but we'll plot one blue circle and one orange circle off of the canvas and label those as "Actual Performance" and "Predicted Performance" respectively. This way, we get a two-member legend of Actual Performance and Predicted Performance without cluttering the canvas. That's a lot of setup, so let's see the code:

```
orange = '#ff7f0e'  # predicted performance
blue = '#1f77b4'    # actual performance
size_of_dots = 11
for team in preds['Team'].unique():
    temp_df = preds[preds['Team'] == team].reset_index()
    predicted = temp_df['Predicted'][0]
    actual = temp_df['Actual'][0]
    if actual != predicted:
        plt.plot([actual, predicted],
                 [actual, actual],
                 color='gray', linestyle='-')
        plt.plot(actual, actual, color=blue, marker='o',
                 markersize=size_of_dots)
        plt.plot(predicted, actual, color=orange, marker='o',
                 markersize=size_of_dots)
    else:
        plt.plot(actual, actual, color=blue, marker='o',
                 markersize=size_of_dots)

    if actual > predicted:
        toplot = actual
    elif predicted > actual:
        toplot = predicted
    else:
        toplot = actual
```

```
    plt.annotate(text=team,
                 xy=(toplot + 1, actual + 0.15),
                 fontsize=7, color='black')
plt.gca().get_yaxis().set_major_formatter(
           FuncFormatter(lambda x, p: format(int(x), ',')))
plt.yticks(np.arange(0, 21, 1))
plt.tick_params(axis='both', which='both',
               bottom=False, top=False,
               labelbottom=False, left=False,
               labelleft=False)
plt.xlim(0.33, 27)
plt.ylim(0.33, 20.66)
plt.gca().invert_yaxis()
plt.plot(27, 27, color=blue, label="Actual Performance",
         marker='o', markersize=size_of_dots)
plt.plot(28, 28, color=orange, label="Predicted Performance",
         marker='o', markersize=size_of_dots)
plt.legend()
plt.title('English Premier League 2018-2019 Cleveland Dot Plot')
plt.show()
```

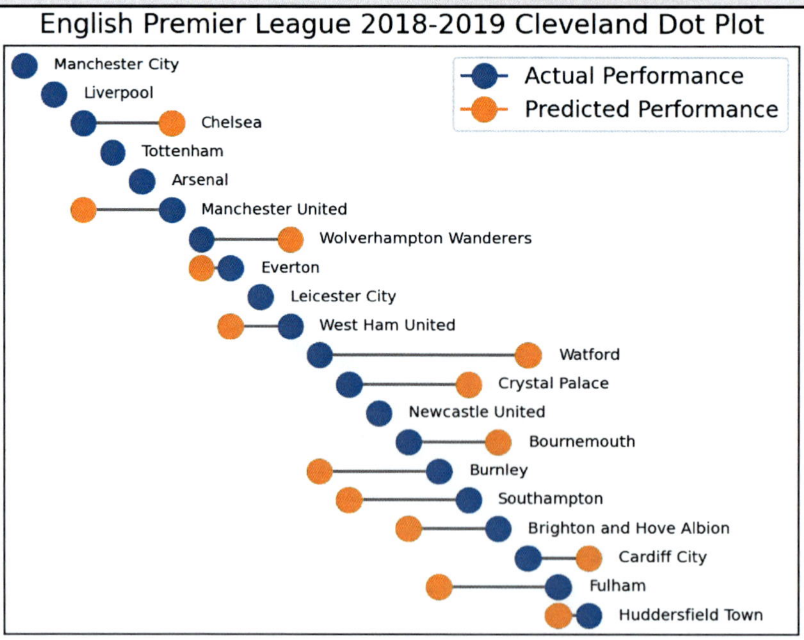

It takes a minute to understand, but these dot plots very quickly show which teams performed as expected (blue dot, no orange dot), which teams underperformed (orange dot then blue dot, going from left to right), and which teams overperformed (blue dot then orange dot, going left to right), at least according to The Guardian.

The figure looks good, but we can improve it with ranking annotations; we don't want the reader to have to count to figure out what place Leicester City achieved, for example. To do this, we need to add annotations to each point. The annotations required a little troubleshooting to appear centered on the dots, so here is the end result:

```
if actual < 10:
    plt.annotate(text=actual,
                 xy=(actual - 0.15, actual + 0.15),
                 fontsize=7, color='w')
else:
    plt.annotate(text=actual,
                 xy=(actual - 0.31, actual + 0.15),
                 fontsize=7, color='w')

if predicted < 10:
    plt.annotate(text=predicted,
                 xy=(predicted - 0.15, actual + 0.15),
                 fontsize=7, color='w')
else:
    plt.annotate(text=predicted,
                 xy=(predicted - 0.31, actual + 0.15),
                 fontsize=7, color='w')
```

This is what the full code looks like:

```
orange = '#ff7f0e'  # predicted performance
blue = '#1f77b4'    # actual performance
size_of_dots = 11
for team in preds['Team'].unique():
    temp_df = preds[preds['Team'] == team].reset_index()
    predicted = temp_df['Predicted'][0]
    actual = temp_df['Actual'][0]
    if actual != predicted:
        plt.plot([actual, predicted],
                 [actual, actual],
                 color='gray', linestyle='-')
        plt.plot(actual, actual,
                 color=blue, marker='o',
                 markersize=size_of_dots)
        plt.plot(predicted, actual,
                 color=orange, marker='o',
                 markersize=size_of_dots)
    else:
        plt.plot(actual, actual, color=blue, marker='o',
                 markersize=size_of_dots)

    if actual < 10:
        plt.annotate(text=actual,
                    xy=(actual - 0.15, actual + 0.15),
                    fontsize=7, color='w')
    else:
        plt.annotate(text=actual,
                     xy=(actual - 0.31, actual + 0.15),
                     fontsize=7, color='w')

    if predicted < 10:
        plt.annotate(text=predicted,
                     xy=(predicted - 0.15, actual + 0.15),
                     fontsize=7, color='w')
    else:
        plt.annotate(text=predicted,
                     xy=(predicted - 0.31, actual + 0.15),
```

```
                      fontsize=7, color='w')

    if actual > predicted:
        toplot = actual
    elif predicted > actual:
        toplot = predicted
    else:
        toplot = actual
    plt.annotate(text=team,
                 xy=(toplot + 1, actual + 0.15),
                 fontsize=7, color='black')
plt.gca().get_yaxis().set_major_formatter(
          FuncFormatter(lambda x, p: format(int(x), ',')))
plt.yticks(np.arange(0, 21, 1))
plt.tick_params(axis='both', which='both',
                bottom=False, top=False,
                labelbottom=False, left=False,
                labelleft=False)
plt.xlim(0.33, 27)
plt.ylim(0.33, 20.66)
plt.gca().invert_yaxis()
plt.plot(27, 27, color=blue, label="Actual Performance",
         marker='o', markersize=size_of_dots)
plt.plot(28, 28, color=orange, label="Predicted Performance",
         marker='o', markersize=size_of_dots)
plt.legend()
plt.title('English Premier League 2018-2019 Cleveland Dot Plot')
plt.show()
```

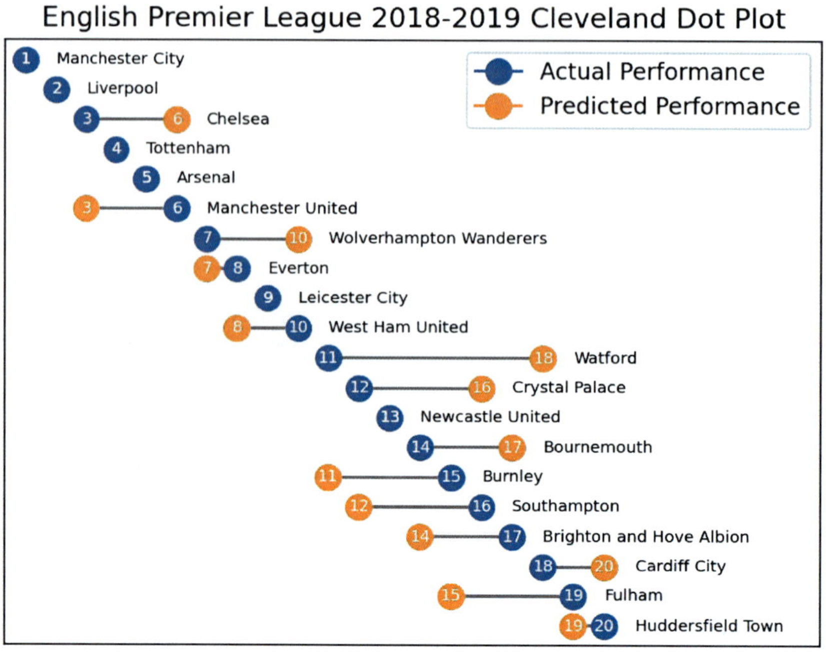

If you wanted to be cruel, you could add red marks to places 18, 19, and 20 to show The Relegation Zone.

Plotly

We can start off with Plotly Express' `scatter()` method, but we are going to need to jump into Plotly Graph Objects to get the required level of customization. We will start with showing the first version of a Plotly Bump Chart.

```
fig = px.scatter(df, x='Matchweek', y='Rank', color='Team')
fig.update_layout({'title':
                   'Premier League 2018-2019 Season Bump Chart'})
fig.show()
```

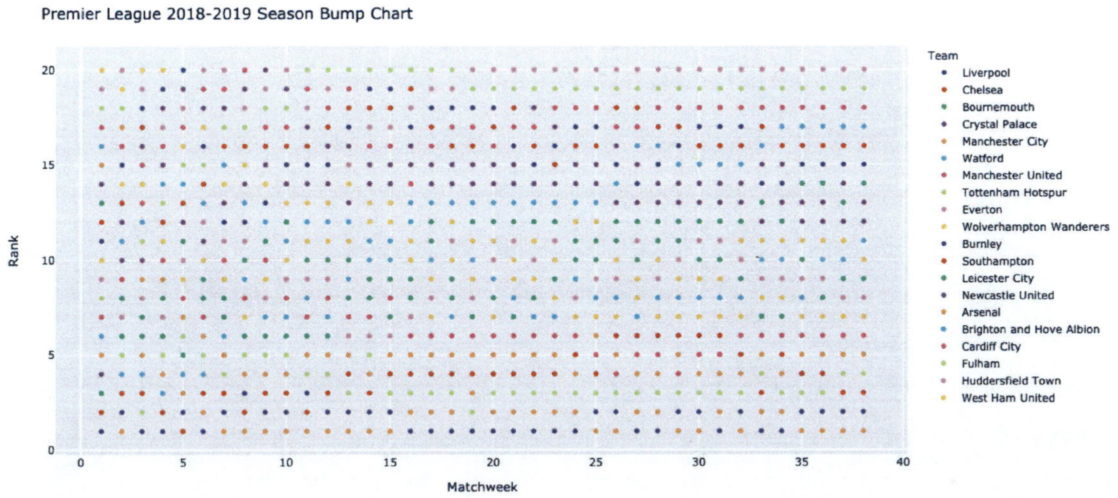

As you can see, the y axis is unflipped, the team colors have been randomly chosen, and the legend detracts from the visualization. Graph Objects, here we come.

The same plan is required for making a bump chart in Plotly as it was for making a bump chart in Matplotlib: we need a line connecting scatter plot markers. We can do this by creating a `Figure()` and then adding a `go.Scatter()` object with both markers and lines. After that, the program flows about the same as with Matplotlib by dynamically adding each team to the figure. Since this is Plotly, we can one-up Matplotlib by adding hover text that says that "{team} was in {place} on Matchweek {number}." In our case, it is easiest to create a new column in the DataFrame of what our desired hover text is. Here is what that function should look like:

```
def ranking_text(df1) -> str:
    place = str(df1['Rank'])
    teamname = df1['Team']
    conversion_dict = {'1': 'st', '2': 'nd', '3': 'rd'}

    if place in conversion_dict.keys():
        return '{} was in {}{}'.format(teamname,
                                       place, conversion_dict[place[-1]])
    else:
        return '{} was in {}th'.format(teamname, place)
```

We can apply it to the rows of the DataFrame as we have previously done:

```
df['Place'] = df[['Rank', 'Team']].apply(ranking_text, axis=1)
```

With the new `Place` column, this is what the rest of the program looks like:

```
size_of_dots = 14
fig = go.Figure()
for team in df['Team'].unique():
    temp_df = df[df['Team'] == team].reset_index()
    fig.add_trace(go.Scatter(x=temp_df['Matchweek'],
                             y=temp_df['Rank'],
                             mode="lines+markers",
                             marker={'size': size_of_dots,
                             'color': temp_df['Color'][0]},
                             line={'color': temp_df['Color'][0]},
                             name="", showlegend=False,
                       hovertemplate='%{text} on Matchweek %{x}',
                             text=temp_df['Place']))
    fig.add_annotation(text=team, x=39,
                       y=temp_df['Rank'].tail(1)[37],
                       showarrow=False, xref='x',
                       xanchor='left',
                       font={'size': 10,
                             'color': temp_df['Color'][0]})


fig.update_yaxes(range=[21, 0],
```

```
                showtickLabels=False, ticks="")
fig.update_xaxes(showtickLabels=True,
                title_text='Matchweek',
                tickmode="array",
                tickvals=[val for val in range(1, 39, 1)])
fig.update_layout({'template': 'simple_white',
                  'plot_bgcolor': '#e6e6e6',
          'title': 'Premier League 2018-2019 Season Bump Chart'},
                 hoverlabel={'bgcolor': '#F3F0EF'})
fig.show()
```

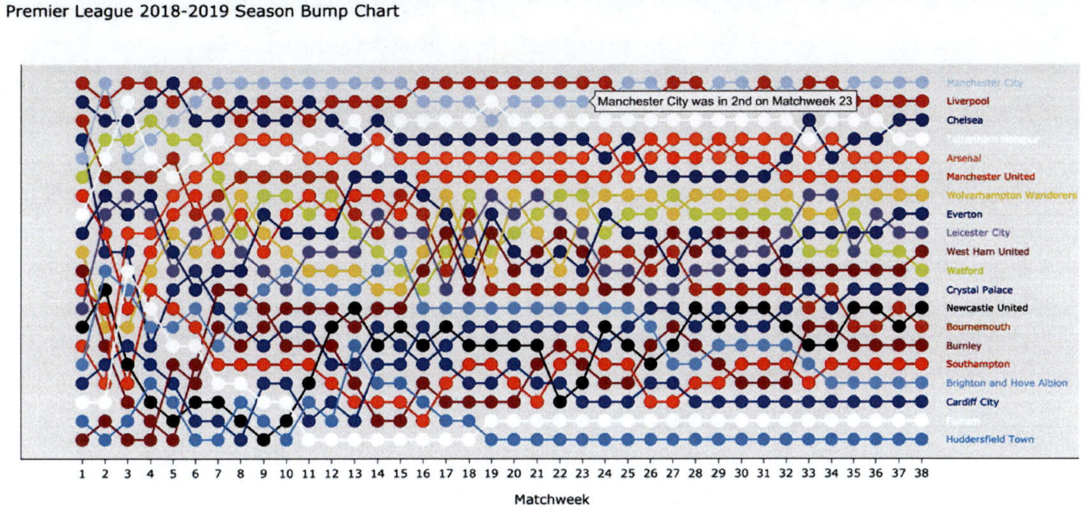

Again, the slope chart is just a simplified version of the bump chart. We make a new DataFrame that contains only matchweeks 19 and 38, and then we follow a similar process as before.

```
mw19 = df[df['Matchweek'] == 19]
mw38 = df[df['Matchweek'] == 38]
slope_data = mw19.append(mw38, ignore_index=True)
def ranking_text(df1) -> str:
    place = str(df1['Rank'])
    teamname = df1['Team']
    conversion_dict = {'1': 'st', '2': 'nd', '3': 'rd'}

    if place in conversion_dict.keys():
        return '{} was in {}{}'.format(teamname,
```

```
                             place, conversion_dict[place[-1]])
    else:
        return '{} was in {}th'.format(teamname, place)

slope_data['Place'] = slope_data[['Rank',
                     'Team']].apply(ranking_text, axis=1)
size_of_dots = 14
fig = go.Figure()
for team in slope_data['Team'].unique():
    temp_df = slope_data[slope_data['Team'] == team].reset_index()
    fig.add_trace(go.Scatter(x=temp_df['Matchweek'],
                             y=temp_df['Rank'],
                             mode="lines+markers",
                             marker={'size': size_of_dots,
                                 'color': temp_df['Color'][0]},
                             line={'color': temp_df['Color'][0]},
                             name="", showlegend=False,
                       hovertemplate='%{text} on Matchweek %{x}',
                             text=temp_df['Place']))
    fig.add_annotation(text=team, x=39,
                       y=temp_df['Rank'].tail(1)[1],
                       showarrow=False, xref='x',
                       xanchor='left',
                       font={'size': 10,
                         'color': temp_df['Color'][0]})

fig.update_yaxes(range=[21, 0],
                 showticklabels=False, ticks="")
fig.update_xaxes(showticklabels=True, title_text='Matchweek',
                 tickmode="array", tickvals=[19, 38])
fig.update_layout({'template': 'simple_white',
                   'plot_bgcolor': '#e6e6e6',
            'title': 'Premier League 2018-2019 Season Slope Chart'},
                  hoverlabel={'bgcolor': '#F3F0EF'})
fig.show()
```

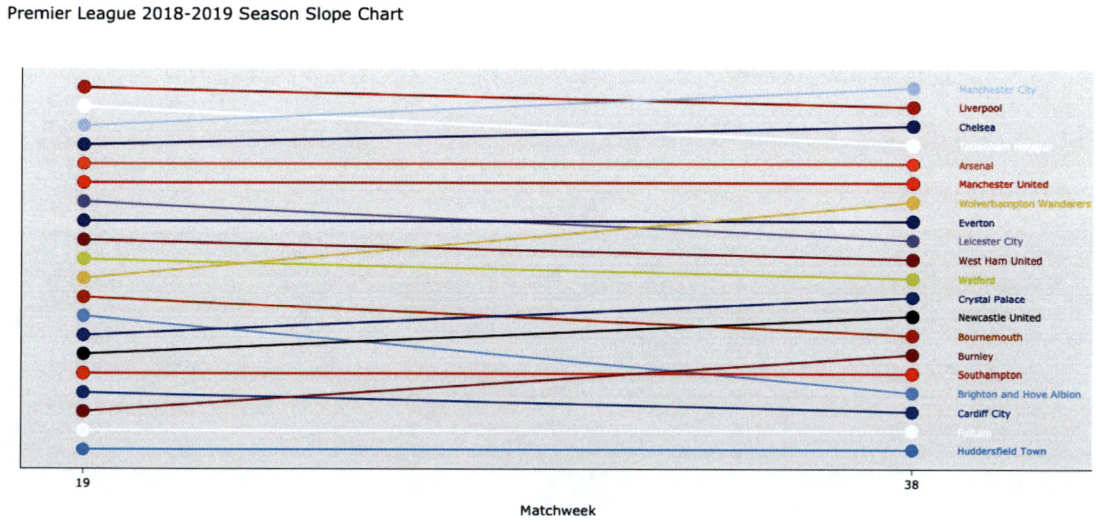

We need to perform the same annotations and coordinate systems for Plotly's Cleveland Dotplot. The syntax is a little different, but the ideas are the same. Here is the completed code:

```
orange = '#ff7f0e'  # predicted performance
blue = '#1f77b4'    # actual performance
size_of_dots = 18
fig = go.Figure(layout={'xaxis': {'mirror': True,
                                  'ticks': 'outside',
                                  'showline': True},
                        'yaxis': {'mirror': True,
                                  'ticks': 'outside',
                                  'showline': True}})

for team in preds['Team'].unique():
    temp_df = preds[preds['Team'] == team].reset_index()
    predicted = temp_df['Predicted'][0]
    actual = temp_df['Actual'][0]
    if predicted != actual:
        fig.add_trace(go.Scatter(x=[actual, predicted],
                                 y=[actual, actual],
                                 mode='lines',
                                 marker={'color': 'gray'},
                                 name="", showlegend=False))
        fig.add_trace(go.Scatter(x=temp_df['Predicted'],
```

```
                                        y=temp_df['Actual'],
                                        mode='markers', name="",
                                        showLegend=False,
                                        fillcolor=orange,
                                        marker={'size': size_of_dots,
                                           'color': orange},
   hovertemplate='Team: %{text}<br>Predicted: %{x}<br>Actual: %{y}',
                                        text=temp_df['Team']))
        fig.add_trace(go.Scatter(x=temp_df['Actual'],
                                        y=temp_df['Actual'],
                                        mode='markers', name="",
                                        showLegend=False,
                                        marker={'size': size_of_dots,
                                                'color': blue},
                                        hoverinfo='text',
    hovertemplate='Team: %{text}<br>Predicted: %{x}<br>Actual:
%{y}',
                                        text=temp_df['Team']))
    else:
        fig.add_trace(go.Scatter(x=temp_df['Actual'],
                                        y=temp_df['Actual'],
                                        mode='markers', name="",
                                        showLegend=False,
                                        marker={'size': size_of_dots,
                                                'color': blue},
    hovertemplate='Team: %{text}<br>Predicted: %{x}<br>Actual:
%{y}',
                                        text=temp_df['Team']))

    if actual < 10:
        fig.add_annotation(text=str(actual), x=actual,
                           y=actual, showarrow=False,
                           font={'size': 10, 'color': 'white'})
    else:
        fig.add_annotation(text=str(actual), x=actual,
                           y=actual, showarrow=False,
                           font={'size': 10, 'color': 'white'})

    if predicted < 10:
        fig.add_annotation(text=str(predicted), x=predicted,
```

```
                         y=actual, showarrow=False,
                         font={'size': 10, 'color': 'white'})
    else:
        fig.add_annotation(text=str(predicted), x=predicted,
                         y=actual, showarrow=False,
                         font={'size': 10, 'color': 'white'})

    if actual > predicted:
        toplot = actual
    elif predicted > actual:
        toplot = predicted
    else:
        toplot = actual

    fig.add_annotation(text=team, x=toplot + 0.38, y=actual,
                       showarrow=False, xref='x',
                       xanchor='left',
                       font={'size': 10, 'color': 'black'})

fig.add_trace(go.Scatter(x=[27], y=[27],
                         mode='markers',
                         name="Actual Performance",
                         showLegend=True,
                         marker={'size': size_of_dots,
                                 'color': blue}))
fig.add_trace(go.Scatter(x=[28], y=[28],
                         mode='markers',
                         name="Predicted Performance",
                         showLegend=True,
                         marker={'size': size_of_dots,
                                 'color': orange}))
fig.update_yaxes(range=[21, 0],
                 showticklabels=False, ticks="")
fig.update_xaxes(range=[0, 25],
                 showticklabels=False, ticks="")
fig.update_layout({'template': 'simple_white',
      'title': 'English Premier League 2018-2019 Cleveland Dot
Plot'},
                  hoverlabel={'bgcolor': '#F3F0EF'})
fig.show()
```

English Premier League 2018-2019 Cleveland Dot Plot

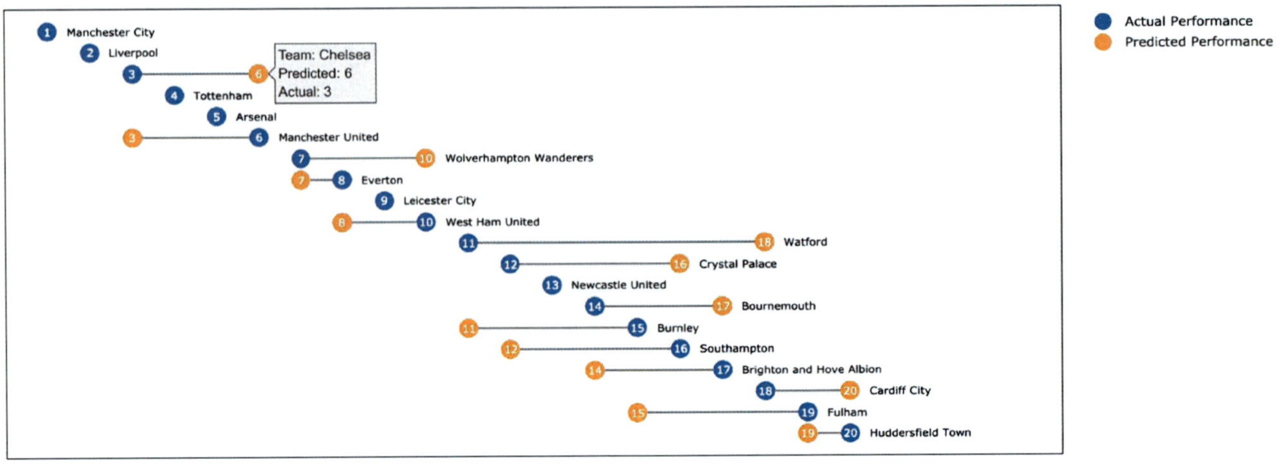

The last section of code is a little long, but we end up with an interactive lollipop chart that quickly shows actual performance compared with predicted performance.

Summary

Bump charts are a great way to show how rankings change over time. They can become a little busy, so take care to ensure that your message is clear. In our case, Arsenal and Manchester United have similar colors, so it can get hard to read when they were fighting for 5th and 6th place. Slope charts could be a way to alleviate the burden on readers if you want to show a change over an even more specific time period. They can also be a good way to show the financial performance of certain categories over a time period. Finally, dumbbell/lollipop/dot plot/Cleveland Dot Plot charts are a good way to show one categorial and two numerical observations; anything more than two observations starts to push more cognitive load onto the reader. In our reference system, the dumbbell chart made it easy to see which teams over- or under-performed according to The

Guardian's predictions. These types of charts have specific use cases, but they can be employed to great effect with careful consideration.

Examples for Each Library

```
import matplotlib.pyplot as plt
from matplotlib.ticker import FuncFormatter
import plotly.graph_objects as go
import pandas as pd
import numpy as np
import plotly.io as pio
pio.renderers.default = "browser"

df = pd.read_csv('https://raw.githubusercontent.com/
                 alexkenan/pyviz/main/datasets/prem.csv',
                 names=['Matchweek', 'Team', 'Rank'], header=0)
preds = pd.read_csv('https://raw.githubusercontent.com/
                    alexkenan/pyviz/main/datasets/predictions.csv',
                    names=['Team', 'Actual', 'Predicted'],
                    header=0)
orange = '#ff7f0e'  # predicted performance
blue = '#1f77b4'    # actual performance
def add_team_color(df1: pd.DataFrame) -> str:
    name = df1['Team']
    colors = {'Bournemouth': '#cc2900',
              'Crystal Palace': "#0000FF",
              'Liverpool': '#CD0206',
              'Chelsea': '#0000CC',
              'Manchester City': '#99CCFF',
              'Watford': '#cccc00',
              'Manchester United': '#FF0000',
              'Tottenham Hotspur': '#FFFFFF',
              'Everton': '#0000CC',
              'Wolverhampton Wanderers': '#EFBE29',
              'Burnley': '#99172B',
              'Southampton': '#FF0000',
              'Leicester City': '#6666ff',
              'Newcastle United': '#000000',
              'Arsenal': '#ff3333',
```

```
            'Brighton and Hove Albion': '#47a5ff',
            'Cardiff City': '#0039e6',
            'Fulham': '#FFFFFF',
            'Huddersfield Town': '#0099FF',
            'West Ham United': '#99182B'
            }

    if name in colors.keys():
        return colors[name]
    else:
        return '#000000'


df['Color'] = df.apply(add_team_color, axis=1)

# Bump chart, Matplotlib
plt.style.use('default')
for team in df['Team'].unique():
    info = df[df['Team'] == team]
    linecolor = info['Color'].unique()[0]
    plt.plot(info['Matchweek'], info['Rank'],
             color=linecolor, linestyle='-')
    plt.plot(info['Matchweek'], info['Rank'],
             color=linecolor, marker='o')
    plt.annotate(text=team,
                 xy=(40, info['Rank'].tail(1) + 0.15),
                 fontsize=7, color=linecolor)

plt.yticks(np.arange(0, 21, 1))
plt.xticks(np.arange(0, 39, 2))
plt.xlim(0.33, 52)
plt.ylim(0.33, 20.66)
plt.gca().invert_yaxis()
plt.gca().get_yaxis().set_major_formatter(
          FuncFormatter(lambda x, p: format(int(x), ',')))
plt.gcf().set_size_inches((9, 6))
plt.xlabel('Matchweek')
plt.title('Premier League 2018-2019 Season')
plt.gca().set_facecolor('#e6e6e6')
plt.show()
```

```
# Bump chart, Plotly
def ranking_text(df1: pd.DataFrame) -> str:
    place = str(df1['Rank'])
    teamname = df1['Team']
    conversion_dict = {'1': 'st', '2': 'nd', '3': 'rd'}

    if place in conversion_dict.keys():
        return '{} was in {}{}'.format(teamname, place,
                               conversion_dict[place[-1]])
    else:
        return '{} was in {}th'.format(teamname, place)


df['Place'] = df[['Rank', 'Team']].apply(ranking_text, axis=1)
size_of_dots = 14
fig = go.Figure()
for team in df['Team'].unique():
    temp_df = df[df['Team'] == team].reset_index()
    fig.add_trace(go.Scatter(x=temp_df['Matchweek'],
                             y=temp_df['Rank'],
                             mode="lines+markers",
                             marker={'size': size_of_dots,
                                 'color': temp_df['Color'][0]},
                             line={'color': temp_df['Color'][0]},
                             name="", showlegend=False,
            hovertemplate='%{text} on Matchweek %{x}',
                             text=temp_df['Place']))
    fig.add_annotation(text=team, x=39,
                       y=temp_df['Rank'].tail(1)[37],
                       showarrow=False, xref='x',
                       xanchor='left',
                       font={'size': 10,
                             'color': temp_df['Color'][0]})

fig.update_yaxes(range=[21, 0],
                 showticklabels=False, ticks="")
fig.update_xaxes(showticklabels=True,
                 title_text='Matchweek',
                 tickmode="array",
```

```
                  tickvals=[val for val in range(1, 39, 1)])
fig.update_layout({'template': 'simple_white',
                    'plot_bgcolor': '#e6e6e6',
             'title': 'Premier League 2018-2019 Season Bump Chart'},
                   hoverlabel={'bgcolor': '#F3F0EF'})
fig.show()

# Slope chart, Matplotlib
plt.style.use('default')
mw19 = df[df['Matchweek'] == 19]
mw38 = df[df['Matchweek'] == 38]
slope_data = mw19.append(mw38, ignore_index=True)

for team in slope_data['Team'].unique():
    temp_df = slope_data[slope_data['Team'] == team].reset_index()
    linecolor = temp_df['Color'][0]
    plt.plot(temp_df['Matchweek'], temp_df['Rank'],
             color=linecolor, linestyle='-')
    plt.plot(temp_df['Matchweek'], temp_df['Rank'],
             color=linecolor, marker='o')
    plt.annotate(text=team,
                 xy=(40, temp_df['Rank'].tail(1) + 0.15),
                 fontsize=7, color=linecolor)
plt.xlim(17, 50)
plt.ylim(0.33, 21)
plt.yticks(range(1, 21, 1))
plt.xticks([19, 38])
plt.gca().invert_yaxis()
plt.gca().get_yaxis().set_major_formatter(
            FuncFormatter(lambda x, p: format(int(x), ',')))
plt.xlabel('Matchweek')
plt.title('Premier League 2018-2019 Season')
plt.gca().set_facecolor('#e6e6e6')
plt.show()

# Slope chart, Plotly
def ranking_text(df1: pd.DataFrame) -> str:
    place = str(df1['Rank'])
    teamname = df1['Team']
    conversion_dict = {'1': 'st', '2': 'nd', '3': 'rd'}
```

```
    if place in conversion_dict.keys():
        return '{} was in {}{}'.format(teamname, place,
                                       conversion_dict[place[-1]])
    else:
        return '{} was in {}th'.format(teamname, place)


slope_data['Place'] = slope_data[['Rank',
                      'Team']].apply(ranking_text, axis=1)
size_of_dots = 14
fig = go.Figure()
for team in slope_data['Team'].unique():
    temp_df = slope_data[slope_data['Team'] == team].reset_index()
    fig.add_trace(go.Scatter(x=temp_df['Matchweek'],
                             y=temp_df['Rank'],
                             mode="lines+markers",
                             marker={'size': size_of_dots,
                                   'color': temp_df['Color'][0]},
                             line={'color': temp_df['Color'][0]},
                             name="", showlegend=False,
                      hovertemplate='%{text} on Matchweek %{x}',
                             text=temp_df['Place']))
    fig.add_annotation(text=team, x=39,
                       y=temp_df['Rank'].tail(1)[1],
                       showarrow=False, xref='x',
                       xanchor='left',
                       font={'size': 10,
                             'color': temp_df['Color'][0]})

fig.update_yaxes(range=[21, 0],
                 showticklabels=False, ticks="")
fig.update_xaxes(showticklabels=True,
                 title_text='Matchweek',
                 tickmode="array", tickvals=[19, 38])
fig.update_layout({'template': 'simple_white',
                   'plot_bgcolor': '#e6e6e6',
              'title': 'Premier League 2018-2019 Season Bump
Chart'},
                  hoverlabel={'bgcolor': '#F3F0EF'})
```

```
fig.show()


# Lollipop chart, Matplotlib
plt.style.use('default')
size_of_dots = 11
for team in preds['Team'].unique():
    temp_df = preds[preds['Team'] == team].reset_index()
    predicted = temp_df['Predicted'][0]
    actual = temp_df['Actual'][0]
    if actual != predicted:
        plt.plot([actual, predicted], [actual, actual],
                 color='gray', linestyle='-')
        plt.plot(actual, actual, color=blue,
                 marker='o', markersize=size_of_dots)
        plt.plot(predicted, actual, color=orange,
                 marker='o', markersize=size_of_dots)
    else:
        plt.plot(actual, actual, color=blue,
                 marker='o', markersize=size_of_dots)

    if actual < 10:
        plt.annotate(text=actual,
                     xy=(actual - 0.15, actual + 0.15),
                     fontsize=7, color='w')
    else:
        plt.annotate(text=actual,
                     xy=(actual - 0.31, actual + 0.15),
                     fontsize=7, color='w')

    if predicted < 10:
        plt.annotate(text=predicted,
                     xy=(predicted - 0.15, actual + 0.15),
                     fontsize=7, color='w')
    else:
        plt.annotate(text=predicted,
                     xy=(predicted - 0.31, actual + 0.15),
                     fontsize=7, color='w')

    if actual > predicted:
```

```
        toplot = actual
    elif predicted > actual:
        toplot = predicted
    else:
        toplot = actual
    plt.annotate(text=team, xy=(toplot + 1, actual + 0.15),
                 fontsize=7, color='black')
plt.gca().get_yaxis().set_major_formatter(
         FuncFormatter(lambda x, p: format(int(x), ',')))
plt.yticks(np.arange(0, 21, 1))
plt.tick_params(axis='both', which='both',
                bottom=False, top=False,
                labelbottom=False, left=False,
                labelleft=False)
plt.xlim(0.33, 27)
plt.ylim(0.33, 20.66)
plt.gca().invert_yaxis()
plt.plot(27, 27, color=blue, label="Actual Performance",
         marker='o', markersize=size_of_dots)
plt.plot(28, 28, color=orange, label="Predicted Performance",
         marker='o', markersize=size_of_dots)
plt.legend()
plt.title('English Premier League 2018-2019 Cleveland Dot Plot')
plt.show()

# Lollipop chart, Plotly
size_of_dots = 18
fig = go.Figure(layout={'xaxis': {'mirror': True,
                                  'ticks': 'outside',
                                  'showline': True},
                        'yaxis': {'mirror': True,
                                  'ticks': 'outside',
                                  'showline': True}})

for team in preds['Team'].unique():
    temp_df = preds[preds['Team'] == team].reset_index()
    predicted = temp_df['Predicted'][0]
    actual = temp_df['Actual'][0]
    if predicted != actual:
        fig.add_trace(go.Scatter(x=[actual, predicted],
```

```
                                y=[actual, actual], mode='lines',
                                marker={'color': 'gray'},
                                name="", showlegend=False))
        fig.add_trace(go.Scatter(x=temp_df['Predicted'],
                                y=temp_df['Actual'],
                                mode='markers', name="",
                                showlegend=False,
                                fillcolor=orange,
                                marker={'size': size_of_dots,
                                        'color': orange},
                                hovertemplate='Team:
                        %{text}<br>Predicted: %{x}<br>Actual: %{y}',
                                text=temp_df['Team']))
        fig.add_trace(go.Scatter(x=temp_df['Actual'],
                                y=temp_df['Actual'],
                                mode='markers', name="",
                                showlegend=False, hoverinfo='text',
                                marker={'size': size_of_dots,
                                        'color': blue},
                                hovertemplate='Team:
                        %{text}<br>Predicted: %{x}<br>Actual: %{y}',
                                text=temp_df['Team']))
    else:
        fig.add_trace(go.Scatter(x=temp_df['Actual'],
                                y=temp_df['Actual'],
                                mode='markers', name="",
                                showlegend=False,
                                marker={'size': size_of_dots,
                                        'color': blue},
                               hovertemplate='Team:
                        %{text}<br>Predicted: %{x}<br>Actual: %{y}',
                                text=temp_df['Team']))
    if actual < 10:
        fig.add_annotation(text=str(actual), x=actual,
                           y=actual, showarrow=False,
                           font={'size': 10, 'color': 'white'})
    else:
        fig.add_annotation(text=str(actual), x=actual,
                           y=actual, showarrow=False,
                           font={'size': 10, 'color': 'white'})
```

```
    if predicted < 10:
        fig.add_annotation(text=str(predicted), x=predicted,
                           y=actual, showarrow=False,
                           font={'size': 10, 'color': 'white'})
    else:
        fig.add_annotation(text=str(predicted), x=predicted,
                           y=actual, showarrow=False,
                           font={'size': 10, 'color': 'white'})
    if actual > predicted:
        toplot = actual
    elif predicted > actual:
        toplot = predicted
    else:
        toplot = actual
    fig.add_annotation(text=team, x=toplot + 0.38, xref='x',
                       y=actual, showarrow=False, xanchor='left',
                       font={'size': 10, 'color': 'black'})
fig.add_trace(go.Scatter(x=[27], y=[27], mode='markers',
                         name="Actual Performance", showlegend=True,
                         marker={'size': size_of_dots,
                                 'color': blue}))
fig.add_trace(go.Scatter(x=[28], y=[28], mode='markers',
                         name="Predicted Performance",
                         showlegend=True,
                         marker={'size': size_of_dots,
                                 'color': orange}))
fig.update_yaxes(range=[21, 0], showticklabels=False, ticks="")
fig.update_xaxes(range=[0, 25], showticklabels=False, ticks="")
fig.update_layout({'template': 'simple_white',
   'title': 'English Premier League 2018-2019 Cleveland Dot Plot'},
                  hoverlabel={'bgcolor': '#F3F0EF'})
fig.show()
```

View this code on GitHub at https://github.com/alexkenan/pyviz/

Resources

[1] https://github.com/jalapic/engsoccerdata/tree/master/data-raw

Hexbinning & US Electoral College

Introduction

When Americans go to the voting booth to elect a President, the winner is not directly decided by a simple majority of votes; rather, electors in each state participate in the Electoral College, with most states having a winner-take-all system. The magic number for Presidential candidates is not 50.1% of the popular vote. Instead, it is 270: there are 538 total electors, so one more than 50% of 538 is 270. The Electoral College has its proponents and its critics; we won't get into that here. What we want to do is answer the simple question: what is the minimum number of states required to win a Presidential election? We will use Plotly to emphasize the required states and to gray out the unneeded states, and we will also experiment with hexbinning to reduce the Alaska effect on a continental US map, where Alaska either distorts the map or gets squished into a frame on the side of the map. With hexbinning, we can represent each state as a hexagon. This shape packs together neatly, and we can mimic the shape of the US without having to scale for the disproportionately large Alaska or the small and faraway Hawaii. In this section, we will only be using Plotly for our graphs because of its ability to easily handle geographical data. Similar visualizations can be made with geoPandas and Matplotlib, but for simplicity, we will stay with Plotly.

Our dataset is simple: we have the state name, the state abbreviation, the number of electors for that state, and the running total. The specific number of electors for each state may vary; every

10 years, after the US census takes place, the number of electors per state is re-calculated to be proportionally representative. This dataset is current for 2020.

Column Name	**Datatype**	**Description**
State	`str`	The full name of the state
Abbr	`str`	The 2 letter abbreviation of the state
Electors	`int`	The number of electors that that state has
Cumulative Count	`int`	The running total of all electors, including the current row

Imports

```
import plotly.express as px
import plotly.graph_objects as go
import pandas as pd
import json
import requests
df = pd.read_csv('https://raw.githubusercontent.com/
                 alexkenan/pyviz/main/datasets/elect.csv')
j_file_str = requests.get('https://raw.githubusercontent.com/

alexkenan/pyviz/main/datasets/geoJSONstates.json').text
j_file = json.loads(j_file_str)
df['Needed to Win'] = df['Cumulative Count'] <= 270
```

The JSON library will be required later to work with the hexbin shape file, and we can use simple math to figure out which state is needed to win: the data is already sorted from largest to smallest, so if the cumulative count is less than or equal to 270, that state is needed to win.

Plotly

As always, we will start with Plotly Express and use its `choropleth()` function. We can pass a `color_discrete_sequence` to show the needed to win states in blue and the not needed to win states in gray.

```
fig = px.choropleth(df, locations=df['Abbr'],
                    locationmode="USA-states",
                    color="Needed to Win",
                    color_discrete_sequence=['#0c68e6', '#f4f4f6'],
                    scope="usa")
fig.update_layout(
          title="Electoral College Minimum States Needed to Win")
fig.show()
```

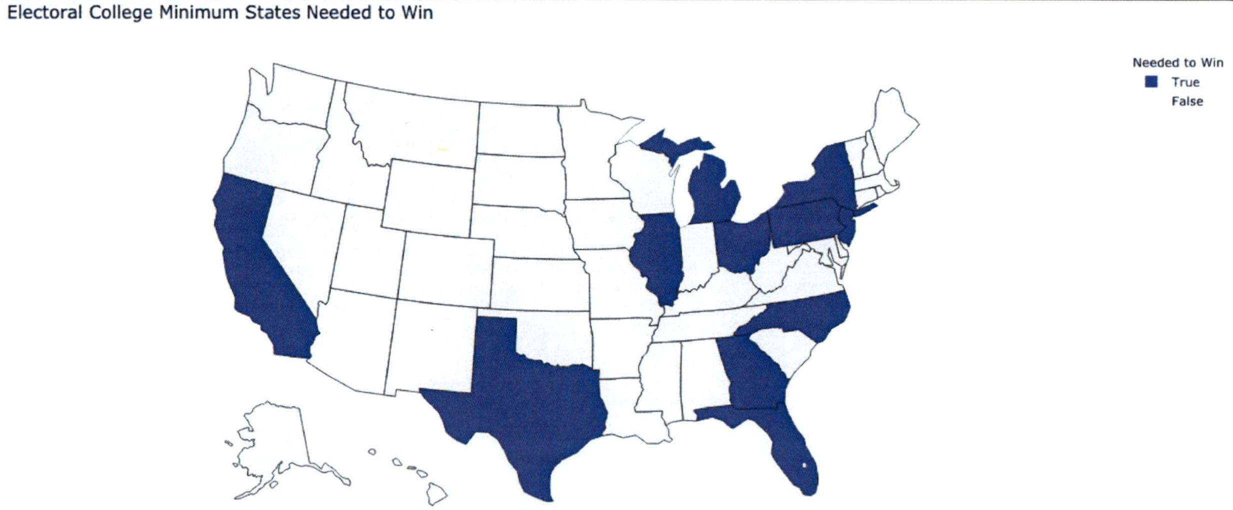

This visualization could be used to support the argument that the Electoral College helps the most populous states; after all, the most populous states have the most electors, and it looks like 11 states could elect a President. (It seems unlikely that both California and Texas would nominate the same candidate.) The state lines still detract from the visual; the states needed to win don't quite draw the viewer's eye.

We can address this by using Plotly's Graph Objects. First, we need to change the `Needed to Win` column into a binary column (which Plotly Express did under the hood for us), and then we need to create a column for some hover text. With the `Needed to Win` column either `True` or `False`, we can create a small function to convert that to `1` or `0`, respectively:

```
def binary_win(row):
    if row['Needed to Win']:
        return 1
    else:
        return 0
```

We can create the new column with `apply`:

```
df['Binary'] = df.apply(binary_win, axis=1)
```

Next, we can create a hover text column that will say either "{State} **is** need to win with {number} electors" or "{State} **is not** needed to win with {number} of electors."

```
def hover_text(row):
    if row['Needed to Win']:
        return '{} <b>is</b> needed to win with {}
                electors'.format(row['State'], row['Electors'])
    else:
        return '{} <b>is not</b> needed to win with {}
                electors'.format(row['State'], row['Electors'])
```

Again, we can create the new column with `apply`:

```
df['Display Text'] = df.apply(hover_text, axis=1)
```

Now, we can get to the actual plotting. We can specify the `marker_line_color` and `marker_line_width` as white and 0.01, respectively, to effectively eliminate the state borders.

```
def binary_win(row):
    if row['Needed to Win']:
        return 1
    else:
        return 0

def hover_text(row):
    if row['Needed to Win']:
        return '{} <b>is</b> needed to win with {}
                electors'.format(row['State'], row['Electors'])
    else:
        return '{} <b>is not</b> needed to win with {}
                electors'.format(row['State'], row['Electors'])


df['Binary'] = df.apply(binary_win, axis=1)
df['Display Text'] = df.apply(hover_text, axis=1)

fig = go.Figure(data=go.Choropleth(locations=df['Abbr'],
                                   locationmode="USA-states",
                                   z=df['Binary'],
                                   colorscale=['#f4f4f6',
                                               '#0c68e6'],
                                   marker_line_color='white',
                                   marker_line_width=0.01,
                                   showscale=False,
                                   text=df['Display Text'],
                                   hovertemplate='%{text}',
                                   name=""))
fig.update_layout(geo_scope='usa',
            title="Electoral College Minimum States Needed to Win")
fig.show()
```

The United States loses some of its shape, but this refined visualization emphasizes how few states are needed to win under the Electoral College. Per our 2014 US States population choropleth earlier, these states represent at least 50.01% of the population, but the contrast is stark. If it makes the reader pause and reflect, you have created a good data visualization!

Lastly, we can see if hexbinning improves our visualization. We need to use a pre-made JSON file with latitude and longitude coordinates that correspond to hexagon vertices. To make use of these hexagons, we will use a Plotly Express `choropleth_mapbox()` that allows choropleth potential overlaid on a world map. These hexagons are centered at the point (0 degrees latitude, 0 degrees longitude), so we will need to project the hexagons on a white background; otherwise, we will have hexagons overlaid on top of Africa (around the point 0 degrees latitude, 0 degrees longitude). Finally, we have to tell Plotly how to link `State` and the hexagon geometry with `featureidkey=" properties.State"`, which helps Plotly decode the JSON and find the hexagon coordinates. Here is the code:

```
fig = px.choropleth_mapbox(df, geojson=j_file,
                           color="Needed to Win",
                           color_discrete_sequence=['#0c68e6',
                                                    '#dadbde'],
                           locations="State",
                           featureidkey="properties.State",
                           center={"lat": 5.0, "lon": 10.0},
                           zoom=4.2,
                           hover_data={'State': True,
                                       'Electors': True,
                                       'Abbr': False,
                                       'Needed to Win': False})

fig.update_layout(margin={"r": 0, "t": 0, "l": 0, "b": 0},
                  mapbox_style="white-bg")
fig.show()
```

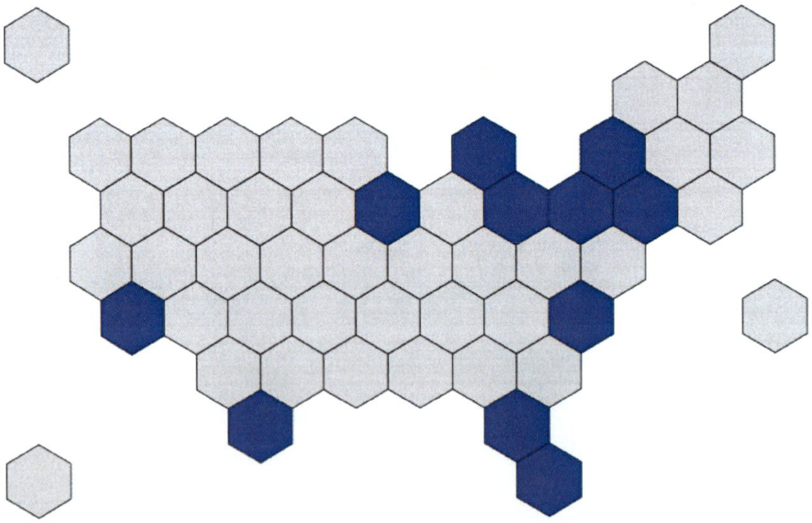

The legend has been cropped out of the screenshot to be able to center the image better. Washington, DC appears as an island in the Atlantic, and the exact shape of the US is lost due to the geometry. Decide for yourself: is hexbinning a better visualization in this case than a choropleth? The use of hexbins can remove geographic bias like the Alaska effect, but it also removes familiar shapes like that of the United States. Hexbinning should be used with care, but it can be a great way to remove geographic outliers. The technique can be difficult to use without pre-defined JSON or .shp files, so you may have to search around the internet to find a suitable hexagon file.

Summary

This chapter shows the necessity of iterating on your data visualization to ensure that it is intuitive and clear. We could have shown a horizontal bar chart, but the choropleth and hexbin approach provides better visualizations that convey geography and geometry. The visualization itself could be used by critics of the Electoral College, just as the state population choropleth could be used by proponents.

Examples for Each Library

```
import plotly.express as px
import plotly.graph_objects as go
import pandas as pd
import json
import requests

df = pd.read_csv('https://raw.githubusercontent.com/
                 alexkenan/pyviz/main/datasets/elect.csv')
j_file_str = requests.get('https://raw.githubusercontent.com/

alexkenan/pyviz/main/datasets/geoJSONstates.json').text
j_file = json.loads(j_file_str)
df['Needed to Win'] = df['Cumulative Count'] <= 270
```

```
def binary_win(row):
    if row['Needed to Win']:
        return 1
    else:
        return 0


def hover_text(row):
    if row['Needed to Win']:
        return '{} <b>is</b> needed to win with {}
                electors'.format(row['State'], row['Electors'])
    else:
        return '{} <b>is not</b> needed to win with {}
                electors'.format(row['State'], row['Electors'])


df['Binary'] = df.apply(binary_win, axis=1)
df['Display Text'] = df.apply(hover_text, axis=1)


# Plotly Express US states needed to win
fig = px.choropleth(df, locations=df['Abbr'],
                  locationmode="USA-states", color="Needed to Win",
                    color_discrete_sequence=['#0c68e6', '#f4f4f6'],
                    scope="usa")
fig.update_layout(
        title="Electoral College Minimum States Needed to Win")
fig.show()


# Plotly GO US map with faded states that aren't needed to win
fig = go.Figure(data=go.Choropleth(locations=df['Abbr'],
                                   locationmode="USA-states",
                                   z=df['Binary'],
                                   colorscale=['#f4f4f6',
                                               '#0c68e6'],
                                   marker_line_color='white',
                                   marker_line_width=0.01,
                                   showscale=False,
                                   text=df['Display Text'],
```

```
                                   hovertemplate='%{text}',
                                   name=""))
fig.update_layout(geo_scope='usa',
       title="Electoral College Minimum States Needed to Win")
fig.show()

# Plotly Hexbin of US Electoral College
fig = px.choropleth_mapbox(df, geojson=j_file,
                           color="Needed to Win",
                           color_discrete_sequence=['#0c68e6',
                                                    '#dadbde'],
                           locations="State",
                           featureidkey="properties.State",
                           center={"lat": 5.0, "lon": 10.0},
                           zoom=4.2,
                           hover_data={'State': True,
                                       'Electors': True,
                                       'Abbr': False,
                                       'Needed to Win': False})

fig.update_layout(margin={"r": 0, "t": 0, "l": 0, "b": 0},
                  mapbox_style="white-bg")
fig.show()
```

View this code on GitHub at https://github.com/alexkenan/pyviz/

Resources

[1] https://plotly.com/python/mapbox-county-choropleth/

Animation & The Birthday Problem

Introduction

The Birthday Problem is a math problem concerning the probability that at least two people share the same birthday (month and day of the month) in a set of randomly chosen people. Surprisingly, there is a 50% chance of this match occurring with 23 people, and 99.9% probability of this occurring with 70 people. 100.0% probability occurs with 367 people (since all 366 days, including February 29th, must be accounted for). This seems surprising since 23 people, at most, would represent only 23 days out of the year. The likelihood comes from the calculation that there are 23 * 22/2 = 253 potential pairings of people, which accounts for a majority of the days in the year. For the rest of this chapter, we will refer to at least two people in a group sharing the same birthday as a match, and to no shared birthdays in a group as no match.

Animation can be an effective tool for data visualization; it draws readers' eyes and is an easy method to guide a reader through your visualization and its story. Animations are incredibly effective at showing changes over time; a popular dataset from Gapminder was used to show how the entire continent of Africa has been left behind in world economic development. Of course, with great power comes great responsibility. Animation can quickly become chart junk, so its use should be carefully considered. For the Birthday Problem, animation is a good way to show how drastically the probability of a match increases with an unintuitively small increase in group size.

We will use Matplotlib and Plotly to create visualizations comparing the likelihood of having at least two people share the same birthday against the likelihood of nobody sharing the same birthday. Ultimately, we will end with a stacked bar chart that shows how the probability changes when you sweep from 2 to 70 people. We will programmatically generate and calculate the probability of a match from each group number, so we don't have a dataset. We will also assume a non-leap year for simplicity.

Imports

```
from math import perm
import matplotlib.pyplot as plt
import matplotlib.animation as animation
import plotly.express as px
import plotly.graph_objects as go
import pandas as pd
import plotly.io as pio
pio.renderers.default = "browser"
```

The `perm()` function was added to the math library in Python 3.8; if you get an `ImportError`, you need to go to the end of this chapter to write the `perm()` function yourself.

Matplotlib

The principle behind the Birthday Problem proof is to calculate the probability of everyone not having a shared birthday, take 1 minus that number, and arrive at the probability of at least two people sharing the same birthday. For 23 people, this means that the probability of not having a match is:

$$P(No\ Match) = \frac{365}{365} * \frac{364}{365} * \frac{363}{365} * \ \dots \ * \frac{343}{365}$$

That is a lot to type out. Fortunately for us, there is a pattern. The numerator in the fraction starts at 365 and ends at (365 – `number_of_people` + 1). We can write a `for` loop to iterate through the range of numbers and keep calculating the probability of no matches. In code:

```
number_of_people = 23
starting_number = 365.0
prob_no_matches = 1.0
for i in range(1, number_of_people):
    prob_no_matches *= (starting_number - i) / starting_number
```

Because `range()` does not give us the last number, we don't have to account for the `+ 1` for the last numerator. This expression can be simplified with permutations and factorials, which we will use later in the chapter. Since we are starting on the proof of concept, let's calculate the probability of a match and `print()` it out.

```
prob_matches = 1.0 - prob_no_matches
print('For {} people, there is a {:.1f}% chance of at least two
      people having the same birthday'.format(
      number_of_people, prob_matches * 100))
```

You should see the statement with 50.7% printed to the console.

Let's experiment with plotting one stacked bar with 23 people. We will use the code from above to generate the data, and we will need to create the two bars, set the axis labels, and tweak the axis limits. We will also multiply all of the probabilities by 100 to get numbers between 0 and 100, not 0 and 1.

```
blue = '#5e83f6'
red = '#df4728'

number_of_people = 23
starting_number = 365.0
prob_no_matches = 1.0
for i in range(1, number_of_people):
    prob_no_matches *= (starting_number - i)/starting_number

prob_matches = (1.0 - prob_no_matches)*100
prob_no_matches *= 100
plt.bar(number_of_people, prob_matches, label='Match', color=blue)
plt.bar(number_of_people, prob_no_matches, label="No Match",
        bottom=prob_matches, color=red)
plt.xlim(number_of_people - 3, number_of_people + 3)
plt.xticks([number_of_people])
plt.ylim(0, 103)
plt.title('Birthday Problem with {}
People'.format(number_of_people))
plt.xlabel('Number of People')
plt.ylabel('Percentage (%)')
plt.legend()
plt.show()
```

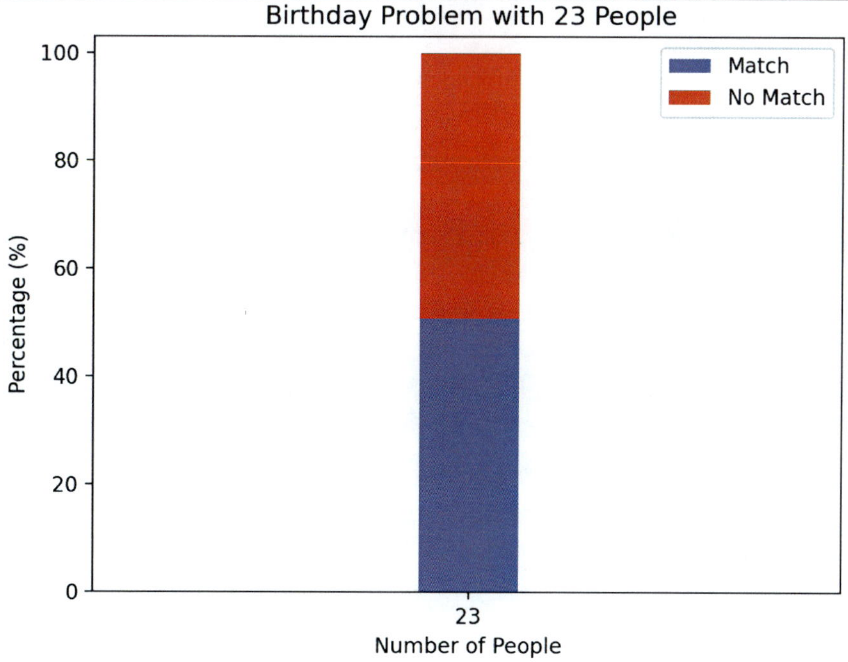

If you want the legend to match the stacked bars (meaning you want "No Match" to be on top in the legend), you could plot the bars with no labels, and then plot a small bar off of the canvas (like at x = 100) with the correct color and label.

Now that we have one bar, let's plot the range of numbers from 2 to 71. This will be the final frame of our animation. We will need to put the probability calculations inside of a `for` loop and add each one to `Lists` to keep track of the probabilities. Since we are adding another `for` loop, we can use a mathematical simplification of the no match probability calculation to avoid having two nested `for` loops. Don't worry, you will be spared the mathematical derivation of this shortcut. As another shortcut, we will put these `Lists` in a DataFrame for easier access and manipulation; we'll have a DataFrame with columns of `Number of People`, `Match Prob`, and `No Match Prob`.

```
blue = '#5e83f6'
red = '#df4728'
num_people = []
matches = []
no_matches = []
upper_limit = 71
for number_of_people in range(2, upper_limit):
    num_people.append(number_of_people)
    starting_number = 365.0
    prob_no_matches = perm(int(starting_number),
        number_of_people)/starting_number ** number_of_people
    prob_matches = 1.0 - prob_no_matches
    matches.append(round(prob_matches*100, 1))
    no_matches.append(round(prob_no_matches*100, 1))

# create df
df = pd.DataFrame(data={'Number of People': num_people,
```

```
                           'Match Prob': matches,
                           'No Match Prob': no_matches})
# plot the data
plt.bar(df['Number of People'], df['Match Prob'],
       label="Match Probability", color=blue)
plt.bar(df['Number of People'], df['No Match Prob'],
        label="No Match Probability",
        bottom=df['Match Prob'], color=red)
plt.title('Visualizing the Birthday Problem')
plt.xlabel('Number of People')
plt.ylabel('Percentage (%)')
plt.gca().set_yticks(range(20, 120, 20))
plt.ylim(0, 120)
plt.legend()
plt.show()
```

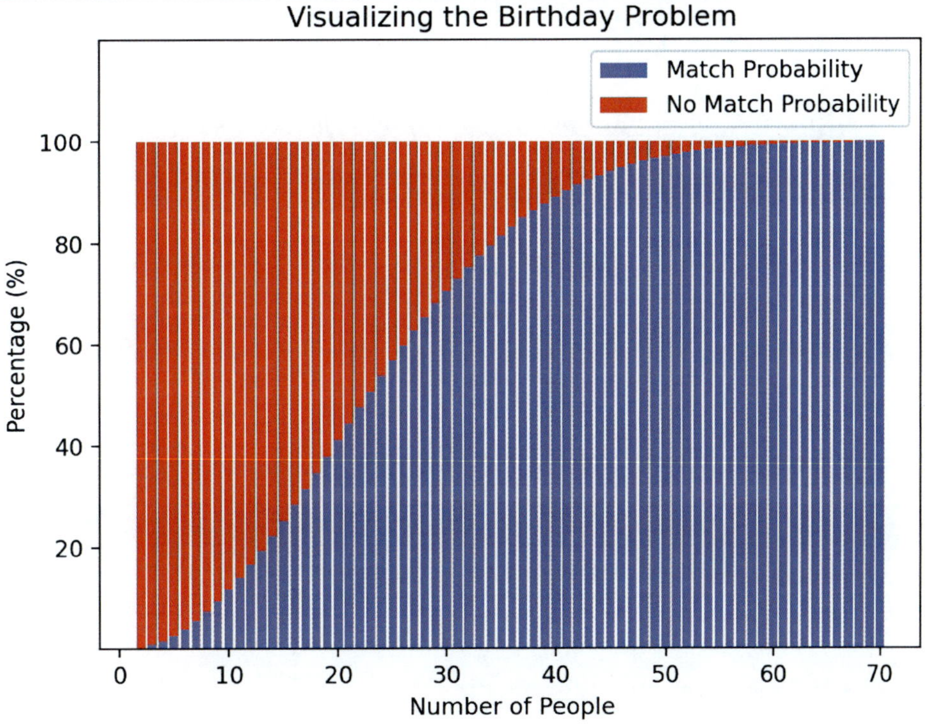

This visualization is a little busy, but it shows the remarkable swing in match and no match probabilities as the size of the group grows between 10 and 30 people. This visualization would be more effective if we could watch the stacked bars change size. This is where Matplotlib animation will help.

Since we have the DataFrame with the number of people and match/no match probability, we want the animation to plot each "number of people in the group" datapoint. We can do this by using Matplotlib's `animation.FuncAnimation()` function which will take a canvas, a `List`-like object, and an interval `i` to iterate through, and display the incremental elements in the `List`-like object. At its simplest, we pass this animation function a figure from `fig, ax = plt.subplots()`, a function to use in the animation, and an interval (length of `df` in our case).

For our purposes, we need to create an `animate_chart()` function that plots that specific interval's number of people. In other words, we will sweep from (0, `len(df)`) and use `iloc` to return that row of the DataFrame. To protect against calling an index that doesn't exist, we have to make sure that we are using an `i` that is less than the length of the `df`. Here is the full function:

```
def animate_chart(i):
    actual_i = min(i, len(df) - 1)
    ax.bar(df.iloc[actual_i]['Number of People'],
           df.iloc[actual_i]['Match Prob'], color=blue)
    ax.bar(df.iloc[actual_i]['Number of People'],
           df.iloc[actual_i]['No Match Prob'], color=red,
           bottom=df.iloc[actual_i]['Match Prob'])
```

We then create and call the animation with this line:

```
myAnimation = animation.FuncAnimation(fig, animate_chart,
                                      interval=len(df), repeat=False)
```

The rest of the code is the usual setup that we did in the last iteration: setting axis labels and axis limits, creating a title, and fixing the legend by plotting bars off of the canvas.

```
blue = '#5e83f6'
red = '#df4728'
fig, ax = plt.subplots()
num_people = []
matches = []
no_matches = []
upper_limit = 71
for number_of_people in range(2, upper_limit):
    num_people.append(number_of_people)
    starting_number = 365.0
    prob_no_matches = perm(int(starting_number),
              number_of_people)/starting_number ** number_of_people
    prob_matches = 1.0 - prob_no_matches
    matches.append(round(prob_matches*100, 1))
    no_matches.append(round(prob_no_matches*100, 1))

# create df
df = pd.DataFrame(data={'Number of People': num_people,
                        'Match Prob': matches,
                        'No Match Prob': no_matches})
def animate_chart(i):
    actual_i = min(i, len(df) - 1)
    ax.bar(df.iloc[actual_i]['Number of People'],
           df.iloc[actual_i]['Match Prob'], color=blue)
    ax.bar(df.iloc[actual_i]['Number of People'],
           df.iloc[actual_i]['No Match Prob'], color=red,
           bottom=df.iloc[actual_i]['Match Prob'])

# Get the labels right by plotting bars off screen with the right
# label and color
ax.bar(upper_limit*100 + 1, 1, color=blue, label="Match
Probability")
ax.bar(upper_limit*100, 1, color=red, label="No Match Probability")

# create animation using the animate() function
myAnimation = animation.FuncAnimation(fig, animate_chart,
```

```
                                            interval=len(df), repeat=False)
plt.title('Animated Birthday Problem')
plt.xlabel("Number of People")
plt.ylabel('Probability (%)')
plt.xlim(0, upper_limit + 1)
plt.gca().set_yticks(range(20, 120, 20))
plt.ylim(0, 120)
plt.legend()
plt.show()
```

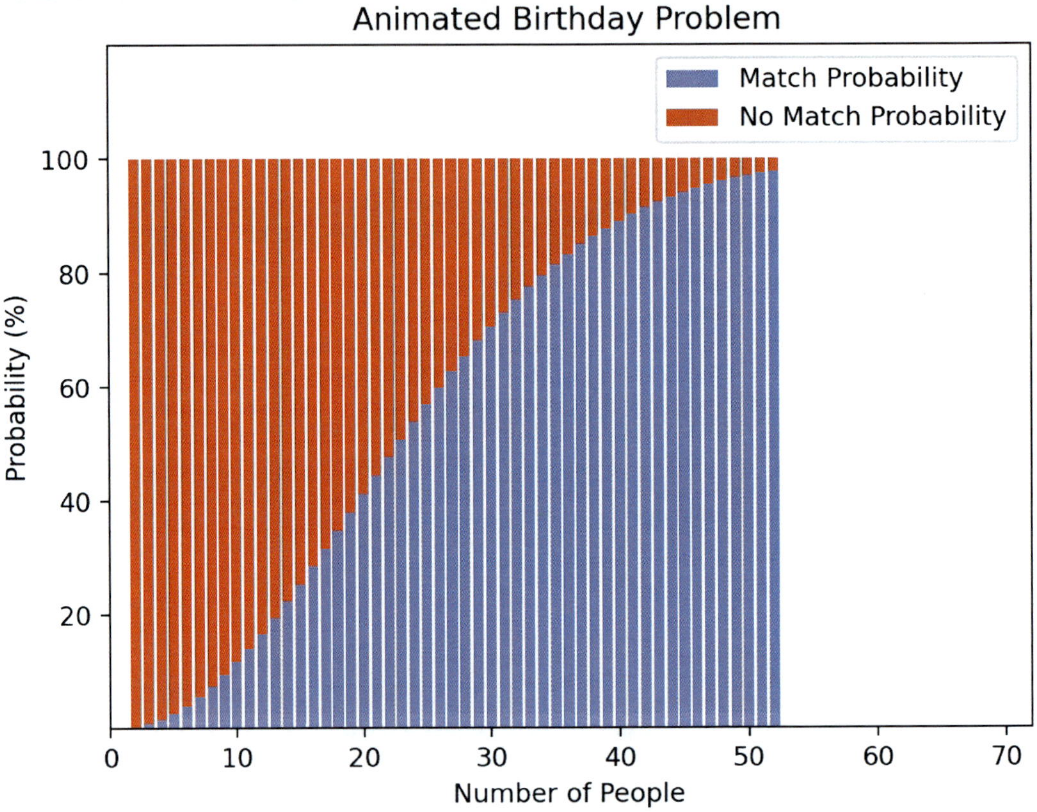

This is just a static screenshot, but the Matplotlib window should show the animation. If you want the animation to repeat forever, change `repeat=False` to `repeat=True`. To save your animation as a gif, use the following code:

```
from matplotlib.animation import PillowWriter
writer = PillowWriter(fps=30)
# code from above without plt.show()
myAnimation.save('/path/to/animation.gif', writer=writer)
```

This will give you a nice gif to share with all your friends so that they can learn about the Birthday Problem, too!

Plotly

Since we have already done the hard work for generating the probalities, we can jump right to a static stacked bar chart in Plotly Express:

```
blue = '#5e83f6'
red = '#df4728'
num_people = []
matches = []
no_matches = []
upper_limit = 71
for number_of_people in range(2, upper_limit):
    num_people.append(number_of_people)
    starting_number = 365.0
    prob_no_matches = perm(int(starting_number),
          number_of_people)/starting_number ** number_of_people
    prob_matches = 1.0 - prob_no_matches
    matches.append(round(prob_matches*100, 1))
    no_matches.append(round(prob_no_matches*100, 1))

df = pd.DataFrame(data={'Number of People': num_people,
                        'Match Prob': matches,
                        'No Match Prob': no_matches})
fig = px.bar(df, x="Number of People",
             y=["Match Prob", 'No Match Prob'],
             color_discrete_sequence=[blue, red],
             title="Visualizing the Birthday Problem",
             labels={'value': 'Probability (%)',
```

```
                                "Match Prob": "Match Probability",
                                'No Match Prob': "No Match Probability"})
fig.show()
```

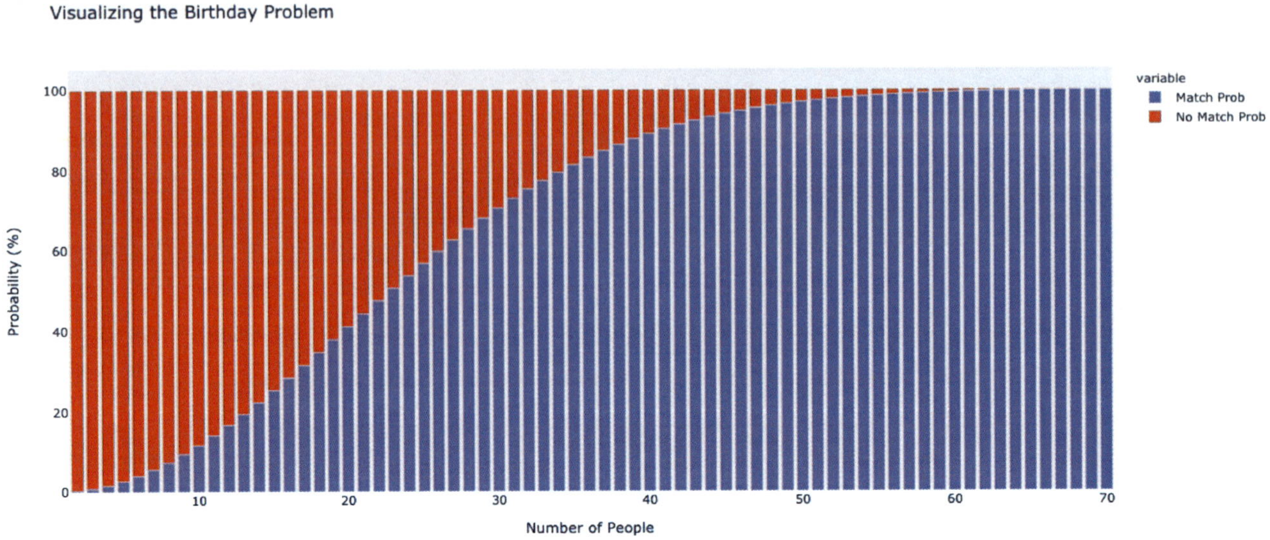

Animation with Plotly Express is incredibly easy: all we need to do is tell the `px.bar()` function which column to animate over, and it will automatically create a slider and a start/stop button. Because the animation will autoscale the axes, we want to specify the `range_x` and `range_y` to force the canvas to be stationary.

```
blue = '#5e83f6'
red = '#df4728'
num_people = []
matches = []
no_matches = []
upper_limit = 70
for number_of_people in range(2, upper_limit):
    num_people.append(number_of_people)
    starting_number = 365.0
    prob_no_matches = perm(int(starting_number),
             number_of_people)/starting_number ** number_of_people
    prob_matches = 1.0 - prob_no_matches
    matches.append(round(prob_matches*100, 1))
    no_matches.append(round(prob_no_matches*100, 1))
```

```
# create df
df = pd.DataFrame(data={'Number of People': num_people,
                        'Match Prob': matches,
                        'No Match Prob': no_matches})
# plot the data
fig = px.bar(df, x="Number of People",
             y=["Match Prob", 'No Match Prob'],
             color_discrete_sequence=[blue, red],
             animation_frame="Number of People",
             range_y=[0, 101],
             range_x=[1, upper_limit],
             title="Visualizing the Birthday Problem",
             labels={'value': 'Probability (%)',
                     "Match Prob": "Match Probability",
                     'No Match Prob': "No Match Probability"})
fig.show()
```

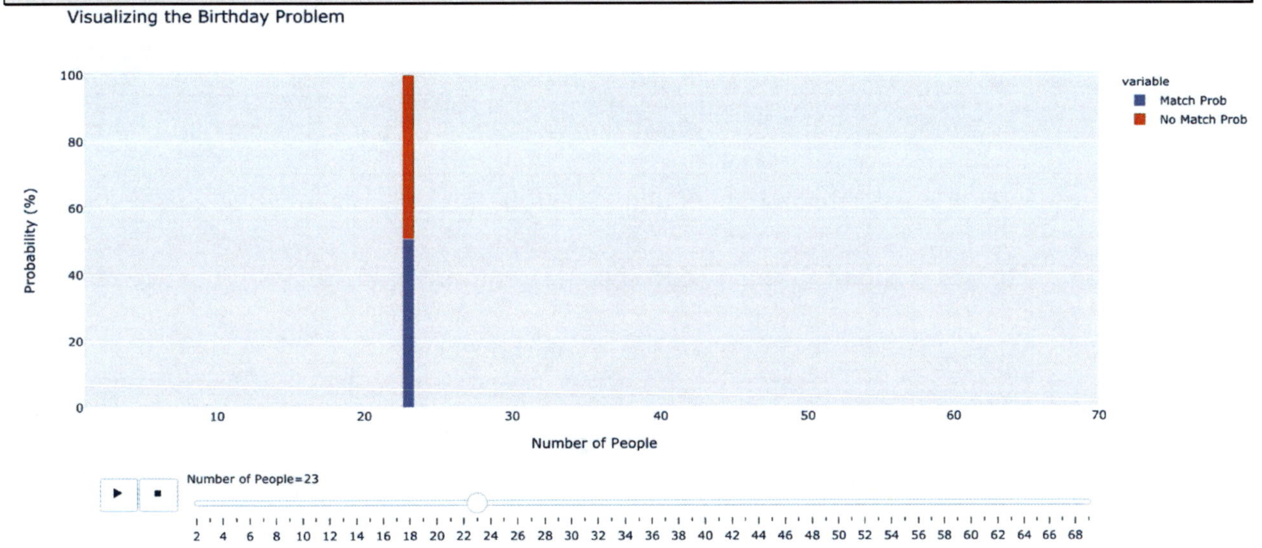

With this animation, you can send the saved HTML instead of having to save a GIF. You should be able to right click in the webpage and Save As … HTML, or you can save the page within your program with `fig.write_html("path/to/file.html")`.

Summary

The Birthday Problem is a counterintuitive theory that shows how the brain is bad at estimating the power of exponents. It also shows how selfish we are, since we automatically think "What is the probability of someone else sharing a birthday with *me*" versus "What is the probability of any two people sharing a birthday." It does, however, allow us to learn how to use animation in Matplotlib and Plotly to drive our point home. The animation reinforces the notion that the probability of having a match drastically increases by only adding a few people to the group, and it also shows that you can have a 50% probability of having a match with only 23 people.

In our analysis of the Birthday Problem, we assumed that each day has an equal probability of someone having a birthday (1/365 or 1/366 if you're counting on a leap year). In reality, more people are born on certain days than others. Oddly enough, this phenomenon **reduces** the number of people required to be certain of a match: since people are more likely to be born on certain days, it is more likely that people in your group were born on those days.

Since we ended up using a lot of the same code to generate the probabilities, the full code examples below show the use of a `calculate_probabilities()` function that returns a DataFrame with the probabilities given the group size upper limit.

```
try:
    from math import perm
except ImportError:
    from math import factorial

    def perm(n, k):
        if n > k:
            return factorial(n)/(factorial(n - k))
        else:
            return 0
import matplotlib.pyplot as plt
import matplotlib.animation as animation
import plotly.express as px
import pandas as pd
import plotly.io as pio
pio.renderers.default = "browser"


blue = '#5e83f6'
red = '#df4728'
upper_limit = 71

def calculate_probabilities(upperlimit):
    num_people_list = []
    matches_list = []
    no_matches_list = []
    for num_people in range(2, upperlimit):
        num_people_list.append(num_people)
        start = 365.0
        prob_no_matches = perm(int(start),
                          num_people)/start ** num_people
        prob_matches = 1.0 - prob_no_matches
        matches_list.append(round(prob_matches*100, 1))
        no_matches_list.append(round(prob_no_matches*100, 1))

    df_calcs = pd.DataFrame(data={'Number of People':
num_people_list,
```

```
                                   'Match Prob': matches_list,
                                   'No Match Prob': no_matches_list})
    return df_calcs

# Matplotlib one stacked bar
number_of_people = 23
starting_number = 365.0
prob_no_matches = 1.0
for i in range(1, number_of_people):
    prob_no_matches *= (starting_number - i)/starting_number

prob_matches = (1.0 - prob_no_matches)*100
prob_no_matches *= 100
plt.bar(number_of_people, prob_matches, label='Match', color=blue)
plt.bar(number_of_people, prob_no_matches, label="No Match",
        bottom=prob_matches, color=red)
plt.xlim(number_of_people - 3, number_of_people + 3)
plt.xticks([number_of_people])
plt.ylim(0, 103)
plt.title('Birthday Problem with {}
People'.format(number_of_people))
plt.xlabel('Number of People')
plt.ylabel('Percentage (%)')
plt.legend()
plt.show()

# Matplotlib all stacked stacked bar chart
df = calculate_probabilities(upper_limit)
plt.bar(df['Number of People'], df['Match Prob'],
        label="Match Probability", color=blue)
plt.bar(df['Number of People'], df['No Match Prob'],
        label="No Match Probability",
        bottom=df['Match Prob'], color=red)
plt.title('Visualizing the Birthday Problem')
plt.xlabel('Number of People')
plt.ylabel('Percentage (%)')
plt.gca().set_yticks(range(20, 120, 20))
plt.ylim(0, 120)
plt.legend()
plt.show()
```

```
# Matplotlib animation
fig, ax = plt.subplots()
df = calculate_probabilities(upper_limit)

def animate_chart(i):
    actual_i = min(i, len(df) - 1)
    ax.bar(df.iloc[actual_i]['Number of People'],
           df.iloc[actual_i]['Match Prob'], color=blue)
    ax.bar(df.iloc[actual_i]['Number of People'],
           df.iloc[actual_i]['No Match Prob'], color=red,
           bottom=df.iloc[actual_i]['Match Prob'])

ax.bar(upper_limit*100 + 1, 1, color=blue,
       label="Match Probability")
ax.bar(upper_limit*100, 1, color=red,
       label="No Match Probability")

# create animation using the animate function
myAnimation = animation.FuncAnimation(fig, animate_chart,
                       interval=len(df), repeat=False)

plt.title('Animated Birthday Problem')
plt.xlabel("Number of People")
plt.ylabel('Probability (%)')
plt.xlim(0, upper_limit + 1)
plt.gca().set_yticks(range(20, 120, 20))
plt.ylim(0, 120)
plt.legend()
plt.show()
"""
To save a gif:
from matplotlib.animation import PillowWriter
writer = PillowWriter(fps=30)

myAnimation.save('myAnimation.gif', writer=writer)
"""

# Plotly Express static bar chart
```

```
df = calculate_probabilities(upper_limit)
fig = px.bar(df, x="Number of People",
             y=["Match Prob", 'No Match Prob'],
             color_discrete_sequence=[blue, red],
             title="Visualizing the Birthday Problem",
             labels={'value': 'Probability (%)',
                     "Match Prob": "Match Probability",
                     'No Match Prob': "No Match Probability"})
fig.show()

# Plotly Express animation
df = calculate_probabilities(upper_limit)

# plot the data
fig = px.bar(df, x="Number of People",
             y=["Match Prob", 'No Match Prob'],
             color_discrete_sequence=[blue, red],
             animation_frame="Number of People", range_y=[0, 101],
             range_x=[1, upper_limit],
             title="Visualizing the Birthday Problem",
             labels={'value': 'Probability (%)',
                     "Match Prob": "Match Probability",
                     'No Match Prob': "No Match Probability"})
fig.show()
```

View this code on GitHub at https://github.com/alexkenan/pyviz/

Resources

[1] https://en.wikipedia.org/wiki/Birthday_problem

[2] https://matplotlib.org/api/_as_gen/matplotlib.animation.FuncAnimation.html

[3] https://plotly.com/python/animations/

Writing the Perm Function

If you are using a version of Python earlier than 3.8.0, `perm()` is not defined in the math library. Fortunately, it is easy to create it yourself. `Perm()` is a probability function short for permutation, and it is commonly abbreviated as `nPr`. It is represented with factorials and can be written in Python as:

```
from math import factorial
def perm(n, k):
    if n > k:
        return factorial(n)/(factorial(n - k))
    else:
        return 0
```

At the top of your program, instead of just writing `from math import perm`, put:

```
try:
    from math import perm
except ImportError:
    from math import factorial

    def perm(n, k):
        if n > k:
            return factorial(n)/(factorial(n - k))
        else:
            return 0
```

Graphical User Interfaces

Introduction

So far, all of our programs and visualizations have been created from a program editor, and any tweaking meant hunting in the code to make a change. Most users are much more comfortable with interacting with a user interface of some sort. Embedding a data visualization within a Graphical User Interface (GUI) can create user interaction for more customized slicing, manipulating, and viewing of data. It can also allow for details on demand, which lets any users decide how much detail they want. If they just want to see the trend, they can look at a summary of the data; if they want to see day by day, they can zoom into that level of detail, too.

Python has many GUI libraries for making customization and interaction easier and prettier. To keep things simple, we will use Tkinter, which ships with Python by default. Matplotlib provides functionality to render and change inside of a Tkinter window; unfortunately, Plotly does not have this same compatibility. Since Plotly already provides a pseudo-GUI in the form of a web browser, we will focus our attention on Matplotlib for this chapter.

We will look at data from the Transportation Security Administration's (TSA) passenger data to see the impact of the COVID-19 pandemic on US air travel. The dataset shows how many passengers were screened at US airport security checkpoints every day between March 1st, 2020 and December 31st, 2020. It also provides a "this day in 2019" number for comparison. We will use this dataset to show a line plot comparing the 2020 and 2019 passenger numbers by day and by week, and we will show an alternate plot showing 2020 passenger numbers by day and week as a percentage of 2019 passenger numbers.

Due to the cyclic nature of air travel, the date in 2019 corresponds to the same day of the week in 2019, not the exact same date. For example, March 1st, 2020 was the 9th Sunday in 2020, so its 2019 comparison is the 9th Sunday in 2019, which was March 3rd, 2019.

Column Name	**Datatype**	**Description**
Date	`str`	Date of the measured datapoint
2020	`int`	Number of passengers counted on that day in 2020
2019	`int`	Number of passengers counted on that day in 2019, adjusted for day of the week

Imports

```
import tkinter as tk
import matplotlib.pyplot as plt
from matplotlib.backends.backend_tkagg import FigureCanvasTkAgg
from matplotlib.ticker import FuncFormatter
import pandas as pd
```

Some IDEs may require an additional two lines to allow Tkinter and Matplotlib to play together nicely:

```
import matplotlib
matplotlib.use("TkAgg")
```

Matplotlib

To start, let's graph the 2020 and 2019 day-by-day comparison in a normal Matplotlib window. Once we have this created, it's easy to convert it to be Tkinter-friendly. Since we will use an aggregating function to compute the "percentage of 2019 passenger numbers" comparison, let's go ahead and set up a `tsa()` function that loads the DataFrame, creates a `yoy` column (for Year Over Year), converts the `Date` column from `str` to `datetime`, and then returns the DataFrame.

```
def tsa(path: str) -> pd.DataFrame:
    dataframe = pd.read_csv(path,
                            names=['Date', '2020', '2019'],
                            header=0, parse_dates=['Date'])
    dataframe['yoy'] = (dataframe['2020'] / dataframe['2019']) * 100
    return dataframe
```

Now, we have to set the figure size, set some line colors, re-format the y axis, and label the axes, and title the plot for our day-to-day comparison.

```
df = tsa('https://raw.githubusercontent.com/
        alexkenan/pyviz/main/datasets/tsa_pax.csv')
blue = "#327ff6"
gray = "#bdb8b6"
plt.figure(figsize=(9, 6))
plt.plot(df['Date'], df['2020'], color=blue, linestyle='-',
        label="2020")
plt.plot(df['Date'], df['2019'], color=gray, linestyle='-',
        label="2019")
plt.legend()
plt.xlabel('Date')
plt.ylabel('Passengers')
plt.title('TSA Passenger Daily Throughput 2019 and 2020')
plt.gca().get_yaxis().set_major_formatter(
            FuncFormatter(lambda x, p: format(int(x), ',')))
plt.show()
```

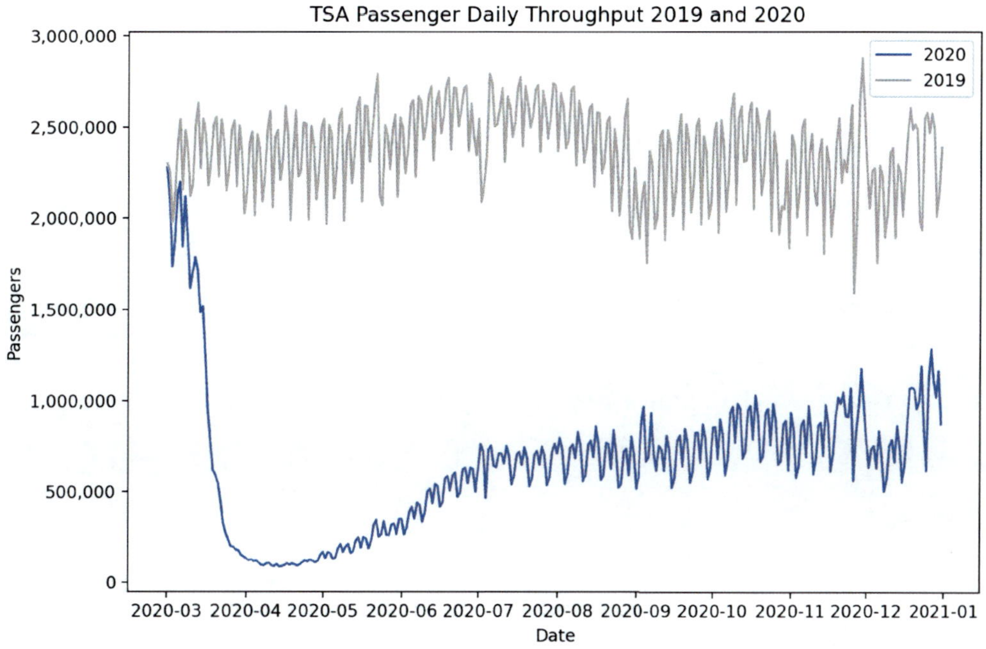

Here, we use gray to show the 2019 numbers, and the blue draws the reader's eye and emphasizes the drastic impact of COVID-19 in 2020. We can also see the cyclical nature of passenger air travel, so week-by-week will show a smoother version of this graph.

Pandas DataFrames have a `resample()` method that allows time-based grouping of data. In essence, we want to group the data by week and sum the datapoints over that week. To make this happen, we have to pass a `rule` (how we want the DataFrame to be grouped) and an `on` parameter (which column in the DataFrame to use for the `rule`). There are more parameters, but the default behavior works for the rest. Our `rule` is `W-Mon` meaning group by `W`eek starting on `Mon`days, and `on` is our `Date` column. Just doing `df.resample('W-Mon', on='Date')` creates a `DatetimeIndexResampler`, so we want to `sum()` it, reset its index with `reset_index()`, and sort it by `Date` with `sort_values(by='Date')`. We can string all of those operations together into one (or two) lines:

```
weekly_data = df.resample('W-Mon',
             on='Date').sum().reset_index().sort_values(by='Date')
```

From here, we can plot `weekly_data` like how we plotted `df`:

```
df = tsa('https://raw.githubusercontent.com/
         alexkenan/pyviz/main/datasets/tsa_pax.csv')
blue = "#327ff6"
gray = "#bdb8b6"
plt.figure(figsize=(9, 6))

weekly_data = df.resample('W-Mon',
              on='Date').sum().reset_index().sort_values(by='Date')
plt.plot(weekly_data['Date'], weekly_data['2020'],
         color=blue, linestyle='-', label="2020")
plt.plot(weekly_data['Date'], weekly_data['2019'],
         color=gray, linestyle='-', label="2019")
plt.legend()
plt.xlabel('Date')
plt.ylabel('Passengers')
plt.title('TSA Passenger Weekly Throughput 2019 and 2020')
plt.gca().get_yaxis().set_major_formatter(
              FuncFormatter(lambda x, p: format(int(x), ',')))
plt.show()
```

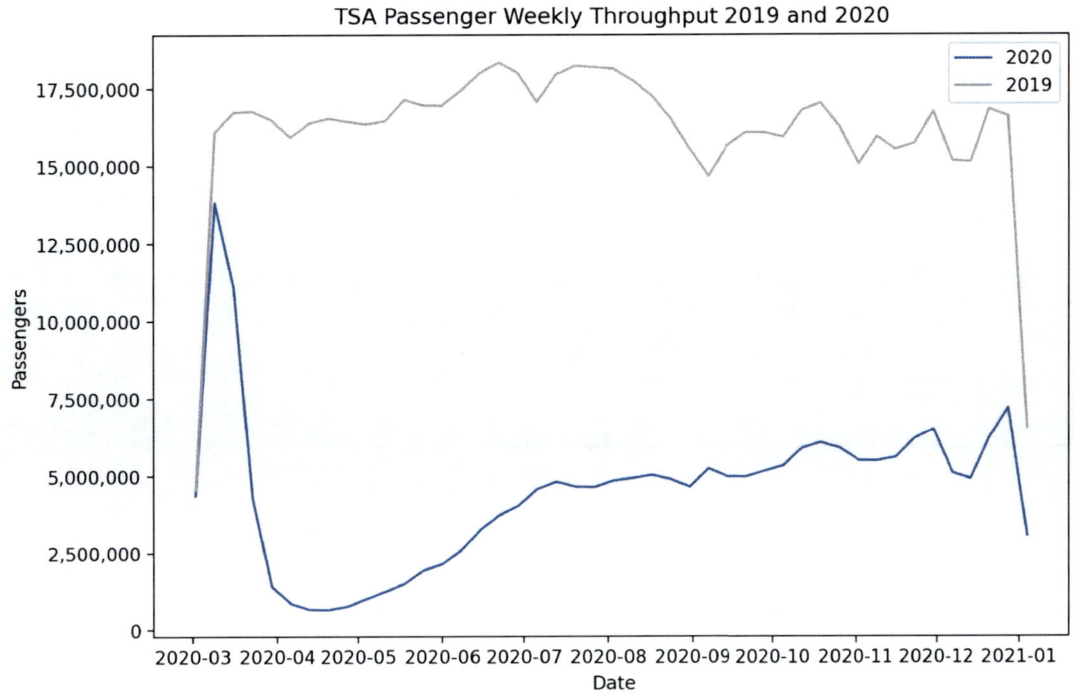

This visualization removes the choppiness but maintains the same message: COVID-19 literally decimated passenger numbers in April, and even by the end of December, the situation had not come close to returning to 2019 levels. If we squint, we can estimate the 2020 passenger number as a percentage of the 2019 passenger number. Let's make a graph showing these percentages.

Since we created the year-over-year percentage in the `tsa()` function, plotting the percentage means passing the `'yoy'` column instead of the `'2020'` and `'2019'` columns. Since the 2019 percentage will just be 100% across the board, let's omit it and just show the 2020 year-over-year column.

```
df = tsa('https://raw.githubusercontent.com/
        alexkenan/pyviz/main/datasets/tsa_pax.csv')
blue = "#327ff6"
plt.figure(figsize=(9, 6))
plt.plot(df['Date'], df['yoy'], color=blue, linestyle='-',
        label="2020")
plt.legend()
plt.xlabel('Date')
plt.ylabel('Passenger Load Factor (%)')
plt.title('TSA Passenger Daily Throughput in 2020 as a Percentage of
          2019')
plt.show()
```

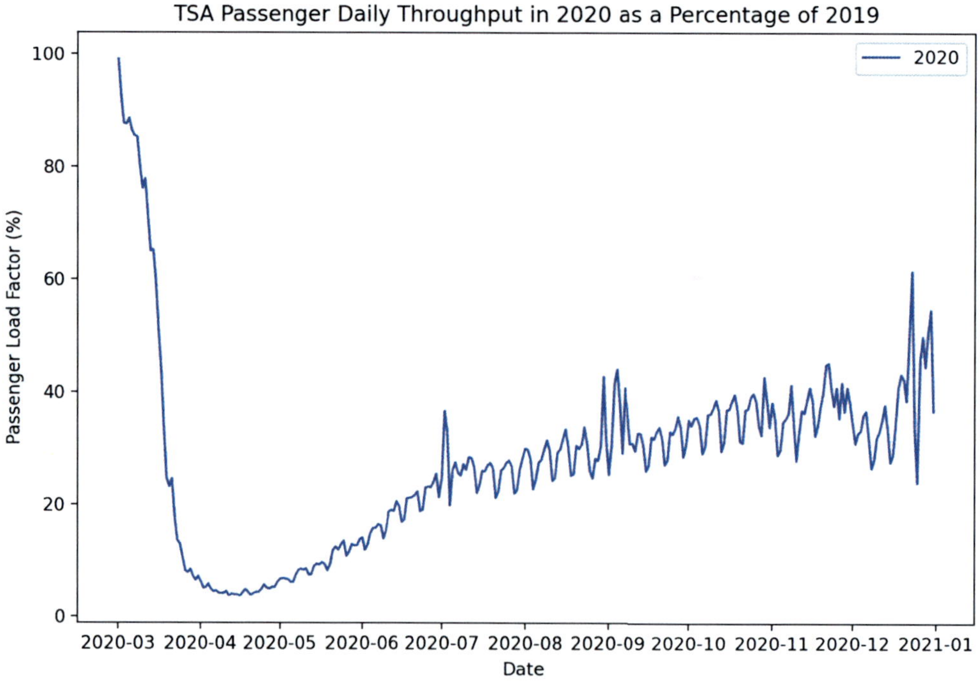

Like before, we can aggregate this and group it by week to get rid of the choppiness. We will have one issue though: our year-over-year percentages will get summed along with the passenger counts. Therefore, we need to re-define the *yoy* column after we resample the DataFrame.

```
df = tsa('https://raw.githubusercontent.com/
        alexkenan/pyviz/main/datasets/tsa_pax.csv')
weekly_data = df.resample('W-Mon',
             on='Date').sum().reset_index().sort_values(by='Date')
weekly_data['yoy'] = (weekly_data['2020']/weekly_data['2019'])*100
blue = "#327ff6"
gray = "#bdb8b6"
plt.figure(figsize=(9, 6))
plt.plot(weekly_data['Date'], weekly_data['yoy'],
        color=blue, linestyle='-', label="2020")
plt.xlabel('Date')
plt.ylabel('Passenger Load Factor (%)')
plt.legend()
plt.title('TSA Passenger Daily Throughput in 2020 as a Percentage of
         2019')
plt.show()
```

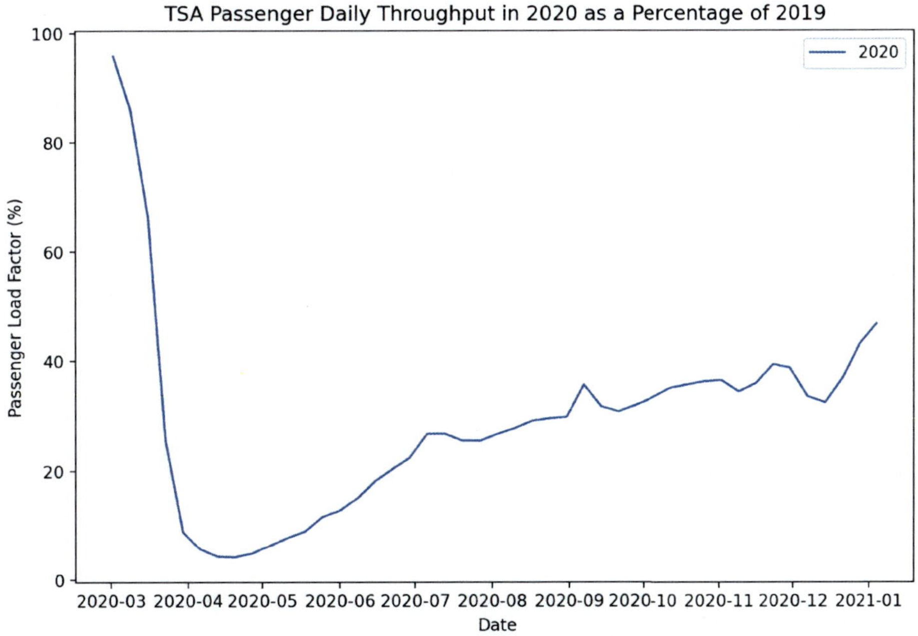

Now that we have all four plotting methods created, we need to set up our Tkinter GUI. We will set up a one-page window that shows a big canvas, has four different radio buttons for the four different visualizations, and a button to quit and close the window. When making a GUI with

Tkinter, you need to decide if you are going to arrange elements by gridding them with `grid()` or packing them with `pack()`. `Pack()` packs the elements sequentially as you create them, while `grid()` allows you to grid according to row number and column number. We will use `grid()` in all of our examples. If you mix `grid()` and `pack()`, your program will either error out, or it will run in an infinite loop but not display anything as it tries to figure out how to display elements that are gridded and packed (hint: it's not possible, so Tkinter will never figure it out).

All of the elements that you can create with Tkinter are still Python objects; they can be manipulated, named, renamed, etc. "Widget" is a popular term that is used to label any object. Below is a table of the common Tkinter widgets:

Tkinter Widget Name	**Description**
`Tk.Label()`	A stage to display text
`Tk.Entry()`	A text box where the user can write text
`Tk.Button()`	A button to click
`Tk.RadioButton()`	A selection radio button. Choose one option only
`Tk.CheckButton()`	A selection checkmark button. Choose as many options as you want
`Tk.OptionMenu()`	A dropdown menu. Choose one option only

There are many more options, but these are usually the most popular widgets. We will only use the `Button()` and `RadioButton()` widgets, and we will also use Matplotlib's `FigureCanvasTkAgg` as our `plt` object. In summary, our GUI should look like this:

<table>
<tr><td rowspan="5"><code>FigureCanvasTkAgg()</code></td><td>Daily <code>RadioButton()</code></td></tr>
<tr><td>Weekly <code>RadioButton()</code></td></tr>
<tr><td>Daily % Year-over-Year <code>RadioButton()</code></td></tr>
<tr><td>Weekly % Year-over-Year <code>RadioButton()</code></td></tr>
<tr><td>Quit <code>Button()</code></td></tr>
</table>

To start, we will create two helper functions: one that closes the GUI window, and one that converts a `plt.figure()` into a `FigureCanvasTkAgg()`.

```
def _quit(main: tk.Tk):
    main.quit()
    main.destroy()
```

This ensures that the window closes without hanging, freezing, or crashing. Next, we will use a `plot_new_canvas()` function to convert a Matplotlib `figure` into something that can be rendered on a Tkinter canvas.

```
def plot_new_canvas(figure: plt.figure, main: tk.Tk) -> None:
    figure.set_size_inches((9, 6))
    canvas = FigureCanvasTkAgg(figure, master=main)
    canvas.draw()
    canvas.get_tk_widget().grid(column=0, row=0, columnspan=2,
                                rowspan=8)
```

The last function we need to create is a plot function that we will call `plot_choice()` that plots the user's choice. We can assign a value to each `RadioButton` (daily is 1, weekly is 2, daily % YoY is 3, and weekly % YoY is 4), and based on the number, `plot_choice()` will plot the choice (nice name, right?) via the `plot_new_canvas()` helper function that we just created.

```
def plot_choice(num: int, plot: plt, df1: pd.DataFrame) -> None:
    plot.clf()  # clears the current figure, just in case
    blue = "#327ff6"
    gray = "#bdb8b6"
    if num == 1:
        # Daily raw pax numbers
        fig, axis = plt.subplots()
        axis.plot(df1['Date'], df1['2020'],
                  color=blue, linestyle='-', label="2020")
        axis.plot(df1['Date'], df1['2019'],
                  color=gray, linestyle='-', label="2019")
        plot.legend()
        plot.xlabel('Date')
        plot.ylabel('Passengers')
        plot.title('TSA Passenger Daily Throughput 2019 and 2020')
        axis.get_yaxis().set_major_formatter(
            FuncFormatter(lambda x, p: format(int(x), ',')))
        plot_new_canvas(fig, root)

    elif num == 2:
        # Weekly raw pax numbers
        weekly_data = df1.resample('W-Mon',
                label='right', closed='right',
```

```
            on='Date').sum().reset_index().sort_values(by='Date')
        fig, axis = plt.subplots()
        axis.plot(weekly_data['Date'], weekly_data['2020'],
                  color=blue, linestyle='-',
                  label="2020")
        axis.plot(weekly_data['Date'], weekly_data['2019'],
                  color=gray, linestyle='-',
                  label="2019")
        axis.get_yaxis().set_major_formatter(
                FuncFormatter(lambda x, p: format(int(x), ',')))
        plot.xlabel('Date')
        plot.ylabel('Passengers')
        plot.legend()
        plot.ylim(0, 20E6)
        plot.title('TSA Passenger Weekly Throughput 2019 and 2020')
        plot_new_canvas(fig, root)

    elif num == 3:
        # Daily YoY percentage
        fig, axis = plt.subplots()
        axis.plot(df1['Date'], df1['yoy'],
                  color=blue, linestyle='-', label="2020")
        plot.legend()
        plot.xlabel('Date')
        plot.ylabel('Passenger Load Factor (%)')
        plot.title('TSA Passenger Daily Throughput in 2020 as a
                    Percentage of 2019')
        plot_new_canvas(fig, root)

    elif num == 4:
        # Weekly YoY percentage
        weekly_data = df1.resample('W-Mon', label='right',
                closed='right',

on='Date').sum().reset_index().sort_values(by='Date')
        weekly_data['yoy'] = (weekly_data['2020'] /
                              weekly_data['2019'])*100
        fig, axis = plt.subplots()
        axis.plot(weekly_data['Date'], weekly_data['yoy'],
```

```
                color=blue, linestyle='-', label="2020")
        plot.xlabel('Date')
        plot.ylabel('Passenger Load Factor (%)')
        plot.legend()
        plot.title('TSA Passenger Daily Throughput in 2020 as a
                  Percentage of 2019')
        plot_new_canvas(fig, root)
```

Lastly, we need to set up the main Tkinter window. We will create the `Tk` instance, set the window width and height, create the variable to hold the `RadioButton` value, create the four `RadioButtons`, create the quit Button, set up the GUI to start with choice #1 (day-by-day comparison of 2020 and 2019 passenger numbers), and then start the GUI. The formatting may look weird because of how the Python code needs to be squished to fit onto the page. If in doubt, double-check in the GitHub repository to make sure you have the correct indentation and code.

```
root = tk.Tk()
root.geometry("1100x750")
root.wm_title("TSA Passenger Throughput")

selection = tk.IntVar()
selection.set(1)
tk.Radiobutton(root, text="Daily", variable=selection, value=1,
               command=lambda: plot_choice(selection.get(),
                            plt, df)).grid(row=1, column=3)
tk.Radiobutton(root, text="Weekly", variable=selection, value=2,
               command=lambda: plot_choice(selection.get(),
                            plt, df)).grid(row=2, column=3)
tk.Radiobutton(root, text="Daily % YoY", variable=selection,
value=3,
               command=lambda: plot_choice(selection.get(),
                            plt, df)).grid(row=3, column=3)
tk.Radiobutton(root, text="Weekly % YoY", variable=selection,
value=4,
               command=lambda: plot_choice(selection.get(),
```

```
                         plt, df)).grid(row=4, column=3)

button = tk.Button(master=root, text="Quit",
                   command=lambda: _quit(root))
button.grid(row=5, column=3)

df = tsa('https://raw.githubusercontent.com/
        alexkenan/pyviz/main/datasets/tsa_pax.csv')
plot_choice(1, plt, df)

tk.mainloop()
```

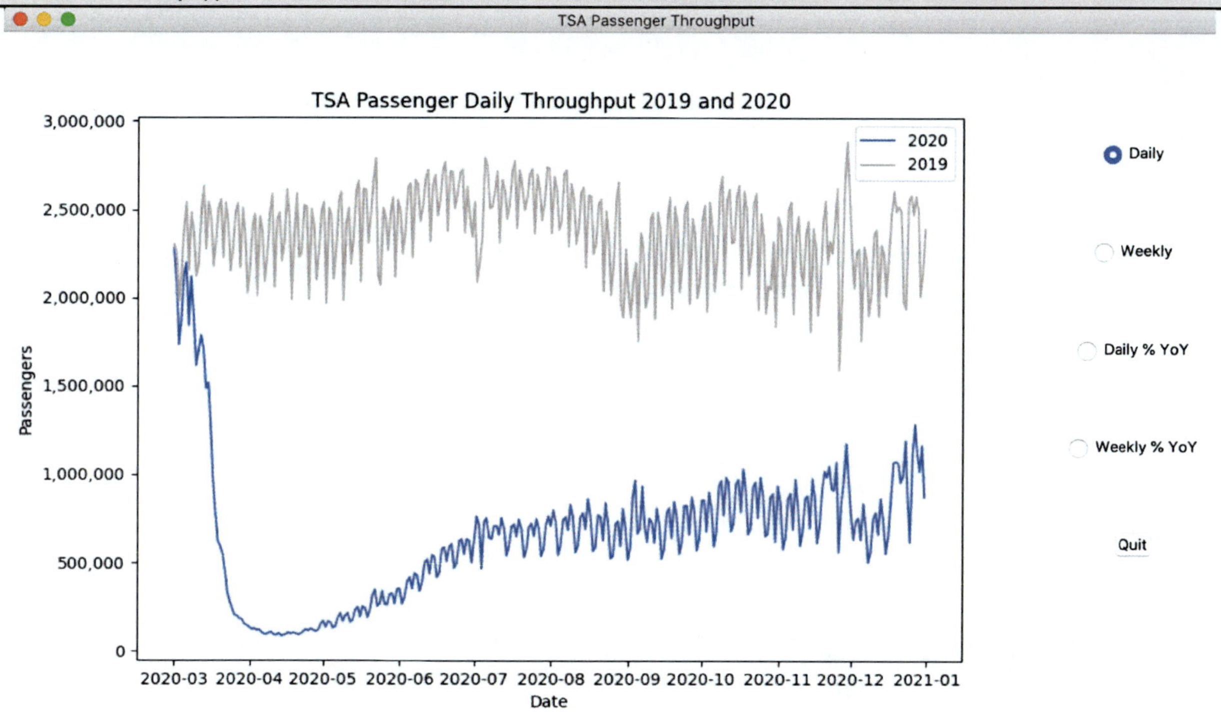

Now you have a GUI for looking at different slices of the same data!

Summary

Different people have different preferences for how they want to see visualizations for raw numbers like the TSA Passenger Throughput data. Some prefer the raw numbers, some prefer a weekly look, and some prefer daily or weekly year-over-year comparisons. With this GUI, you can let the user pick their favorite. While this GUI does not look like a polished Tableau dashboard, it does show you how you can use Python to create interactive displays that allow a user to select their preference for data display. There are certainly better ways to make the GUI more visually appealing, but it shows that more advanced GUIs are possible with Python.

Even though Plotly is left out of this section, it can be used to a similar effect by creating multiple HTML files and placing them in a folder. Plotly's interactive nature lets it stand further apart since a distributed HTML file is already more interactive than a static image. Plotly encourages the use of its own framework called *Dash* for analytical work and visualization in Python. It may be a good vehicle for accomplishing similar results.

Examples for Each Library

```
import tkinter as tk
import matplotlib.pyplot as plt
from matplotlib.backends.backend_tkagg import FigureCanvasTkAgg
from matplotlib.ticker import FuncFormatter
import pandas as pd
#import matplotlib
#matplotlib.use("TkAgg")


def _quit(main: tk.Tk):
    main.quit()
    main.destroy()
```

```
def tsa(path: str) -> pd.DataFrame:
    dataframe = pd.read_csv(path,
                            names=['Date', '2020', '2019'],
                            header=0, parse_dates=['Date'])
    dataframe['yoy'] = (dataframe['2020'] / dataframe['2019']) * 100
    return dataframe

def plot_new_canvas(figure: plt.figure, main: tk.Tk) -> None:
    figure.set_size_inches((9, 6))
    canvas = FigureCanvasTkAgg(figure, master=main)
    canvas.draw()
    canvas.get_tk_widget().grid(column=0, row=0,
                           columnspan=2, rowspan=8)

def plot_choice(num: int, plot: plt, df1: pd.DataFrame) -> None:
    plot.clf()
    blue = "#327ff6"
    gray = "#bdb8b6"
    if num == 1:
        # Daily raw pax numbers
        fig, axis = plt.subplots()
        axis.plot(df1['Date'], df1['2020'],
                  color=blue, linestyle='-', label="2020")
        axis.plot(df1['Date'], df1['2019'],
                  color=gray, linestyle='-', label="2019")
        plot.legend()
        plot.xlabel('Date')
        plot.ylabel('Passengers')
        plot.title('TSA Passenger Daily Throughput 2019 and 2020')
        axis.get_yaxis().set_major_formatter(
                FuncFormatter(lambda x, p: format(int(x), ',')))
        plot_new_canvas(fig, root)

    elif num == 2:
        # Weekly raw pax numbers
        weekly_data = df1.resample('W-Mon', label='right',
             closed='right',
             on='Date').sum().reset_index().sort_values(by='Date')
```

```
        fig, axis = plt.subplots()
        axis.plot(weekly_data['Date'], weekly_data['2020'],
                  color=blue, linestyle='-',
                  label="2020")
        axis.plot(weekly_data['Date'], weekly_data['2019'],
                  color=gray, linestyle='-',
                  label="2019")
        axis.get_yaxis().set_major_formatter(
                 FuncFormatter(lambda x, p: format(int(x), ',')))
        plot.xlabel('Date')
        plot.ylabel('Passengers')
        plot.legend()
        plot.ylim(0, 20E6)
        plot.title('TSA Passenger Weekly Throughput 2019 and 2020')
        plot_new_canvas(fig, root)

    elif num == 3:
        # Daily YoY percentage
        fig, axis = plt.subplots()
        axis.plot(df1['Date'], df1['yoy'],
                  color=blue, linestyle='-', label="2020")
        plot.legend()
        plot.xlabel('Date')
        plot.ylabel('Passenger Load Factor (%)')
        plot.title('TSA Passenger Daily Throughput in 2020 as a
                   Percentage of 2019')
        plot_new_canvas(fig, root)

    elif num == 4:
        # Weekly YoY percentage
        weekly_data = df1.resample('W-Mon', label='right',
                      closed='right',
              on='Date').sum().reset_index().sort_values(by='Date')
        weekly_data['yoy'] = (weekly_data['2020'] /
                              weekly_data['2019'])*100
        fig, axis = plt.subplots()
        axis.plot(weekly_data['Date'], weekly_data['yoy'],
                  color=blue, linestyle='-',
                  label="2020")
        plot.xlabel('Date')
```

```
        plot.ylabel('Passenger Load Factor (%)')
        plot.legend()
        plot.title('TSA Passenger Daily Throughput in 2020 as a
                   Percentage of 2019')
        plot_new_canvas(fig, root)

root = tk.Tk()
root.geometry("1100x750")
root.wm_title("TSA Passenger Throughput")

selection = tk.IntVar()
selection.set(1)
tk.Radiobutton(root, text="Daily", variable=selection, value=1,
               command=lambda: plot_choice(selection.get(),
                                  plt, df)).grid(row=1, column=3)
tk.Radiobutton(root, text="Weekly", variable=selection, value=2,
               command=lambda: plot_choice(selection.get(),
                                  plt, df)).grid(row=2, column=3)
tk.Radiobutton(root, text="Daily % YoY", variable=selection,
value=3,
               command=lambda: plot_choice(selection.get(),
                                  plt, df)).grid(row=3, column=3)
tk.Radiobutton(root, text="Weekly % YoY", variable=selection,
value=4,
               command=lambda: plot_choice(selection.get(),
                                  plt, df)).grid(row=4, column=3)

button = tk.Button(master=root, text="Quit",
                   command=lambda: _quit(root))
button.grid(row=5, column=3)
df = tsa('https://raw.githubusercontent.com/
         alexkenan/pyviz/main/datasets/tsa_pax.csv')
plot_choice(1, plt, df)

tk.mainloop()
```

View this code on GitHub at https://github.com/alexkenan/pyviz/

Resources

[1] https://docs.python.org/3/library/tkinter.html

[2] https://matplotlib.org/stable/gallery/user_interfaces/embedding_in_tk_sgskip.html

[3] https://pandas.pydata.org/pandas-docs/stable/reference/api/pandas.DataFrame.resample.html

[4] https://pandas.pydata.org/pandas-docs/stable/user_guide/timeseries.html#resampling

[5] https://dash.plotly.com/introduction

Data Visualization Rules

Introduction

This is the last chapter of the book, and it will look a little different than the previous chapters. So far, we have discussed a lot of data visualization methods and how to make them in Matplotlib, Seaborn, and Plotly. In each section, there were some rules of thumb for what to do and what not to do with that data visualization. This chapter has some of these guidelines outlined below. While the specific visualization method with Matplotlib, Seaborn, Plotly, or another library may be temporary, the general idea behind the data visualization is more permanent.

Data Visualization Rules

Scatter plots

- Typically used to compare two numerical variables (with an optional categorical or numerical variable as color)
- Don't overplot and clutter the canvas. Considering grouping, reducing the plotted sample size, using transparency, or something else to de-clutter the canvas
- Perform some exploratory data analysis to see if you have any subgroups in your data. Using different categorical colors or using transparency can help visualize and find any groups
- Remember, correlation does not equal causation
- Only connect datapoints if they are related

Line plots

- Typically used to compare two numerical variables (with an optional categorical or numerical variable as color) with the x-axis being time
- Usually used to emphasize a trend over time
- Don't overplot and clutter the canvas. Again, consider a method to summarize or otherwise declutter the canvas
- Adjust axis limits with care. Excessively zoomed-in y-axes can exaggerate small changes, and excessively zoomed-out y-axes can hide large changes
- Don't invert the y-axis (unless you are plotting rankings)
- Don't use a cumulative sum as an axis unless you have very good reason to do so

Histogram

- Typically used to show the representation and distribution of one numerical variable
- Ensure that you have explored different bin sizes. Large bin width (meaning a small number of bins) will often hide groups and insight
- Use the same bin width for each bin (e.g. having groups from 80-89, 90-99, etc and not 80-85, 86-99)
- Usually, more than 3 histograms on the same canvas is too much

Box plots and violin plots

- Typically used to summarize the distribution of a numerical variable for one or more groups
- Violin plot also shows a graphical distribution on the side of the box
- Box plots can hide the distribution of datapoints if you are showing multiple groups. By showing the distribution, violin plots can mitigate this distortion
- Order the boxes or violins by median for maximum intuitiveness

Bar charts

- Typically used to represent one categorical variable and one numerical variable
- Don't truncate the y-axis! Always show 0
- Use a uniform bar area. Don't use area to convey a message
- Sort the bars from largest to smallest (or vice versa) if you have multiple categories
    - Exception: Leave dates in chronological order
- Use color to emphasize certain bars to present your story

Pie charts

- Typically used to represent one numerical variable and one categorical variable
- Typically misused to represent almost anything

- Use with care
- Keep the number of slices to about 5 or fewer
- Ensure that percentages sum to 100%
- No donut charts and no 3D pie charts

Joint plots and pair plots

- Typically used to show distributions in the margins of a scatter plot and to show relationships between all numerical variables, respectively
- Be careful with overcluttering. Don't present all of the data and hope that the reader understands. Guide the reader through the visualization, the relationship, and why you are showing a joint plot or pair plot
- Don't use these visualization types just because you can

Choropleths

- Typically used to show a numerical or a categorical variable overlaid on a geographic variable
- Use color intuitively

Use of Color

- More color means more of what you are measuring
- Use a common-sense colorscale for the situation

    - If you are plotting a continuous variable like population, use a continuous color scale like `Blues`, `Greys`, `Reds`, etc
    - If you are plotting a variable like profit, which can have very negative or very positive values, use a bivariate continuous color scale like red to black
    - If you are plotting a categorical variable, use distinct colors for each category
    - If you are using color to show parts taken out of a whole (like income tax taken out of income), the part should be a lighter color, and the whole (or remainder) should be a darker color. This is an extension of "more color means more of what you are measuring" from above
- Use the same color, except to highlight differences or to highlight data
- Use a neutral background color
- Avoid cute chart junk

Welcome to the zen of good, effective, and truthful data visualization!

About the Author

Alex Kenan is a Senior Analyst at Delta Air Lines in the SkyMiles loyalty program, focusing on data analysis and program strategy. He uses Python, SAS software suite, and Oracle Hyperion to build models of future customer behavior, creates consumer insight from past customer behavior, and performs ad-hoc analyses for frequent flyer population impact. He provides instruction to new hires on data analysis in SAS software suite, Oracle Hyperion, Microsoft Access, and Python. He also has used Python to catch and prevent fraud in the SkyMiles program by identifying and blocking fraudulent redemptions and identifying hacked customer accounts.

Alex previously worked as a Propulsion Engineer for Delta TechOps where he oversaw a jet engine portfolio of nearly 200 Rolls-Royce BR-715 engines, and nearly 900 CFM56-5A, CFM56-5B, and CFM56-7B engines before that. He was responsible for the overall engine reliability for in-flight shutdown rate, unscheduled engine removal rate, and delays attributed to engine issues. He used Python to correlate engine component failure with FADEC faults which improved engine component troubleshooting and reduced engine component repair and overhaul costs.

Alex holds a Bachelor of Science degree in Aerospace Engineering from the University of Virginia and a Master of Business Administration from Emory University's Goizueta Business School.

Copyright Explanation

Acknowledgments

A sincere thank you to the following people:

- Adi
- Will R

Also by Alex Kenan

Python for Mechanical and Aerospace Engineering

Learn how the Python programming language can make mechanical and aerospace engineering modeling, simulation, data analysis, and visualization simple and easy.

https://www.alexkenan.com/pymae/

What did you think?

Please rate and review this book on Amazon!

https://www.amazon.com/dp/B08XQ26LDX

Made in United States
North Haven, CT
04 November 2026

21725028R00146